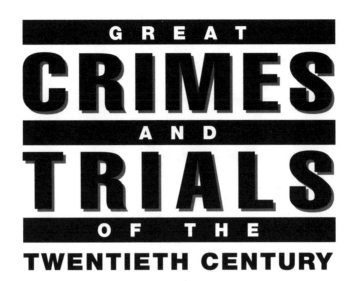

GREAT
CRIMES
AND
TRIALS
OF THE
TWENTIETH CENTURY

Dr. Crippen

John George Haig

Al Capone

Neville Heath

Jack Murphy

The Kray Twins

John Dillinger

John Gacy

The Yorkshire Ripper

GREAT
CRIMES
AND
TRIALS
OF THE
TWENTIETH CENTURY

Paul Begg & Martin Fido

LONDON NEW YORK SYDNEY TORONTO

THIS IS A CARLTON BOOK

For Keith

This edition published in 1994 by BCA by arrangement with Carlton Books Limited

CN 1539

'Great Crimes and Trials of the Twentieth Century' © 1993 Nugus/Martin Productions Ltd

Text and design copyright © 1993 Carlton Books Limited

Project Editor: Honor Head
Project Art Director: Bobbie Colgate Stone
Design: Simon Wilder
Editor: Mary Morton

Printed and bound in Great Britain by Mackays of Chatham plc

CONTENTS

INTRODUCTION

I N RECENT YEARS there has been a marked increase in the number of true crime programmes on television and in output and sales of true crime books. The difference between true crime and crime fiction - apart from the latter being almost traditionally dominated by female writers and the former by male - is that crime fiction most often concentrates on the good guys, the private detective in pursuit of the bad guys, or the local policeman patiently pieceing together the clues.

True crime writing is almost exclusively concerned with the criminal. For example, authors study at length the criminal psychology, motives and methods of the likes of Charles Manson and the Yorkshire Ripper, but the detectives who were instrumental in tracking them down or the police force who sifted through endless clues and leads over a period of years, are very rarely mentioned and even then only in passing. However the background information telling us how a criminal was caught, the methods used and even the mistakes made are all equally fascinating.

Great Crimes and Trials of the Twentieth Century is the book of a series of television programmes which investigates not only the criminal mind but also the detection and subsequent trials of some of the most bizarre and outrageous crimes since the turn of the century, as well as reconstructing cases which have become legendary in legal history around the world. Much of the material used in the series is taken from archive material never before seen on television. This book reproduces many of these images, taken from film footage and video tapes, as screenshots, and consequently the quality may not be as sharp as that of conventional photographs. But the fact that they have never before appeared in book form as still images makes them a must for any book that is to appeal to fans of true crime and crime detection.

Today, much of the interest in true crime is surely born of fear. Crime hasn't greatly changed, but our perception of it has. Today we seem to feel a need to understand crime and protect ourselves against criminals. Times have changed. Murder cases fifty years ago were mainly domestic, spiced by scandalous love affairs or other strong emotions. Or else they were mob related. Today inner city living is a regular night-time howl of police sirens.

TODAY MUCH OF THE INTEREST IN TRUE CRIME IS SURELY BORN OF FEAR.

The domestic murder, with its passions and motives, or even mob killings which usually only involved mob members, have been replaced by the seemingly motiveless serial killings of men like Ted Bundy. A straightforward murder committed in a moment of hate, rage or jealousy and probably regretted ever after, is replaced by mutilation and torture for the sake of inflicting pain and seemingly enjoyed by the perpetrator.

Society has changed, so has crime. As a consequence law keeping has had to change, too. *Great Crimes and Trials of the Twentieth Century* details how crime and criminal justice has evolved over the last century. It makes fascinating if not disturbing, reading.

THE CASE OF
DR. CRIPPEN

In the annals of British criminal history

Dr. Crippen probably ranks second only to Jack the

Ripper. His capture also marked the end of the

career of one of Scotland Yard's earliest superstar

detectives, Chief Inspector Walter Dew.

Crippen is infamous, yet his crime was a sordid,

domestic affair, hardly deserving the notoriety it

achieved. It is hard not to feel sympathy for him

and perhaps even admiration for the courage he

displayed throughout his trial and as he plunged

through the gallows' trapdoor.

■

HAWLEY HARVEY CRIPPEN was born in 1862, in Coldwater, Michigan, USA, where his father, Myron, was the wealthiest man in town and his uncle, Bradley, was the local physician. His future nemesis, Walter Dew, was born the following year, 1863, across the Atlantic in Far Cotton, Northampton. Dew joined the Metropolitan Police in 1882. In 1887 he was transferred to H Division, which covered the parishes of Whitechapel and Spitalfields in the East End of London. This meant that in 1888, as a young constable, he was involved in the hunt for the notorious prostitute killer, Jack the Ripper.

In 1888 Crippen was married to Charlotte Bell, a devoutly Catholic student nurse he had met when serving an internship at a hospital in New York City. The marriage was not successful, though in the year of the Ripper murders she gave birth to his son, Otto. Four years later, while pregnant with a second child, Charlotte died of apoplexy in Salt Lake City, Utah. Otto went to live in California with his grandparents while Crippen returned to New York. It was six months later, in July 1892, that Dr. Crippen met 19-year-old Cora Turner. Cora's real name was Kunigunde Mackamotzki, but, as a would-be opera singer, she realized that her birth name wouldn't look good in lights.

Crippen romanced the young girl and in six weeks they married. Almost immediately the couple encountered financial problems. Cora was forced to abandon her opera lessons and Crippen, at his wife's urging, soon joined a quack doctor, "Professor" Munyon, a purveyor of patent remedies, in New York. The patent medicine business was, in the main, a massive fraud. The medicines were advertised as cures for every human ill except death. Pills, ointments and liquids promised cures for ailments from asthma, through rheumatism, to all manner of skin disease and they netted millions of dollars. Crippen became very successful at pushing these medicines. Munyon promoted him to general manager of the Philadelphia office, then entrusted him with opening an office in Toronto, and finally, in 1897, put him in charge of the London office. Crippen was paid $10,000, which in 1897 was a very handsome salary.

By now Cora had abandoned all hope of a professional career in opera and had turned her sights to vaudeville. Going to London with her husband and using the stage name Cora Motzki, she made her debut at the Old Marylebone Music Hall. She lasted only a week. Unfortunately, she had gained a great deal of weight and there were quite a few unkind comments about her.

She blamed Crippen, but Crippen had in fact neglected his work for the bogus professor in order to help promote his wife's theatrical aspirations. Moreover, Munyon's attention had been drawn to a playbill which described Crippen as Acting Manager for Vio and Motzki's American Bright Lights Co.

Munyon thought this ill fitted Crippen's role as a purveyor of patent medicines and promptly sacked him.

Crippen's fortunes declined even further. Cora, now known as Belle Elmore,

IT OUGHT TO BE SAID THAT NOBODY DESERVES TO DIE, BUT CORA CRIPPEN CERTAINLY CAME AS NEAR TO DESERVING IT AS IT WAS POSSIBLE TO COME.

Cora, Crippen's troublesome wife.

had begun to drink heavily, frequently displayed a violent temper, and had taken up with a good-looking former boxer, Bruce Miller, who was doing the music hall circuit. As Crippen's marriage collapsed around him, with Cora never missing an opportunity to humiliate and belittle him, he threw himself into work. A patent pill company employed him, but went bust within a year and Crippen

tried to market a patent remedy of his own. This endeavour failed and, in 1901, Crippen joined the Drouet Institute.

This company was responsible for an incredible scam, a massive fraud that sold a plaster which, it was said, if stuck behind the ear would cure deafness. The Drouet Institute is said to have spent as much as £30,000 a year on advertising which, given the purchasing power of the pound in 1901, is an indication of how much money the scam was pulling in. It was at the Drouet Institute that Dr. Hawley Harvey Crippen first set eyes on a young lady named Ethel Le Neve.

Ethel Neve – the "Le" was an affectation and the original spelling of her surname was Neave – was in her late teens and lived with her parents in London's Camden Town. Her elder sister, Nina, was Crippen's secretary at the Drouet Institute. When Nina got married and left work, Ethel got her sister's job. Over the next five years she and Crippen gradually fell in love. For Crippen, who seems to have genuinely loved Le Neve, the relationship was a much-needed release from his stunting, demoralizing marriage to Cora.

In April 1904, Bruce Miller had returned to his wife and children in America. Cora had never hidden her affair with Miller from Crippen and may, indeed, have taken pleasure in rubbing his face in it, so when Miller went back to the States, Cora openly expressed her wish to return also. She began increasingly to attack Crippen. She was also extremely extravagant, acquiring from Crippen a fine jewellery collection and, at a time when he was in financial difficulties and needed her support, she bought a new wardrobe of clothes. The purchase was made to hurt him.

The Crippens moved to 39 Hilldrop Crescent. Cora, having abandoned her music hall career, nevertheless threw her energies into a social whirl that was helped considerably by her committee work with the Music Hall Ladies' Guild, which brought her into contact with some of the greatest names in music hall of the day.

In 1906, Cora began to take in paying guests at Hilldrop Crescent. Within a few months she started an affair with one of them, a German student named William Ehrlich. In November 1906, this development came to the attention of Crippen when he discovered the lovers in bed together. Ehrlich later described life in the Crippen household, particularly commenting on how Cora never missed an opportunity to deride and berate her husband and how Crippen had displayed extraordinary self-control in not retaliating, either verbally or physically. The reality, though, is that Crippen had probably stopped caring about what

Ethel Le Neve was in her late teens when she went to work for Crippen.

Cora said or did and, not caring, couldn't be hurt by her behaviour, especially as now he had the respect and love of Ethel Le Neve to sustain him.

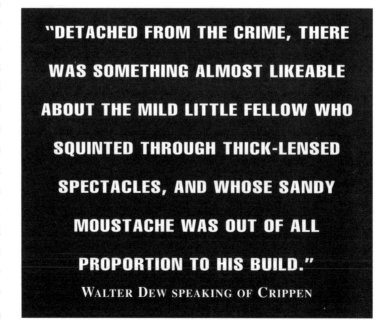

"DETACHED FROM THE CRIME, THERE WAS SOMETHING ALMOST LIKEABLE ABOUT THE MILD LITTLE FELLOW WHO SQUINTED THROUGH THICK-LENSED SPECTACLES, AND WHOSE SANDY MOUSTACHE WAS OUT OF ALL PROPORTION TO HIS BUILD."
WALTER DEW SPEAKING OF CRIPPEN

By 1908 Crippen and Cora barely talked. Crippen had gone into partnership with Dr. Gilbert Rylance, an American, and formed The Yale Tooth Specialists. Rylance later claimed that

Crippen merely handled the day-to-day business affairs but Ethel Le Neve said that Crippen carried out tooth extractions himself. Le Neve had less reason to lie than Rylance and, since she worked closely with Crippen, was in a position to know the truth.

Cora knew about Crippen's affair with Le Neve and was desperately jealous of it. In particular she believed Le Neve had encouraged Crippen to set up The Yale Tooth Specialists and that it was a cheap business which would never bring in the kind of money Cora wanted. It didn't have the aura of upper-middle-class respectability Cora desired and, in her opinion, would probably fail and ruin them all anyway.

Poor Crippen was also under pressure from Ethel Le Neve. Understandably, she wanted Crippen to leave Cora as she herself wanted marriage and respectability. In 1909, Ethel became pregnant. It could have forced Crippen's hand and been the reason he'd needed to finally break away from his wife, but in March 1909 Ethel suffered a miscarriage. Cora was delighted. She spread the rumour that Ethel had had an abortion and she even claimed that the child's father was unknown. It ought to be said that nobody deserves to die, but Cora Crippen certainly came as near to deserving it as it was possible to come.

William and Burroughs chemists in London's New Oxford Street were often used by Crippen. On January 19, 1910, he visited their premises and purchased five grains of hyoscine.

On January 31, 1910, he and Cora had dinner at Hilldrop Crescent with some friends, Paul and Clara Martinetti. The next day he went to his office and left a short note on Ethel Le Neve's typewriter to the effect that Cora had gone to America and that he and Ethel could have a pleasant evening together. On March 12 Ethel moved into Hilldrop Crescent and began openly living with Crippen. She even accompanied Crippen to a social occasion where a number of Cora's friends and acquaintances were present, many of them noting that Ethel was wearing some of Cora's jewellery.

After several months of sheer relief and pleasure, including holidays in Dieppe and Boulogne, Crippen sent friends the news that Cora had died in America. The friends were less than convinced by this story and some went so far as to pay a call on the police.

WALTER DEW

Born near Northampton, Walter Dew moved with his family to London in 1878. His father worked as a guard on the railway and young Walter wanted to follow in his footsteps. However, in 1881 he'd gone to work in a solicitor's office, then as a clerk for a seed merchant, who sacked him. Walter Dew then joined the police. He made rapid

progress through the ranks, and was eventually transferred to the CID (Criminal Investigation Department) in 1887, became involved in the Jack the Ripper hunt in 1888, and worked through the various grades from sergeant to inspector, until, in November 1906, he was promoted to Chief Inspector.

On March 31, 1910, Scotland Yard received a visit from a Mrs. Louise Smythson. She was concerned, she said, about a good friend of hers named Cora Crippen – her husband claimed she had gone to America. What worried Mrs. Smythson was that Cora hadn't intimated to anyone that she planned on making such a journey, nor had anyone received any sort of communication from Mrs.

A police dig in the garden of Crippen's home at Hilldrop Crescent revealed nothing suspicious.

Crippen since her departure. A short time later, explained Mrs. Smythson, Cora's husband reported that she had been taken ill in America and, a week later, to have died there. An obituary notice for Cora had even been published in the theatrical newspaper *Era*.

Worse still, Crippen's behaviour seemed very odd indeed to Cora's friends. He didn't seem to know where his wife had been, showed no intention of going to America to attend to his wife's funeral and claimed that Cora was to be cremated, something Cora's friends doubted that Catholic Cora would have wanted or sanctioned. Moreover, Crippen was openly consorting with his secretary, who had actually moved into the Crippen home and was wearing Cora's prized jewellery.

Dew was less than persuaded by the story. However, a few months later a Mr. and Mrs. John Nash paid a call on Scotland Yard, visiting a personal friend, Superintendent Frank Froest, a balding, round-headed, Teutonic-looking policeman. Having only recently returned from a tour of the United States – Mrs. Nash being a vaudeville performer whose stage name was Lil Hawthorne – they had been shocked to discover that Cora Crippen had died. They had, of course, visited her husband, but had found him somewhat evasive.

Dew records in his autobiography the visit made by Mr. and Mrs. Nash to Scotland Yard and recites how Superintendent Froest turned to him and said: "'Well, Mr. Dew, that's the story. What do you make of it?' Without a second's

hesitation, I replied: 'I think it would be just as well if I made a few inquiries into this personally.'"

Dew goes on lamely to explain that he could have passed the inquiries over to the uniformed police, but that they would have treated it as a simple missing person case and done nothing unless there was something suspicious.

Dew interviewed many people, then paid a call at Hilldrop Crescent. "I am Chief Inspector Dew of Scotland Yard," he introduced himself to Ethel Le Neve, who, at his prompting, agreed to accompany him to Crippen's offices. Dew, Le Neve and a Sergeant Mitchell caught a bus (this was 1910 and police cars were a thing of the future) from Hilldrop Crescent to Tottenham Court Road, from where they walked to New Oxford

The telegram sent by Captain Kendall of the S.S. Montrose, alerting police to the whereabouts of Crippen and Le Neve.

Captain Henry Kendall of the S.S. Montrose.

Ethel Le Neve, still disguised as a boy, under arrest.

Street. Crippen's office was on the third floor and Ethel Le Neve, concerned for the reputation of the business, rushed ahead of Dew and returned moments later with Crippen.

" 'This is Dr. Crippen,' Miss Le Neve announced, and I found myself looking into the shortsighted eyes of the man who was already a murderer.

"My thoughts have often gone back since to that first meeting between Crippen and myself on the stairs of Albion House. What a moment it must have been for him! The police had come. How much did they know? His mind must have been in a torment of anxiety. Yet he was as calm as I was."

So wrote Walter Dew of their first meeting. Crippen's statement to Dew was open and frank. It took about five hours, which included a break for lunch at an Italian restaurant near Albion

House, where, according to Dew, Crippen ordered a steak and ate with relish, as if he hadn't a care in the world. Moreover, Crippen's story was convincingly direct and seemingly honest. He openly admitted that his relationship with Cora had deteriorated to the point where he'd ceased to sleep or share any intimacy with her, and he freely declared that Ethel Le Neve was his mistress. He added that the account of his wife's illness and death was indeed a lie. She had, in fact, gone off to America, but to join a former lover named Bruce Miller, and the story of her death was an invention because he, Crippen, was ashamed of his wife's infidelities and the failure of his marriage. Dew was fairly satisfied with Crippen's story, especially after a cursory search of Hilldrop Crescent revealed nothing suspicious. Before Dew left the house he urged Crippen to make every

effort to contact his wife in America. Crippen drafted an advertisement to be placed in a US newspaper.

Dew was not unduly suspicious, even when, on re-reading Crippen's statement, he noted several inconsistencies. Just to clear up a few small details, the following Monday morning Dew visited Hilldrop Crescent, but found the house empty. He then went on to Crippen's office. He found it closed up. Alarmed, Dew ordered Crippen's home in Hilldrop Crescent to be thoroughly searched. Nothing was found. Dew then had the garden dug up. Nothing was found.

Dew turned his attention to the dusty coal cellar. There was a little pile of coal and some wood for burning, but nothing to arouse suspicion. Dew ran his finger between two bricks on the flooring. The mortar was old and crumbly. Dew was able to lever a brick free, revealing the clay below. He pulled away a few bricks, then a nauseating smell suddenly filled the small room. Dew and his sergeant reeled out of the house and took a breath of fresh air. A little further investigation discovered a low pit dug in the clay. In it was the remains of a woman, covered with lime. Whether or not it was the body of Cora Crippen, Dew now very much wanted to talk further with the mild-mannered Dr. Crippen and his young lover, Ethel Le Neve.

TAKING FLIGHT

At Hilldrop Crescent Crippen had told Le Neve that their lives would be made a misery by gossip and questions from Cora's friends. It was best that they run away and start a new life together. They mustn't be traced, he said, and it was decided that Ethel should dress as a boy. They went to Liverpool Street station and caught the train to Harwich, from where they sailed on the night boat to Rotterdam in Holland. From Rotterdam they went to Brussels and stayed for 10 days in the Hotel des Ardennes. On July 15 he read in the Belgian newspapers that human remains had been found in the cellar at Hilldrop Crescent. Crippen immediately booked tickets to sail aboard the S.S. *Montrose* to Canada on July 20. He and Le Neve travelled as John Philo Robinson and Master John Robinson.

Although they tried not to draw attention to themselves, Ethel Le Neve did not make a very convincing boy and, on those occasions when the couple had to mix with other passengers, they attracted attention. Among those whose attention was attracted was Henry Kendall, captain of the *Montrose*, and after lunching with the couple his suspicions were heavily aroused. Glancing through some back numbers of the *Daily*

Mail, he came across photographs of Crippen and Le Neve. Studying both photographs with great care the conviction grew that the Robinsons were the wanted couple.

The following day Captain Kendall sent a telegram from the ship. In part the unpunctuated telegram read: "...have strong suspicion that Crippen London cellar murderer and accomplice are

amongst saloon passengers moustache taken off growing beard accomplice dressed as boy voice manner and build undoubtedly a girl both travelling as Mr. and Master Robinson." This message was passed to Scotland Yard and eventually reached the eyes of Walter Dew.

Dew made some inquiries and discovered that he could sail aboard the White Star liner *Laurentic* and actually reach Quebec first. Dew went to his superior, Sir Melville Macnaghten, and requested authority to sail. It was a huge, reputation-risking decision for both Dew and Macnaghten. The press was certain to find out and the criticism of Dew, Macnaghten, and Scotland Yard would be harsh if Kendall was wrong. Nevertheless, Macnaghten sanctioned Dew's request, though the chase was to be conducted in utmost secrecy, not even Dew's wife being informed of his trip or its purpose. Under the adopted name of Dewhurst, the inspector boarded the *Laurentic*.

Meanwhile, Captain Kendall was supplying a stream of information back to the press in Britain and daily the newspapers not only described the latest news from aboard the *Montrose*, but showed the relative positions of Crippen's and Dew's vessels. The chase became something like a modern daily soap opera and attracted thousands of readers on both sides of the Atlantic. Crippen, of course, knew nothing of what was going on. Instead, he watched his beard grow while Ethel continued her masquerade as a boy.

> ## "...HAVE STRONG SUSPICION THAT CRIPPEN LONDON CELLAR MURDERER AND ACCOMPLICE ARE AMONG SALOON PASSENGERS..."
>
> TELEGRAM FROM CAPTAIN KENDALL TO WALTER DEW

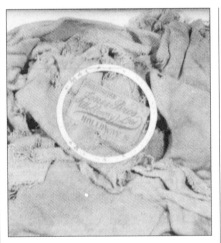

The pyjama top in which the remains of Cora Crippen were wrapped.

"GOOD MORNING, MR. DEW"

Dew reached Canada before the S.S. *Montrose*. Disguised as a pilot in a brass-buttoned jacket and accompanied by a Canadian policeman, Dew boarded the *Montrose* and approached his quarry.

"Poor Crippen was still in ignorance of the fate so close at hand. My pilot's uniform was proving an effective disguise. He had not yet recognized me.

" 'Good morning, Dr. Crippen,' I said. The little man gave a start of surprise, and a puzzled look came into his eyes as they scanned me. For a second longer doubt and uncertainty were registered on his face. Then a sudden twitching of his Adam's apple told me that recognition had come to him.

"Even though I believed him to be a murderer, and a brutal murderer at that, it was impossible at that moment not to feel for him a pang of pity. He had been caught on the threshold of freedom. Only 12 hours more and he would have been safely in Quebec.

" 'Good morning, Mr. Dew,' Crippen replied, and his voice was as calm and quiet as it had been on the occasion of our first meeting at Albion House." So wrote Inspector Dew.

Dew returned with Le Neve and Crippen to London, where they arrived on August 28, 1910. Throughout the journey and afterwards Crippen's only concern was for Ethel Le Neve.

In London Crippen unwittingly accepted an offer to be defended by Arthur Newton, not knowing that Newton was widely known as a dishonest solicitor. Nevertheless, at first Newton approached Edward Marshall Hall, probably the most flamboyant and famous defence counsel of the time (or since).

Properly defended, Crippen might have been saved from the hangman's noose, but Hall was on holiday and Newton instead approached Alfred Tobin, who accepted. Unfortunately, Tobin lacked experience and had little or no courtroom flair, and his client, Crippen, did nothing to help his own defence. He steadfastly maintained that the body in Hilldrop Crescent was not that of Cora Crippen.

The evidence against Crippen was overwhelming: a metal curler found with the remains bore dark brown hair dyed blonde, as was Cora Crippen's; part of the dismembered body bore a scar matching one on Cora Crippen; traces of hyoscine were found in the remains, and Dr. Crippen was shown to have purchased this poison only a short time earlier; the remains were wrapped in a pyjama top which it was shown could not have been done before the Crippens moved to Hilldrop Crescent. Crippen was found guilty and sentenced to death.

On the morning of Wednesday, November 23, 1910, Hawley Harvey Crippen left his cell at Pentonville Prison and stepped onto the gallows. The hangman, James Ellis, placed a hood over Crippen's head and fastened his wrists. The noose in place, the platform gave way beneath Crippen's feet....

As Crippen plunged into eternity, Ethel Le Neve boarded the liner *Majestic* and sailed to New York and into obscurity. She would return to England under an assumed name, marry – her husband never knowing anything about her relationship with Crippen – and have children. She died in Dulwich in 1967.

Walter Dew retired from the Metropolitan Police a few months after the arrest of Crippen and became a private detective. He died in 1947.

Over the years sympathy for Crippen has increased, a sympathy which was undoubtedly felt by Dew and others who came to know the man.

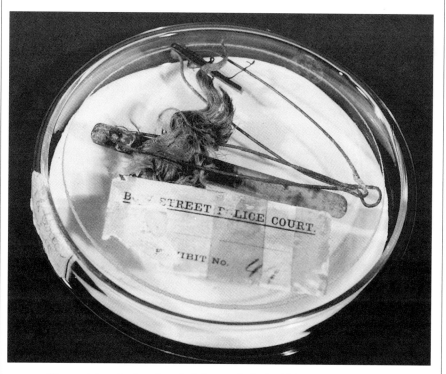

The metal curler bearing dark brown hair dyed blonde, as was Cora's.

THE MASSACRE OF THE TSAR

From his capital in St. Petersburg the Tsar governed the vast Russian Empire. The last of the Tsars was Nicholas II. Cousin to Kaiser Wilhelm of Germany and nephew of Edward, Prince of Wales (the future Edward VII), Nicholas had succeeded his father in 1894 and, like his predecessors, was an autocrat. But revolution was in the air. Russian society was backward and deliberately kept so by the Russian Orthodox Church and the small landed aristocracy. Ideas, though, could not be crushed. They spread.

■

Then Russia engaged in a disastrous war against Germany. It had the manpower but not the resources and the government gradually collapsed, leading to the abdication of Nicholas II and the birth of a mystery.

Russia was a huge country that had not kept pace with the industrialization of the West. In World War I it was able to mass an army of about 15 million men, but lacked the factories to supply the troops with weapons, ammunition, food and adequate clothing. Moreover, the rail network was incapable of getting to the troops such provisions as were available, and the withdrawal of men from the countryside to fight in the army caused a massive decline in agricultural production. Unsupplied, often unarmed, Russian troops died in unprecedented numbers, their losses probably greater than those sustained by any country in any previous war.

On the civilian front, the dramatic decline in agricultural production led to food becoming scarce and prices going through the roof. By 1917 many of the larger Russian cities, their populations swelled with thousands of refugees from the front, faced famine. There was considerable discontent among the people, exacerbated by the knowledge that their suffering was not even being rewarded by military victory.

The Russian imperial government was disinterested, uncaring, and dismissive of the protests lodged by the Duma, the Russian parliament. There were fears within the Duma that existing policies could lead to revolution. Even within court and government circles there was treasonable talk as leaders, recognizing that the Tsar was completely out of touch with reality, discussed ways of averting revolution. As early as November 1916, the Duma warned Emperor Nicholas II that a constitutional form of government should be instituted, but he ignored them and carried on as usual.

Nicholas II was an autocrat by teaching, upbringing and history. He had no contact with his people and his advisors were servants. Telling the Tsar he was wrong was like telling God that He was in error, except the Tsar was less forgiving and his punishment more immediate. It was often impossible to get him to see reason, especially when advice conflicted with the opinions of his wife, Empress Alexandra. In turn, she was heavily influenced and perhaps even dominated by a peasant monk named Rasputin. As senior members of the court circle discussed the very real possibility of revolution within the palace, a group of young aristocrats led by Prince Feliks Yusupov (who didn't die until 1967) hoped that if the influence of Rasputin were removed the Tsar would "wake up" to what was happening

> **RASPUTIN BECAME A WANDERING HOLY MAN AND HIS REPUTATION FOR HEALING STEADILY GREW, AS DID HIS REPUTATION AND APPETITE FOR DEBAUCHERY.**

in his country. Accordingly they assassinated Rasputin in late December 1916. It did no good – Nicholas merely turned to Rasputin's supporters.

Grigory Yefimovich Rasputin was born in 1872, in Pokrovskoye, Siberia. He received little, if any education, but claimed mystical powers and won a reputation as a faith healer. In 1901 he became a wandering holy man and his reputation for healing steadily grew, as did his reputation and appetite for debauchery.

His wanderings brought him to St. Petersburg in 1905. By now his reputation for healing had even reached the court and Rasputin was introduced to the Tsarina, Empress Alexandra. For some reason Rasputin was able to relieve the suffering of her son, Alexis, who was a haemophiliac. Within a short time Rasputin was exercising a sinister influence over Alexandra and, through her, over Nicholas II. With the outbreak of World War I, Nicholas took command of the army at the front and Rasputin became the effective ruler of Russia through his influence in the government – many

Rasputin, who was hated for his womanizing and for the influence he exerted on the Tsar and Tsarina.

holders of high office had been recommended by Rasputin, but most of his appointees were wholly incompetent.

Considerable ill-feeling toward Rasputin, called "the Mad Monk" – and through him, towards Nicholas and Alexandra – was generated by his scandalous orgies and rumours that he was in the pay of Germany. He became such a hated figure that his assassination, at the hands of a group of disaffected noblemen, on December 29–30, 1916, was greeted with relief.

REVOLUTION

Successive demonstrations in St. Petersburg (soon to be known as Petrograd) in February 1917 led to a mass turn-out, on March 8, of 90,000 people. Further demonstrations took place on the following day. Among the cries to be heard and the slogans to be seen on banners was "Down with autocracy!" There was increasing violence and the authorities called in troops to break up the demonstrations. The Cossacks, though, seemed disinclined to confront the people; some, indeed, seemed to support them. The uprising grew and the troops were ordered to quash it. There was some firing, but overall the troops wavered. On March 12 and 13 about 150,000 men from the Petrograd garrison joined the people. It was revolution. The government in Petrograd fell to the Petrograd Soviet of Workers' and Soldiers' Deputies and to a group formed by a provisional committee of the Duma.

The Soviet concentrated initially on solving the immediate problem of food shortages. Then the Tsar's ministers were arrested and official news was published in a new newspaper named *Izves-*

The daughters of Tsar Nicholas: Maria, Tatiana, Anastasia and Olga.

tia, which means news. However, overall the revolutionaries were unprepared for the success of their revolution. It was not until Vladimir Ilyich Lenin, leader of the Bolsheviks, arrived in Russia in April that any real agenda was put forward. But while the Bolsheviks had a loud voice in Lenin, they were a small party, outnumbered by groups like the capitalist and democratic Mensheviks and the peasant Socialist Revolutionaries.

The revolution spread. Eventually the provisional government of the Duma placed its representatives, or commissars, in charge. They demanded that

Nicholas abdicate, and on March 15 he gave up the throne to his brother, Grand Duke Mikhail Aleksandrovich. At this point in the revolution the government, with the exception of the minister of justice, the moderately socialist leader Aleksandr Fyodorovich Kerensky, still consisted of landowners in the mould of figurehead prime minister Prince Georgy Yevgenyevich Lvov.

Under heavy guard Nicholas was taken to his former summer residence at Tsarkoe Selo. From there he and his family were moved to a variety of locations. In the main they were looked after well and enjoyed a degree of freedom, but in July 1918, at their final "prison", a house in the town of Ekaterinburg, the situation changed.

BOLSHEVISM TRIUMPHS

Fuelled by the success in Petrograd, revolution spread throughout the country, but the government had no real power and the loose coalition of political groups began to split, eventually degenerating into open conflict. Meanwhile, following his return to Russia from exile, Lenin had persuaded the minority Bolshevik party to resist joining the other political groups in a scramble for power, but instead to engage in a campaign of propaganda, advocating the seizure of the land by the peasants. In the middle of May Lenin was joined by Leon Trotsky, who had returned to Russia from exile in the United States.

Amid a deepening economic and social crisis, discipline broke down following a major defeat in the continuing bloody and costly war against Germany. Millions of soldiers streamed home from the front to escape further fighting. In the meantime opposition among workers and soldiers in Petrograd to the continuing military campaign led to a mammoth demonstration of about 400,000 Petrograd workers. The views expressed by the demonstrators revealed a wholly unexpected support for Bolshevik ideology. The demonstration was followed by 500,000 armed soldiers of the city garrison and sailors of the nearby naval fortress of Kronstadt joining the workers. The Bolshevik leadership, taken wholly by surprise by their support, responded by placing itself at the head of the movement. The government responded with force and Lenin, denounced as a German agent, fled to Finland. Trotsky and other Bolsheviks were arrested.

Had the Kerensky government been able to overcome the worsening economic situation, it is likely that they might have prevented a resurgence of Bolshevik influence. The problem lay with a dissident named Kornilov, who planned to take over the Kerensky government. The government massed its own support in Petrograd. Surprisingly, its supporters were led by Bolsheviks. Kornilov's force was defeated and the Bolsheviks assumed great influence and some power within the Kerensky government.

As the political situation deteriorated still further, Lenin advocated an armed insurrection and seizure of power. The Bolshevik committee approved the policy on October 23 and on the night of November 6–7 supporters stormed the Winter Palace, headquarters of the provisional government, and seized power.

Nicholas and Alexandra had five children: Maria, Olga, Tatiana, Anastasia, and son Alexis, who was born in 1905 and proved to be a haemophiliac. With them was the Tsar's personal doctor, a valet and a maid. In charge was a

The Tsar and his family in captivity at Tobolsk.

man named Yakov Yurovsky, a member of the CHEKA (secret police), who had only recently been appointed to take charge of the Imperial family.

DEATH OF THE TSAR

At midnight on July 16, 1918, Yurovsky had the family and their servants roused from their sleep and told to dress. They were then taken to a small, unfurnished room. Twelve armed men were in the room, each instructed to assassinate a specific member of the family and their staff. As the family entered the room, Yurovsky told them that they were to be executed. The guards opened fire. The Tsar fell in the first fusillade, but his daughters suffered only wounds or the shots missed altogether. They screamed and ran around the room, but eventually they died and were bayoneted. This was when it was discovered that they had jewellery sewn into their underclothes, which had deflected many of the shots.

Young Alexis, the haemophiliac son, was badly wounded and groaning. Yurovsky had him shot three times.

Yurovsky sent a message to Moscow in which he announced that the execution had been carried out. He then set about disposing of the bodies. A classified report gave an account of the crimes, but local rumour asserted that acid had been poured over the bodies, that the remains had then been burnt, and that whatever was left over had been dumped in a disused mineshaft. Troops investigated the spot in 1919 and found remnants of the family's belongings, which seemed to confirm the rumour.

Yet stories persisted that all or some of the family had survived. One story concerned a man who claimed to be Alexis, but the most famous and persistent claim was that made by supporters of Anna Anderson, who in 1920 was pulled out of a canal. Mentally disturbed, she claimed that she was Anastasia.

ANNA OR ANASTASIA?

For six weeks the rescued girl lay in hospital, refusing to say a word about herself, and was then transferred to the Dalldoff Insane Asylum. She lived there for two years, never showing much interest in what was happening around her, barely speaking to anyone and mostly spending her time in bed. Her physical health broke down. The authorities thought she was an illegal immigrant from Russia whose silence was caused by a fear of repatriation. A fellow patient named Clara Peuthert thought differently. When she was discharged from the asylum she visited Captain Nikolai von Schwabe at the Russian embassy church in Berlin. She told him that she thought the Grand Duchess Anastasia was among the patients at Dalldoff, explaining that she had once lived in Moscow and seen the Imperial Family when there.

Captain von Schwabe passed what he had heard on to various White emigrés and many of them visited the patient. Among them was Baroness Buxhoeveden, who reluctantly visited at the insistence of others and, when the patient refused to talk or properly show her face, left the hospital denying that the young girl was Anastasia.

For some time, though, a former provincial police official from Russian Poland, Baron Arthur von Kleist, had befriended the girl and to some degree won her confidence. He petitioned the authorities to have the girl released into his care and they eventually consented. Von Kleist later claimed that in June, 1922, the girl told his wife and himself that she was Grand Duchess Anastasia.

According to von Kleist, at the time of the shooting "Anastasia" had been

The Tsar with other prisoners working in the fields at Tsarskoe Selo.

standing behind one of her sisters, had been grazed by a bullet and fallen unconscious. She had awakened to find herself in the home of a soldier, Alexander Tschaikowsky, who had rescued her. The soldier's family had taken her to Romania and she had become pregnant by Tschaikowsky, bearing him a son. Tschaikowsky, she said, had been killed in a street fight in Bucharest and her son had been taken from her and put in an orphanage. From Romania, she said, she had gone on alone to Germany.

Baron von Kleist soon broke the news that she claimed to be Anastasia. Lots of people came to visit as a result of this revelation, much to "Anastasia's" great annoyance, and her health began to fail. She recovered and left the von Kleist household, spending the next few years moving from one home to another, going in and out of various hospitals, and receiving visits from various members of the royal houses of Europe.

What the various visitors thought is, in many cases, obscured by later wranglings, but many remained convinced. Among them was Tatiana Botkin, daughter of the doctor to the Tsar. She had spent time in exile with the Russian royal family and been one of the last people known to have seen Anastasia alive. She was totally convinced that "Anastasia" was a fraud – until she met her. Then she became certain, as did other people, that this was, indeed, Anastasia. But equally attempts were made to discredit her story and prove she was someone else.

THE FINAL CHAPTER

In 1977 the house in Ekaterinberg, known officially as "The House of Special Purpose" was destroyed. Over a

Tsar Nicholas shortly before his murder.

decade later, in 1989, *glasnost* swept through the Soviet Union. Among the previously suppressed material released was the report by Yakov Yurovsky. This stated that the bodies had not been dumped in the mine, as previously thought, but taken to a nearby forest. The trucks carrying them had become stuck in the mud, though, and a pit was hastily dug. An attempt was made to burn the bodies of Alexis and Anastasia, but it wasn't successful and their bodies were left beside the pit. The other corpses were thrown in the pit, acid poured over them and then covered with rubble.

In July 1991, a team of archaeologists and other experts were sent from Moscow to investigate the site. They found the pit, as described by Yurovsky, and discovered a mass of bones. There followed a hugely detailed investigation and analysis of the remains. There was little doubt that the Tsar and his family had been found. One of the world's greatest mysteries had been solved.

Or was it? There are still people who question the findings and believe that members of the Tsar's family survived the murderous assault made on them. Support for Anna Anderson lives on.

THE STORY OF
AL CAPONE

In 1920 Prohibition outlawed the sale and consumption of alcohol in the USA – but people still wanted to drink. Mobster Al Capone made Chicago the bootlegging capital of the USA, eliminating all competition for this lucrative business. His most famous takeover bid became known as the St. Valentine's Day Massacre. Bribery bought him the law. To bring him down needed policemen who were incorruptible – the Untouchables. In the end, though, it was the more ponderous taxman who toppled Scarface Al.

■

In 1673 the French explorers Jacques Marquette and Louis Jolliet trudged along an area of swampland on the south-western shore of Lake Michigan. It smelt of wild onions and the Potawatomi Indians called the region "Checagou". The area remained sparsely settled until the 1830s, when a township called Chicago began to develop. It was almost a short-lived township. In 1871, nearly one-third of central Chicago was destroyed in a great fire, but the city was quickly rebuilt and in 1885 the world's first skyscraper was built there.

By the 1920s Chicago was divided into the North, West, and South Sides, with the downtown retail district known as "the Loop", because of the rail-line that encircled it. The city was a vibrant and exciting place.

Chicago's celebrated saloon and brothel district, known as the Levee, was on the South Side. In 1895 Luigi Colosimo settled there with his three sons and two daughters. One of the sons was aged 17 and named James. James Colosimo (Big Jim) was big and strong. Sometimes he did legitimate work, sometimes criminal work. He took up pimping until the authorities closed him down and he was forced to clean the streets for a living.

In 1902 he met Victoria Moresco, madam of a down-market brothel. Colosimo married Victoria and took over the brothel, turning it into a success. Then he acquired another establishment, then a third. Gradually, he extended his interests into other criminal activities and in 1909 invited his nephew to move to Chicago from New York and become his business manager.

The nephew was a 31-year-old gangster named Johnny Torrio who years

Ingenious hiding places were found for bootlegged booze during Prohibition.

In April 1920, Colosimo divorced Victoria and married his mistress, Dale Winter, with whom he had been openly living since 1917. Torrio, a strict Roman Catholic who didn't believe in divorce, didn't approve. He also got a little worried about the talk on the streets that Colosimo had gone soft. On May 11 he asked Colosimo to attend to some business at his restaurant – Colosimo's Café, at 2126 South Wabash Avenue. Big Jim went along. As he stood in the restaurant two shots rang out. One bullet missed. The other went through his head.

TORRIO THE BOSS

Among those questioned about the killing of Big Jim were Johnny Torrio and a fellow who in 1919 at Torrio's invitation had come to Chicago from New York. He called himself Al Brown, but at other times he answered to Al Capone. Both men were elsewhere when Colosimo was shot and Torrio was openly overcome with grief. Boarding a train, though, and ready to leave Chicago after staying a week, was a New Yorker named Frankie Yale. Nothing could be proved, but there were some folk who favoured the opinion that Yale had killed Colosimo at Torrio's behest.

Frankie Yale (his real surname was Uale) was a Sicilian gangster who had many criminal interests but specialized as a hit man. He was also a prestigious member of the Unione Siciliane, which had begun life as a legitimate organization, but in New York had become perverted by a man called Ignazio Saietta, also known as "Lupo the Wolf". A cold-hearted man who could kill with impunity, Saietta turned the Unione into a criminal organization.

John Torrio, with whom Capone ran Chicago's Southside in the 1920s.

later would be described as "the father of modern American gangsterdom". Within a few years Torrio had expanded Colosimo's operations – any opposition tending suddenly to contract lead poisoning – and Big Jim became a multi-millionaire, wielder of almost king-like power over his South Side district.

In 1915 William Hale "Big Bill" Thompson was elected mayor of Chicago. He had an appetite for money and Colosimo freely donated large quantities of dollar bills to Thompson's campaign fund. Some of the money found its way into Thompson's personal bank account.

Capone had rival gang leader Hymie Weiss dispatched with ruthless efficiency.

Bloody feuds between mobsters were a fact of life in 1920s Chicago, exemplified by the St. Valentine's Day Massacre.

Frankie Yale hired the young Al Capone as a bouncer and barman at his Harvard Inn on Coney Island. It was there that Al Capone made an offensive remark to a young lady, the sister of a small-time hood named Frank Galluccio. Galluccio carved Capone's face with a pocket knife, the visible remains of which altercation resulted in Al being nicknamed "Scarface". It was not a name by which the cautious referred to him personally. Capone hated it, as he hated most nicknames. He just about tolerated "Snorky", which meant smart dresser.

Al Capone was the son of Gabriel and Teresa Caponi. They had left Naples in 1893 to begin a new and better life in the United States. They were not alone. A great wave of immigrants had surged from southern and eastern Europe through Ellis Island and into the north-eastern United States at the turn of the century and settled in the slums of the great cities. The Caponis settled in New York.

Alphonse Caponi was big, sullen, and violent with a vicious temper. He possessed no noticeable intellectual gifts and left school aged 13 to work for local gangland boss Johnny Torrio. Capone was soon a member of Torrio's dreaded Five Points Gang and quickly rose to be a bouncer in Frankie Yale's bar. He also carried out a few minor contract killings on the side.

Gang warfare in New York began to get extremely vicious in the 1920s. Torrio, who'd been giving a lot of part-time help to uncle Jim Colosimo in Chicago, decided to leave the Big Apple for the Windy City permanently. Capone stayed on in New York for a while, then joined Torrio. He didn't have much time to get to know Big Jim before somebody put a bulletthrough his head.

One reason why Big Jim Colosimo had to die was his unwillingness to expand his operations. Torrio, probably

"A REAL GODDAMN CRAZY PLACE. NOBODY'S SAFE IN THE STREET."
LUCKY LUCIANO TALKING ABOUT CHICAGO

Capone: one big fish looking to land others.

one of the cleverest of all the gangsters, may have recognized the massive potential of a tantalizingly lucrative new venture looming on the horizon.

PROHIBITION

January 16, 1920, is not a date that appears in school history books, but in social history it's about as important as the dates of any war, inauguration of any

president or succession of any monarch. As the clock ticked nearer to midnight, Americans downed their last legal alcoholic drinks. As the last chime of midnight faded, the National Prohibition Act, popularly known as the Volstead Act, became law. America became dry, Prohibition began, and, like a vine on the wall of a building, gangsterism was given the chance to firmly attach itself to the brickwork of society. When Prohibition officially ended, on April 7, 1933, organized crime was firmly embedded, its tentacles having spread across and beyond the United States.

The first known violation of the Volstead Act took place in Chicago. At 12.59am six masked man broke into two freight cars and stole $100,000 worth of whiskey stamped FOR MEDICINAL USE. With Canada just over the border, Chicago enjoyed a perfect geographical location for receiving imported liquor. It had also been a centre of brewing in the United States, so there were plenty of people in the City with brewing experience. The Mayor of Chicago, "Big Bill" Thompson, positively encouraged bootlegging within his mayoral domain.

Many people thought Prohibition was a stupid law and treated it as little more than a joke. A small sector of the "business" community, who upheld the principle of supply and demand, recognized that bootlegging was a lucrative business to add to their already established businesses of prostitution, gambling and dope. Johnny Torrio was among them.

The victims of the St. Valentine's Day Massacre being removed from the garage on Clark Street.

However, against this background of bootlegging a vicious gang war was brewing. The trouble could be put down to one man, Dion O'Banion. From his florist shop, O'Banion ran the North Side. He supplied a reasonable whiskey to his customers, but in 1924 a bid for his business was made by the Sicilian Genna family who started moving their inferior but cheaper rotgut into North Side bars. O'Banion responded by hijacking Genna whiskey shipments. The Gennas wanted to kill him, but the head of the local Unione Siciliane, Mike Merlo, said no.

O'Banion then paid a call on Torrio and Capone. They all had a stake in a brewery, but O'Banion said he wanted out and was willing to sell his share for $500,000. Torrio and Capone agreed. A little later the brewery was raided by the cops and closed down. It turned out that

O'Banion had known well in advance about the raid and thus conned Torrio and Capone out of their money.

Finally, O'Banion quarrelled with Angelo Genna over a gambling debt. "Tell them Sicilians to go to Hell," said O'Banion to his trusted lieutenant Hymie Weiss. Angelo Genna went to see fellow Italians Torrio and Capone. On November 10 four men pulled up in a car outside O'Banion's shop. Angelo Genna was driving. Mike Genna and two other men, Albert Anselmi and John Scalise, went into the shop. O'Banion stepped forward to shake hands with Mike Genna and, as he did so, Anselmi and Scalise opened fire. O'Banion would henceforth be pushing up daisies instead of using them in floral tributes.

Hymie Weiss succeeded O'Banion and, with support from Irish, Jewish and Polish gangs, began to make a bid for

overall control of gangland Chicago. He tried to kill Capone, pretty nearly did kill Torrio, and, together with George "Bugs" Moran, succeeded in killing Angelo Genna (whom Frankie Yale had appointed head of the Unione Siciliane). Mike Genna fell next, along with Anselmi and Scalise, this time to the law. And Tony Genna was shot down in the street, some thought at Capone's behest.

On January 23, 1925, Johnny Torrio went shopping with his wife. On their return home, as Torrio left the car and headed for the house, two men leapt from a cruising Cadillac, each clutching an automatic. There were two shots and Torrio fell to the ground. Two more shots hit him in the arm and groin. Meanwhile, two men with sawn-off shotguns strafed Torrio's car. A gunman then stood over Torrio and levelled his automatic at the gangster's head to deliver the *coup de grâce*. He pulled the trigger. His gun was empty. He began to reload, but someone in the Cadillac hit the horn to sound a warning and the gunmen ran back to the car. Torrio valiantly crawled to his wife who managed to drag him indoors to safety.

Torrio knew the men who'd tried to kill him, but he never named them. One witness to the shooting, though, picked out a fellow named Bugs Moran as one of the would-be killers. Nine months later, after a prison sentence, Torrio announced his retirement from Chicago. He was too shrewd – and maybe didn't have the stomach – to get involved in the brutal gang warfare. Into Torrio's shoes stepped Al Capone.

In August, 1926, Capone ordered two attempts on Hymie Weiss's life which failed. Then Weiss struck back. Ten cars drove past the Hawthorne Inn, where Capone was eating, and strafed the frontage with machine-gun fire. Capone wasn't hurt, but one of his gunmen and four bystanders were injured. Their hospital bills were paid for by Capone.

On October 11, following an abortive peace plan rejected by Capone (Weiss agreed to stop the war if Anselmi and Scalise were killed, which Capone refused to order: "I wouldn't do that to a yellow dog," he said), Hymie Weiss and several companions were gunned down outside the Holy Name Cathedral.

Hymie Weiss's North Siders were now taken over by George "Bugs" Moran. He put up a $50,000 contract on Capone's life. There were several takers, though none succeeded. Meanwhile, a group of brothers, the Aiellos, stepped into the shoes left by the Gennas. By January 1929, Moran was hijacking the

trucks carrying Capone's booze, bombing Capone's bars, and killing Capone's employees. "Machine Gun" Jack McGurn, Capone's head gunman, was ambushed in a phone booth. He lived, but only just. Eventually Capone decided to put an end to Bugs's competition and summoned some killers to his palatial winter home on Palm Island, Florida.

On the morning of St. Valentine's Day, February 14, 1929, Al Capone ostentatiously made his presence known in Florida – so establishing an alibi. Meanwhile, in Chicago, Bugs Moran had received a telephone call from a man who said he'd hijacked a truckload of whiskey. Moran told him to deliver it to his warehouse at 2122 North Clark Street at 10.30am. Six members of Moran's gang went to the warehouse to receive delivery. Moran himself was late. He got to the warehouse in time to see a car draw up and two men in police uniform get out. Moran walked away.

Inside the warehouse were James

Clark, alias Albert Kashallek, Bugs's brother-in-law; Adam Heyer, alias John Snyder, the gang's accountant; John May, a safe cracker who was in charge of cars and trucks; Al Weinshank, controller of the unions in Moran's pay; and the brothers Frank and Pete Gusenberg, trigger-men who had been responsible for nearly killing "Machine Gun" Jack McGurn. With these gang members was Rheinhard Shwimmer, who liked to hang around with gangsters because it gave him a thrill.

The two men in police uniform whom Bugs had seen, along with two men in civilian clothes, went into the warehouse. There were gunshots, then the cops emerged with the other two men at gunpoint. All four got into a car and drove away. Inside the warehouse seven men lay sprawled in their own blood, dead or dying. Frank Gusenberg had 14 gunshot wounds. He lived long enough to tell the police: "Nobody shot me."

Nobody really doubted that Capone,

The Untouchables, the tight-knit group of incorruptible FBI agents who would be given the tough assignment of destroying Al Capone.

who threw a St. Valentine's Day party in Florida, had ordered the killings, but no case could be proved. Even a reward of $100,000 failed to produce information and the massacre found its way into the police "unsolved" file.

With Bugs Moran out of the way the only threat to Capone now came from the Unione Siciliane. Its head Mike Merlo, who had stopped the Gennas from killing O'Banion, died of cancer in November 1924. Frankie Yale had appointed Angelo Genna his successor, but Genna was killed by Hymie Weiss and was succeeded by gang member and professional musician Samoots Amatuna. He too was soon killed.

His successor was Capone appointee Tony "The Scourge" Lombardo. Meanwhile, Frankie Yale had been gunned down in New York, apparently by a killer who'd got his machine-gun in Chicago. Lombardo was succeeded by another Capone nominee, Joe Giunta who appointed as his vice-executives Albert Anselmi and John Scalise. "We're the big shots now," Anselmi announced.

Three months later Capone held a banquet in honour of Giunta, Anselmi

> ## "YOU'RE GOING TO JAIL, AL."
> JOHNNY TORRIO TO AL CAPONE AT THE ATLANTIC CITY MEETING

and Scalise. Everyone was supposed to be friends and left their guns outside. Food and wine flowed. Then, at a signal from Capone, his men overpowered the Sicilians and tied them up. Capone walked behind the trio with a baseball bat. Then he unleashed a vicious assault, beating them until they were unconscious, calling them traitors. A bodyguard then brought a gun and Al finished them off. It was a kind of coronation, confirming Capone as king of Chicago.

FROM JAIL TO SOUP KITCHENS

In 1929, there was a momentous event, in its own way as important historically as any war or peace pact. In Atlantic City – then under the control of Enoch "Nucky" Johnson – some of the biggest gangsters in the United States had a meeting. Lucky Luciano and others arrived from New York. Capone came from Chicago. There were mobsters from Kansas City, Philadelphia, Cleveland, Detroit... in the chair sat Johnny Torrio. The meeting was the brainchild

Capone (second from left), still smiling, even in court, but the net was closing.

of Lucky Luciano and its purpose was for the gangs to form a nationwide brotherhood, that is a National Crime Commission. The first decision was that Al Capone should go to prison because he was attracting too much attention to himself and turning both the authorities and the public against the bootleggers.

Capone laughed in disbelief at the suggestion that he go to prison, then stormed from the meeting. Two days later Al Capone was arrested on the faintly ludicrous charge of carrying a gun. He went to prison for ten months, and on his release worked hard to change his public image, setting up soup kitchens for the victims of the Depression then ravaging the States. He provided good soup, too. Someone told a news camera, "This is the finest soup I ever tasted in my life." Capone actively courted good publicity. He used Jake Lingle, a reporter on the *Chicago Tribune*, as his public relations consultant.

In return for $60,000 a year, Lingle filed story after story that made Capone look like Mother Teresa – then Lingle was found shot dead in a subway. The murder caused a sensation, largely because the press didn't like to see one of their own get hurt. Nobody knew exactly why Lingle had been hit, though it was known that he'd fallen out with Capone, had maybe even double-crossed him, and on the eve of his shooting was about to meet with federal agents.

ELLIOT NESS AND THE UNTOUCHABLES

The shooting of Jake Lingle was the last straw for new US President Herbert Hoover. He ordered J. Edgar Hoover, the ambitious young head of the FBI, to put

Alcatraz Prison. The luxury-loving Capone had a tough time in this notorious penitentiary. Attacked and abused by his fellow prisoners, he eventually fell seriously ill.

Capone behind bars, permanently.

The assault on Capone was two-pronged. The Justice Department formed a tight-knit group of incorruptible agents, known as the Untouchables, headed by a young University of Chicago graduate named Elliot Ness. Their mission was to destroy Capone's business, but the authorities knew that Ness's activities amounted to little more than an irritant to Capone. The real assault on the gangster and his empire was led by Frank Wilson of the Internal Revenue Service.

An IRS agent named Mike Malone worked his way into Capone's inner circle and made the financial secrets of the gang his business. The information he gained first brought down Ralph Capone, Al's brother, who was shown to have handled $8 million and not paid a cent in tax. He went down for three years. Next was Jake "Greasy Thumb" Guzik, Capone's treasurer, who drew five years in jail. Finally, Frank Wilson traced

Capone's bookkeeper, who agreed to give evidence in exchange for immunity from prosecution. In June 1931 Al Capone was charged on 23 counts of tax evasion. He was found guilty and sentenced to 11 years. He was first sent to Cook County jail, then to the Federal Penitentiary at Atlanta, Georgia, and in 1934 to Alcatraz in San Francisco Bay.

Capone had a tough time in prison, was given cleaning jobs, and was stabbed in the back when he refused to join a prisoners' strike. After a while his mind began to wander, and tests showed he had syphilis. The illness grew worse, eventually paralyzing him. In 1939 he was released for treatment. For seven years he lived behind the walls of his palatial Florida home, where, in 1947, he died from a stroke, aged 47.

Capone had built up a $27 million fortune, personally killed about 40 men and is thought to have ordered the deaths of a staggering 400 other victims.

JOHN DILLINGER

Historians like to give dates to things, so they reckon the Old West ended at Coffeyville, Kansas, in 1892, with the Dalton Gang shoot-out. Maybe it did. Or maybe the gunslingers and bank robbers lived on into the 1930s. Maybe the successors of Jesse James and Billy the Kid traded horses for cars and got names like Bonnie and Clyde, Pretty Boy Floyd, Al Carpis and Ma Barker, and – most famous of them all – John Dillinger.

■

JOHN DILLINGER ROBBED BANKS. The banks were unpopular and robbing them made John Dillinger a hero of the Great Depression. People said he never shot and killed anyone. That's probably not true. And when he was apparently gunned down by G-Men – federal agents – people thought he was dead. That was possibly wrong too.

John Wilson Dillinger was a grocer and landlord in the middle-class Oak Cliff district of Indianapolis. He was married – his wife's name was Molly – and he had two children. The eldest was Audrey, who was born in 1890. Thirteen years later, on June 22, 1903, their son, John Herbert, was born. Three years later Molly Dillinger died and Audrey took over the raising of young John Herbert, but she married and moved away, leaving the boy in the care of his father, a strict disciplinarian and committed Christian who was afraid of showing emotion and was generally preoccupied with work. In 1912 he married again and the following year fathered another son, Hubert. His wife, Elizabeth Fields, tried to be nice to John Herbert, but he resented her and his father.

By the age of 12, John H. Dillinger was the leader of a street gang known as the Dirty Dozen. Among their varied activities, the gang raided trucks in the railroad yards, stole coal and sold it locally. They were eventually caught, but the judge was lenient and let them off with a caution. John Dillinger was a curious teenager, given to breaking into factories and running the machinery. Anxious to leave school, which he did at the age of 16, he was nevertheless a diligent and reliable worker. His father, worried by his son's running with gangs and staying out all night, punished him fiercely, but without result, and eventually took the desperate step of taking his son from Indianapolis to live on a farm some 18 miles away, near the sleepy town of Mooresville. Dillinger went to high school, but didn't work and soon left, returning to his factory job in Indianapolis, commuting from the farm each day by motorbike.

But Dillinger was on a downward slope. By 1923 he'd lost his job, taken to hanging around pool halls and consorting with prostitutes. In July that year he stole a car so he could visit a girl. The police suspected him of the theft but couldn't prove anything so made no charge against him. Nevertheless John H. thought it best to make himself scarce. He enlisted in the United States Navy as a fireman. He soon discovered how unenjoyable life on the ocean wave

could be and went absent without leave. On his return he was given 10 days in solitary confinement. In December 1923 his ship, the *Utah*, docked in Boston. John H. left the vessel, never to return.

Back in Mooresville, he married, moved in with his in-laws and seemed to

> ## "WILL NOBODY HELP THE WIDOW'S SON?"
> GROCER B. F. MORGAN, BEATEN BY DILLINGER

settle down, even joining the town baseball team. Here, though, he met Ed Singleton (who would die in 1937 after falling asleep on a railway track), who told him that a grocer named B.F. Morgan visited the barber shop once a week and always took his day's takings with

him. Singleton and Dillinger decided to rob him. On September 6, 1924, Morgan set off for the barber shop, but stopped off at his home to leave his takings. The would-be robbers didn't know this. Dillinger, drunk, armed with a pistol and a heavy bolt wrapped in a handkerchief, suddenly confronted Morgan and hit him over the head with the bolt – the wound required 11 stitches. Morgan fell to his knees, but shouted a Masonic distress call: "Will nobody help the widow's son?" Whether or not most who heard this cry understood its meaning, it brought help. Or maybe people came running from several directions because Morgan had grabbed at Dillinger's gun and it had gone off. Even drunk, Dillinger recognized that the best course of action for a prudent man was to get the hell out of there. He fled.

On September 8 he was arrested. What happened next was a decision that shaped Dillinger's life and the lives of many other people and which started a legend. Dillinger was promised a lenient sentence if he pleaded guilty, but he refused, maintaining instead that he was innocent. Then, confronted by his father, he broke down and confessed. He was told that a lawyer would be unnecessary if he pleaded guilty and therefore acted without legal advice. His father, disgusted, left Dillinger to face his punishment alone, and the judge, far from being lenient, as promised, decided to make an example of Dillinger and sentenced him to 10 years in jail.

He was sent to Pendleton Reformatory. His wife, Beryl, tried to stay with him, but on June 20, 1929, she divorced

John Wilson Dillinger, John H.'s stern, God-fearing father.

him. Four months later Wall Street crashed, heralding the worst economic crisis in US history – businesses went bust, failing banks called in mortgages, ordinary people lost their jobs and many lost their homes.

Meanwhile, Dillinger was transferred to the Indiana State Penitentiary in Michigan City. He kept his nose clean and the authorities listened when, in 1933, some 200 citizens of Mooresville, Indiana, signed a petition requesting that John Dillinger's parole application be given an early hearing, on the grounds that his step-mother was dying. Among the names on the petition was that of B.F. Morgan, the man Dillinger had attacked. On May 22, 1933, John Dillinger walked from the Indiana State Penitentiary a free man. He had nothing but the clothes he stood up in and five dollars in his pocket. He got home too late, though – his step-mother had died.

In prison Dillinger learned a lot and made some valuable friends, among them Harry Pierpont and Homer van Meter. "Handsome" Harry Pierpont, a year older than Dillinger, was a former mental patient. Struck on the head with a baseball bat as a child, he was thereafter prone to sudden, violent rages. At the age of 19, in the process of trying to steal a car, he had been surprised by the arrival of the car's owner and shot him. Later he was involved in a bank robbery. In prison he was a hard man, able to take punishment and solitary without worry. He hated authority, and any symbol of it, with a passion bordering on obsession, and would kill without compunction. Russell Lee Clark, a friend of Pierpont's from Detroit, was a bank robber, though he had a record which included convic-

Dillinger's girlfriend, Evelyn "Billie" Frechette.

tions for crimes as varied as attempting to foment revolt and attempted murder. Other fellow inmates included John "Red" Hamilton and Charles Makley.

Dillinger's release was ideal for these friends. They were planning an escape and quickly accepted Dillinger's offer to help them from the outside – his job was to smuggle some guns into the prison.

DILLINGER STRIKES OUT

Pierpont had given Dillinger the names of some contacts and supplied a list of banks and businesses suitable for robbing. First Dillinger contacted an associate of Pierpont's called Noble Claycomb, who in turn introduced him to a teenager named William Shaw. That night the three men robbed a supermarket. It wasn't a particularly smooth operation, but nobody was caught and no suspicion fell on Dillinger.

Next, on June 10, he picked up two men recommended by Pierpont and

headed for the National Bank at New Carlisle, Ohio, which he robbed of $10,600. Back in Indianapolis, that evening he and Shaw robbed two stores, but Shaw and the driver they used, Paul "Lefty" Parker, were so amateurish that the gang was twice almost caught.

Two weeks later, Dillinger and Shaw tried something more ambitious. They attempted to steal the payroll at Marshall Field's Thread Mills in Monticello. The whole episode was a farce. They made themselves so obvious that the man taking the money to the bank, Fred Fisher, was warned and took a route different to his normal one. Dillinger and Shaw then tried to gain entry to the mill, where Fisher was counting money into wages envelopes. Shaw got in, but Fisher wrestled his gun from him and Shaw fled. As he and Dillinger drove away, Dillinger fired at Fisher, but the bullet ricocheted, hitting the mill manager in the leg, though not seriously injuring him.

The fleeing bandits hadn't mapped out an escape route and consequently found themselves on a dirt track. They drove for 50 miles, eventually finding themselves only a little over 10 miles from the scene of the attempted robbery. Two attempts to salvage the day proved disastrous: one planned robbery wasn't possible because the recession-hit business had closed down; the other netted a meagre $175. Someone also threw a milk bottle at them.

John Dillinger committed a series of robberies over the next three or four weeks – no fewer than 10 banks in five states. Meanwhile, Claycomb and Shaw had been arrested. On July 17, Dillinger went with two others to the Commercial Bank in Daleville. It was lunchtime and Margaret Good was the teller, the cashier being out for his midday meal. Dillinger asked to see the bank president, but was told he wasn't there. "Well, honey," said Dillinger, "this is a hold-up". Margaret Good found herself staring down the barrel of a gun. Dillinger gracefully leapt over a six-foot counter, in the manner of his screen hero, Douglas Fairbanks, and set the seal on his fame. He became known as "the Leaping Bandit", also as "Desperate Dan".

Dillinger had been an industrious robber and, true to his word, had invested his share of the proceeds from the robberies in guns. These he managed to smuggle into the Indiana State Penitentiary. Ten of his friends – including Pierpont, Makley, "Red" Hamilton, Clark, and two other men, Jenkins and Shouse – shot their way out. Meanwhile, ironically, Dillinger found himself arrested and on his way back to prison. He was held in Lima, Ohio.

When Pierpont, Makley and Clark heard that Dillinger was back in prison they determined to effect his release.

They went to Lima and, posing as police officers, asked to see Dillinger. Sheriff Jess Sarber became suspicious and asked to see their credentials. "Here they are," said Pierpont, unworried and smiling. Sarber saw Pierpont's gun, and maybe even heard the explosion as Pierpont pulled the trigger. Sheriff Sarber did not die immediately, but suffered further violent abuse and pistol-whipping from Pierpont and Makley as they demanded the keys to the cells. Sheriff Sarber's wife, horrified at what was being done to her husband, pleaded with the gangsters to stop while she got the keys. They unlocked Dillinger's cell. "What kept you?" he asked casually.

Pierpont, Makley, Clark and "Red" Hamilton formed the nucleus of the Dillinger gang, though to call them the Dillinger gang is an error. Pierpont was the leader, though even this has been questioned, some authorities maintaining that the gang didn't have a leader, each member instead contributing his own area of expertise. Their first raids were on police gun-rooms in Auburn and Peru, towns in Indiana. Then they hit a lucrative target, robbing the American Bank and Trust Company in Racine, Wisconsin. The haul was $27,000.

Joined by Dillinger's girlfriend, Evelyn "Billie" Frechette, and Pierpont's, Mary Kinder, the gang made for East Chicago, Indiana, where Dillinger and "Red" Hamilton robbed the First National Bank. They were scooping $20,000 into bags when the police arrived. Grabbing hostages to use as shields, the robbers made a dash for their car. One of the hostages managed to jump aside, however, and Patrolman William Patrick O'Malley fired four shots at Dillinger.

The exploits of Dillinger exemplified, to the authorities, the crime wave sweeping the mid-West and threatening to engulf the whole nation.

According to some sources, Dillinger shouted, "You asked for it!" and shot the policeman dead. Others say he fired at O'Malley's legs and that O'Malley fell into the line of fire. Either way, Dillinger had shot his first man. Or had he? Dillinger maintained he'd been in Florida when the robbery happened and Mary Kinder supported the story until her death, maintaining that Dillinger heard of the robbery over the radio while he was in Daytona Beach. Dillinger even swore to his family that he was not involved in the hold-up. On the other hand, a great many witnesses positively identified Dillinger, and some of the money from the robbery was found in his possession.

The gang criss-crossed the mid-Western states and committed a series of robberies. These were the Depression years and people were disillusioned, many having lost everything they possessed. The banks charged huge interest rates and most people knew at least one family who had been turned out of their homes when the banks foreclosed on

"WHAT KEPT YOU?"

JOHN DILLINGER TO PIERPONT, MAKLEY AND CLARK, AFTER THEY HAD POSED AS POLICE OFFICERS TO SECURE HIS RELEASE FROM LIMA PRISON

loans. The banks symbolized the rich, symbolized an authority which had failed the people. Most people then, as now, were too afraid to step outside the law, but they admired the men who did, the men who refused to be ground down and who fought back. John Dillinger, athletic and looking like popular movie star Humphrey Bogart, became a hero. President Roosevelt, apparently horrified by the widespread public support for Dillinger, announced that the bank robber would be caught. The swathe of hits by the Dillinger gang and others "can be stopped," said the President, "and it will be stopped."

In January 1934 the Dillinger gang were staying at the Congress Hotel. There was a fire and firemen were tipped $12 to rescue a special trunk – which contained a small armoury of guns and ammunition. The tip was extremely generous and the firemen remembered their benefactors. Later they saw pictures of the gang and recognized them. A local posse then went after the gang and, remarkably, caught them.

The events that followed were extraordinary. Every state in which Dillinger and his gang had committed a crime was anxious to get hold of them. Some exciting legal battles loomed on the horizon, but Indiana moved like lightning and, before a writ of habeas corpus could be granted to keep the gang in Arizona, Indiana's lawyers had laid on an aircraft to get Dillinger securely back there to be tried for murder. He became one of the first prisoners to be transported by air. To this day prisoners in the United States are routinely moved by rail or road.

Even Dillinger must have been surprised by his reception in Chicago. A convoy of 13 police cars and 12 motorcycle outriders – a total of 85 policemen! – met him at the airport and thousands of people lined the streets in the hope of catching a glimpse of the notorious bank robber. A judge had refused to sign

A 40-man FBI hit squad was formed to "get" John Dillinger.

papers authorizing Dillinger to be taken to Michigan City Penitentiary. Instead he was taken across the state line to Crown Point Jail, Indiana, where Lillian Holley, the lady sheriff, was waiting. Lillian Holley was completing the term of office for her late husband, a sheriff who had been murdered. She – along with prosecuting attorney Robert Estill – was excited to be involved in looking after the nation's most celebrated criminal and they willingly posed for photographs with him. "There are eight locked doors between Dillinger and freedom," she said, and posted a small army of shotgun-toting deputies in the grounds in case he did indeed make it that far.

And yet Dillinger did escape. Later he said he had fashioned a replica gun out of wood, colouring it with boot polish. Others say he got his lawyer, Louis Piquett, to bribe a corrupt judge to smuggle him a gun. However he managed it, he obtained a gun and at 8.30am on March 3, 1934, Dillinger stuck it in the ribs of a guard and allowed himself to be escorted from the building, collecting some machine guns from a locked closet and releasing a fellow prisoner en route. With the guard as hostage, Dillinger and his fellow con walked out through a side entrance, through the prison garage to freedom. They took a leisurely stroll down a side alley and into a garage next door to the prison. A man named Ed Saager was in charge of the garage and, after being forced to hand over the keys to a car, he joined the guard as a hostage and was driven quietly out of town.

Amazingly, a mailman named Robert Volk had watched the escape take place and telephoned the police. He wasn't believed. Then he ran to the Criminal

America's most wanted man, John Dillinger, is finally caught, but by a local police posse, not Hoover's famed FBI.

Court building and told a guard there, but the guard didn't believe him either. In desperation, Volk went to the prison and rang the doorbell. He told somebody that Dillinger had escaped, and wasn't believed... until somebody took the trouble to check his cell. During the drive out of town, Dillinger sang "I'm heading for the last round-up".

Meanwhile, Pierpont, Clark and Makley were being extradited to Ohio to face trial for the murder of Sheriff Sarber, whom they'd killed when they'd sprung Dillinger from Lima Jail. They were taken by train and met in Ohio by armed guards then taken to prison. Extra guards were mounted. Policemen were assigned to protect the prison governor in case Dillinger kidnapped him and used him to force the gang's release.

But Dillinger couldn't do anything to help his former mates. The gang were tried. Pierpont was sentenced to death

and died in the electric chair; Makley, who was also sentenced to death, was shot during a prison break; Clark was sentenced to life imprisonment.

Dillinger was alone. Also, he had made a powerful, new enemy. He'd driven a stolen car across a state line. This was a federal offence and it brought Dillinger up against the FBI.

FBI

The FBI – Federal Bureau of Investigation – an agency of the US Department of Justice, began life in 1908, when it was called the Bureau of Investigation. It later became the Division of Investigation and acquired the title Federal Bureau of Investigation in 1935. The FBI was created to investigate crimes related to national security, such as espionage and subversion. Today it has jurisdiction in more than 180 areas, including organized crime, terrorism, drug trafficking,

Cool customer – Dillinger posing with a Colt .38 and a submachine gun.

kidnapping, and so on. However, it does not have and never has had jurisdiction when it comes to activities like counterfeiting that violate financial laws; such crimes are investigated by agents of the Treasury Department – the men who eventually put away Al Capone. Violations of the postal laws are the jurisdiction of the US Postal Service, whose agents were responsible for much of the evidence that put away Public Enemy Number One, Alvin Carpis.

By the 1930s the FBI was headed by John Edgar Hoover. He had joined the US Department of Justice in 1917, the same year as he was admitted to the bar. Born in Washington, DC, on January 1, 1895, and a student of law at George Washington University, in 1919 he was appointed a special assistant to the US Attorney General and in 1924 became head of the Justice Department's Bureau of Investigation. His title was changed to Director when the Bureau became the Federal Bureau in 1935. He was never far from controversy, often being accused of exceeding his jurisdiction. He died on May 1, 1972, in Washington, DC. It was Hoover who nominated John Dillinger Public Enemy Number One and authorized the formation of a special 40-man team to "get" John Dillinger. It was put under the leadership of agent Melvin Purvis.

Born in 1903 in South Carolina, the boyish-faced Purvis won the hot-seat job as head of the FBI's Chicago office in 1927. He resigned in July 1935, apparently because of friction with Hoover, and lent his name to an advertising deal with Post Toasties, a breakfast cereal that sponsored the "Melvin Purvis Junior G-Men". A semi-send-up movie about him was made in 1974, called *Melvin Purvis: G-Man*, which starred Dale Robertson in the title role. A movie well worth watching, it spawned a sequel, *The Kansas City Massacre*, which broadened Purvis's story to have the lawman pitting his wits against other baddies from the Public Enemy era: Pretty Boy Floyd, John Dillinger, Baby Face Nelson, and Alvin Carpis. Melvin Purvis committed suicide in 1960.

Dillinger formed a new gang after his escape in March 1934. This set-up included a very nasty character named Lester Gillis. He had tried to give himself an imposing nickname, calling himself Big George Nelson. His youthful face resulted instead in the unflattering tag of Baby Face Nelson. He was a nasty piece of work who liked killing people just for the fun of it. Nelson's approach to robbing banks was crude in the extreme. Dillinger would walk in, politely tell everyone to raise their hands, then go through the rigmarole of asking for the safe to be unlocked and so on, all the time having to watch that the hands stayed raised. Nelson, by contrast, thought it more expedient to enter a bank firing a Tommy gun, kill everyone in sight, take the money and run.

The new Dillinger gang embarked on a fresh spree of bank-robbing. The first robbery was at Sioux Falls, South Dakota, where Baby Face Nelson killed an off-duty policeman. There followed raids in Mason City, Iowa, where $34,000 was netted; in Minneapolis, where the gang escaped a police trap; in Carthage, Illinois; and Mankato, Minnesota. Dillinger then settled down in St. Paul, in an apartment rented with "Billie" Frechette. Unfortunately, Dillinger had a face people recognized and neighbours soon became suspicious. They called the FBI, who then paid a call on Dillinger. In the

"THERE ARE EIGHT LOCKED DOORS BETWEEN DILLINGER AND FREEDOM."
SHERIFF HOLLEY, PRIOR TO DILLINGER'S ESCAPE FROM CROWN POINT JAIL

Dillinger behind bars - but not for long. On March 3, 1934, he made a daring escape from Crown Point Jail.

ensuing showdown, Dillinger was shot in the leg, but still managed to escape.

THE LAST ROUNDUP

On April 5, 1934, he returned to Mooresville, where he made up with his father, introduced "Billie" Frechette as his future wife, and enjoyed a Sunday lunch. The FBI were watching the farm, but evidently not very well. They were wholly unaware he was there. His father later denied that Dillinger had been expected and that a party had been held in his honour. He also expressed his belief that Dillinger had been credited with much he hadn't done and said, "I think if he's given a chance he would go straight."

On April 13, Dillinger, with long-time colleague Homer van Meter, drove north. They'd lost their cache of arms in St. Paul and were now desperate to replace them. In Warsaw, Indiana, they discovered that the police station armoury had only one man on duty. It seemed an ideal opportunity. Their raid, though, was witnessed by a local fireman, who later told reporters that he was not allowed to leave his post and therefore had no alternative but to watch Dillinger and van Meter break in. On duty the two robbers

Dillinger in court in Indiana, his attorney, Joseph Ryan, on one side and Sheriff Holley, to whom he is manacled, on the other.

found Officer Pettinger. At first he refused to hand over the keys, so Dillinger attempted to take them from him. Van Meter had a gun and wanted to shoot Pettinger, but couldn't for fear of hitting Dillinger. In the end, after a violent struggle, van Meter managed to bludgeon the stubborn policeman over the head several times with his gun.

The gang now decided to have a holiday. With some women in tow, they went to the isolated Little Bohemia Lodge, on the banks of Little Star Lake, near Mercer in Wisconsin. Dillinger,

"Red" Hamilton and friends stayed in the main building, while Baby Face Nelson, van Meter and wives were settled in a cabin at the lakeside.

The lodge was owned by Emil Wanatka, who soon guessed the identity of his guests and got a message out to the FBI. Agents quickly descended on the lodge and surrounded it, but guard dogs alerted those inside to the presence of strangers. The FBI opened fire too quickly. They shattered the lodge's windows and wounded innocent guests and staff. Nelson killed an FBI agent, Carter

Baum. Though the gang had to leave their cars, guns and women behind, they managed to escape, stealing a car from a Mr. and Mrs. Lang who lived nearby.

The FBI operation was a fiasco – like a good many conducted by the FBI; when dozens of agents, led by J. Edgar Hoover himself, arrested Alvin Carpis they discovered nobody had thought to bring any handcuffs. Hoover was not a happy man and more determined than ever to put John Dillinger out of business, permanently.

John Dillinger's last heist took place

on June 30, 1934, eight days after his 31st birthday, at South Bend, Indiana. He robbed the Merchants' National Bank. The robbery cost a traffic policeman his life and six bystanders were wounded. Van Meter also took a bullet, but survived – he'd die later in another shootout. And for all this the take was a miserable $24,000. This wasn't enough for Dillinger, who now realized that his face was as well-known as a movie star's and that he couldn't go anywhere without being recognized. Even plastic surgery hadn't helped. He knew his future lay in South America, but for that he needed lots of money.

Dillinger disappeared after the bank raid. In Chicago a man named Jimmie Lawrence began dating a waitress and part-time prostitute named Polly Hamilton. Sometimes Polly worked for a madame named Anna Sage. Sage, an illegal immigrant, recognized Jimmie Lawrence as John Dillinger and paid a call on the police. She was put in touch with the FBI and apparently did a deal. Lawrence, Polly Hamilton and Anna Sage had planned to go to the Biograph Cinema. Anna Sage said she'd wear something bright so the FBI agents outside could recognize her – good as her word, she wore a bright red dress. In return she wanted to stay in the US and not be returned to Romania, her home country. In the event she was deported, given only $5,000 reward money, and died in Timisoara in 1947.

What happened that night has been the subject of lasting controversy which shows no signs of being resolved. According to a contemporary newsreel, Dillinger/Lawrence came out of the cinema. Maybe sensing that something was wrong, he drew or attempted to draw his gun. An FBI agent fired, hitting him in the face. The robber nevertheless managed to run into an alley, but he was shot twice more and fell. Rushed to hospital, he was dead on arrival. In his pocket the investigators said they found a watch containing a photograph of Billie Frechette. The body was put in a wicker basket and, watched by a crowd of 5,000 people, it was taken for burial in Crown Point Cemetery.

But was it John Dillinger? The photograph in the watch wasn't of Billie Frechette but of Polly Hamilton. The dead man had brown eyes; Dillinger's were blue. The dead man wasn't marked by scars; Dillinger was. The dead man's heart showed that he'd had rheumatic fever, a disease from which Dillinger had never suffered. The dead man wore prescription glasses, Dillinger never wore glasses in his life.

Many people think that these anomalies point to the fact that Dillinger escaped and lived out his life in Los Angeles. We shall probably never find out what really happened to him.

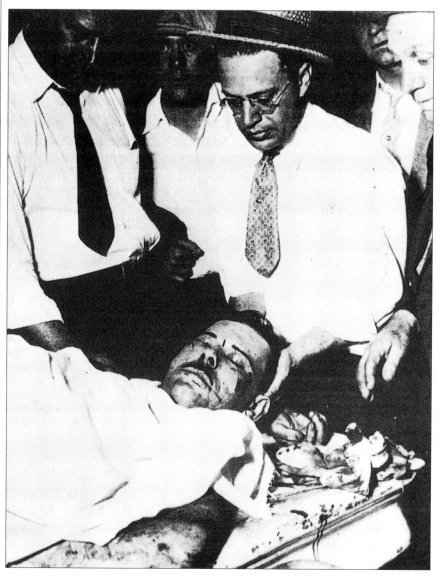

A sight for J. Edgar Hoover's sore eyes: Dillinger dead. But was he?

LUCKY
LUCIANO

Forget John Dillinger. Forget Al Capone and his

operation in Chicago. They pale in comparison to

the **capo de tutti capi**, *the boss of all the bosses,*

the most powerful man in the American Mafia.

This man was Salvatore Lucania – known in the

States as Charles "Lucky" Luciano.

Lucky Luciano was instrumental in creating "The

Mob", by bringing together gangsters from around

the States and forging links based on common

interests. Luciano's legacy is with us today.

■

THE MAFIA HAD BEGUN in New York in the 1880s. It was not, as widely and commonly believed, the successor to a group of cheap extortionists known as the Black Hand, but grew out of it and several other groups and organizations such as the Unione Siciliane, plus the numerous street gangs that grew up in New York and other cities. Simply, these gangs, later called themselves a "family". One of the main families was the Morellos, the last leader of which – Peter Morello – died in the late 1920s. One of the other leaders was Ignazio "the Wolf" Saietta, noted for torturing and murdering his enemies. He is one of the few Mafia bosses to retire, open a legitimate business and die a natural death, which he did in 1944. And then there was Johnny Torrio, the bridge between the old Mafia and the new, the latter being represented by Lucky Luciano and Al Capone.

In February, 1942, just 60 days after the United States had entered World War II, the French liner *Normandie* sailed into New York harbour to be fitted out as a troop ship. Suddenly there was an explosion and the *Normandie* was engulfed in flames. Within hours the magnificent ship, pride of the French passenger fleet, winner of the blue riband, was a burnt-out hulk.

The chiefs of naval intelligence believed the destruction of the *Normandie* to be the work of Nazi agents, who must have infiltrated the harbour. The harbour authorities were approached to work out a plan to prevent it happening again, but they reluctantly confessed that the waterfront was really controlled by the Mafia. Nothing could happen in the docks without their agreement.

Swallowing their pride, naval intelligence turned to Joe "Socks" Lanza, the notorious boss of the Fulton Fish Market, which supplied New York with seafood. Lanza, who retained control of the fish market until the 1960s, had to admit that his empire did not extend to the docks. That was the domain of another boss. Whatever went on in the docks, he told them, was controlled by a tough hombre named Luciano.

Luciano was in prison, doing 30 to 50 years in the notorious Sing Sing for extortion and running prostitution. So a few weeks later the US government authorities met with Luciano and racketeers Frank Costello and Meyer

Lansky to see if Luciano would be a sport and see if he could make sure no more Nazi agents destroyed ships needed for the United States' war effort. Luciano

> ## "I DON'T KNOW WHERE, WHAT, NOTHING. I'M PALS WITH EVERYBODY."
> LUCIANO AFTER BEING ALMOST MURDERED BY JACK DIAMOND'S GANG

was doubtful and reluctant at first, but came round to the authorities' way of thinking and a deal was struck. Luciano would protect ships in the docks; the United States government would release

him from prison at the end of the war. True to his word, Luciano protected the docks and there was no more sabotage.

Born on November 24, 1897, in a village in the hills overlooking Palermo, Italy, Salvatore Lucania was the third of Antonio and Rosalie Lucania's five children. The Lucania family left Italy in 1906, as part of the vast migration of Italians and Jews who hoped to start a new life in the United States. With hundreds of other immigrant families they settled on New York's Lower East Side, where the streets were ruled by gangs.

Salvatore – now known as Charles – joined them and did a few jobs for older

Frank Costello who, under Luciano's "restructuring" of the Mob, was supremo of the gambling end of the operation.

criminals. By the age of 14 he knew how to handle guns as well as his fists, was taking opium, and running a protection racket over kids at school (a place he rarely visited personally). He'd also received a beating from his father and taken to sleeping rough.

The streets of this area of New York, known as Little Italy, were effectively ruled by two men, Giuseppe "Joe the Boss" Masseria and the Jewish mobster Monk Eastman. Lucania, or Luciano as we'd better start calling him, began working for Masseria. He was employed as a hit man and carried out maybe as many as 20 killings. In these early days he met Frank Costello, Joe Adonis, Vito Genovese, and Meyer Lansky. Later he would join the Five Points Gang as a full member together with Al Capone, Frankie Yale and Johnny Torrio.

Luciano had his own gang and, like many gangsters before and since, launched his business career by running a protection racket. He specialized in protecting New York brothels from being smashed up by members of his gang and so began taking over the brothels. Eventually he controlled five thousand women. He also entered the lucrative business of drug smuggling. By this time America was in the grip of Prohibition and Luciano became involved with both Italian and Jewish bootleggers.

A prominent man, his empire was the envy of other gangsters, among them a rogue named Jack "Legs" Diamond. In 1919 Luciano was kidnapped by Diamond's gang. He was beaten up, knifed, and dumped on the street bleeding profusely. By some miracle he survived. Questioned later by the police, Luciano said: "I don't know where, what, nothing. I'm pals with everybody.'

Throughout the Roaring Twenties, when women got the vote, raised their skirts and drank in speakeasies, Luciano's career moved along very pleasantly. He was earning an estimated $800,000 a year and lived in a suite in the lush Barbizon Plaza Hotel. Later he moved into the newly-built Waldorf-Astoria. By 1931 Lucky Luciano was the trusted right-hand man of "Joe the Boss" Masseria. Indeed, it has been said that Masseria thought of Luciano as a son. However, in April, 1931, Luciano had Masseria killed.

On April 15, 1931, Masseria was dining at the Villa Tammaro Restaurant on Coney Island with Luciano and Vito Genovese. By the middle of the afternoon Masseria and Luciano were alone in the restaurant, Genovese having left to attend to some business. When Luciano went to the lavatory, a black sedan pulled up outside. Out got Genovese, Joe Adonis, Albert Anastasia and Bugsy Siegel. Between them they fired 20 bullets into Masseria. He died – quickly. Luciano returned to the restaurant and called the police. He knew nothing, had seen nothing and heard nothing.

The king is dead. Long live the king. Masseria's successor as king of the New York Mafia was Salvatore Maranzano, who'd been with the Italian Mafia before coming to the United States in the 1920s. With the killing of Masseria, Luciano rose to be Maranzano's right-hand man.

Maranzano's contribution to Mafia history was that he devised the set-up of families which has, with modifications, lasted to the present. He set himself up as the leader, a sort of latter-day Julius Caesar – whom, it was said, Maranzano greatly admired – of his own Roman Empire; below him were families, each family having a boss; below the boss there would be a lieutenant; below the lieutenant a district leader; and below the

New York mayor Jimmy Walker was in the pay of Luciano, as was his chief of police, Grover Warren.

Luciano survived a savage assault by the "Legs" Diamond gang.

district leader came the troops who were grouped into tens (a *capo* regime).

He was a distrustful man, though, and soon became suspicious of some of his associates. According to Joe Valachi – Maranzano planned to eliminate Al Capone, Frank Costello, Luciano, Vito Genovese, Joe Adonis, Dutch Schultz, and a few others. He brought in Vince "Mad Dog" Coll to remove Luciano and Genovese, but they discovered the plan and asked Meyer Lansky to provide a couple of gunmen. In his office near Grand Central Station, Maranzano was shot four times and stabbed six times, then his throat was cut. He didn't live. Now Charles "Lucky" Luciano was the boss of bosses, the *capo de tutti capi*.

WHO CONTROLLED WHAT?

To call Luciano *capo de tutti capi* is a slight misnomer. Luciano and his cohorts were the new breed of gangsters. Men like Masseria and Maranzano were old-fashioned, mentally still stuck in the sun-dried hill villages of Sicily. They were rigidly bigoted. They didn't allow mainland Italians into their gangs; they certainly didn't allow non-Italians into the gangs; and they were averse even to doing business with the Irish and Jewish gangs. This rigid attitude led to warfare – and, as men like Luciano and Genovese realized, to a loss of business.

Luciano restructured the Mob and, in so doing, laid down the foundations for modern organized crime. Rather than being boss of all the bosses, Luciano saw himself as a chairman of the board. He also held on to prostitution and drugs. The garment industry and the unions were given to Louis "Lepke" Buchalter. Gambling went to Frank Costello. Liquor was given to Dutch Schultz. Albert Anastasia got the docks and Murder Incorporated (the heavy mob run by Abe "Kid Twist" Reles). Meyer Lansky was the banker, responsible for laundering their vast incomes, and also ran the gambling concessions of Florida and the Bahamas. Gambling in California and Nevada went to Meyer's partner, "Bugsy" Siegel.

The Mafia also moved into politics. Luciano didn't go to the trouble of nominating himself for Mayor of New York or Commissioner of Police, then having to go through the tedious process of election. He simply bought the politicians he needed. The Democratic Club, Tamany Hall, became synonymous with corruption. Mayor Jimmy Walker took Mafia money. So did Police Chief Grover Warren. Soon it was clear even to the most ill-informed man in the street that the gangs governed. However by 1933 an anti-Mob campaign was sufficiently effective to get Fiorella LaGuardia elected as mayor.

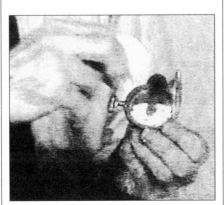

Luciano took total control of drugs and prostitution.

Honest Mayor LaGuardia declared war on the Mob, seizing their weapons.

Beer baron Dutch Schultz pays the price of disobeying a majority decision.

LaGuardia moved against the gangs almost immediately by confiscating and smashing gaming machines. He also sought to seize illicit arms which resulted in a huge cache being dumped in New York harbour. But LaGuardia's chief aim was to crush the gangs and the main weapon in his armoury was Thomas Edmund Dewey.

Dewey was born in Owosso, Michigan, in 1902, and, after an education at the University of Michigan and Colum-bia University, by 1933 was serving as an attorney for the southern district of New York. The following year he became special assistant to Attorney General Homer Cummings, and in 1935 got the job of busting the Mob in New York. He'd later go on to become district attorney of New York County (Manhattan), governor of New York State, and twice a Republican presidential candidate (he was defeated first by Roosevelt, then by Truman).

Dutch Schultz was Dewey's first target and he was soon brought to trial in Albany, New York, for bootlegging and income tax evasion. A mass of evidence against Schultz was accumulated and presented to the court, but the jury – who had been intimidated by the Mob – found Schultz innocent. It cannot be said that Dewey left the courtroom a happy man. In fact, he was very angry and, perhaps rashly, announced that he was going to get "the Dutchman" for murder.

Schultz was just a little alarmed by this and, at a meeting of the syndicate, he demanded that Dewey be killed. Luciano vetoed the killing and Schultz stormed out, saying he'd kill Dewey with or without permission. This declaration was dangerous for the Organization. They couldn't allow one of their own to disobey the majority decision and they couldn't allow Dewey to be killed and maybe have the whole US legal machine brought down on their heads. From the moment he left that meeting, Schultz was booked for a hearse and a burial suite.

The job was assigned to Charlie "the Bug" Workman, one of Luciano's bodyguards. On October 23, 1935, Schultz and three of his men were shot in the Palace Chophouse at Newark, New Jersey. Schultz clung to life for a day. He never said who'd killed him.

With Schultz out of the way, Dewey turned his eyes towards Luciano, who, with a string of racehorses and netting more than $1 million a year, was looking more like a tycoon businessman than a gangster. His up-market air was just that, though – once he opened his mouth, Luciano revealed his Lower East Side origins. Nevertheless, he was safely ensconced in his Waldorf-Astoria suite, leaving it only to make untapped phone calls and to wine and dine his mistress, Gay Orlova. Russian-born, Gay Orlova eventually married a theatre usher, but remained an undesirable in the United States. In 1937 she went to Europe and on returning to the United States found she was *persona non grata* in the eyes of immigration officials.

One thing about being a gangster is that you make enemies. Gangsters make so many enemies they forget a lot of them. However, time and again these forgotten enemies turn out to be the ones to bring down even the biggest gangster. So it was with Luciano. Dewey's agents talked to employees and ex-employees of Luciano, many of whom talked back. Soon, enough evidence was amassed, especially from veteran prostitutes, to have a grand jury indict Luciano on 99 counts of running a vice business.

Luciano had tried to avoid Dewey by moving his operations to Arkansas. Getting Luciano extradited from Arkansas proved to be a tough battle, but Dewey eventually won and Luciano was brought back to New York, where, in May, 1936, he found himself addressed as Charles Lucania in a New York court before Judge Philip J. McCook. Dewey personally prosecuted.

The case against Luciano was weak, though Dewey very effectively showed that Luciano was a mobster. There was one amusing exchange during the trial. Luciano was pressed into admitting that he carried in his car two pistols, one shotgun and 45 rounds of ammunition. He was asked why he carried this small armoury in his car. "To shoot birds with," he replied. "What kind of birds?" asked Dewey. "Peasants," said Luciano.

Dewey's case may have been weak, but the jury found Luciano guilty and he was sent down for 30 to 50 years. This was the heaviest jail sentence ever given for vice offences. Luciano holidayed briefly at Sing Sing, where he was diag-

ONE THING ABOUT BEING A GANGSTER IS THAT YOU MAKE ENEMIES — SO MANY YOU FORGET THEM.

nosed as syphilitic and a drug addict, before being moved to Dannemora on the Canadian border. Convicts called Dannemora "Siberia".

Dewey then turned his attention to Vito Genovese. Born in 1897, he was a killer without any compunction – in 1932 he had cheerfully shot dead the husband of a woman he'd fallen in love with. With Luciano out of the way, Genovese tried to take his place. But he found the hot seat a little too hot and thought it prudent to get out of the kitchen. He went to Italy.

THE CANARY THAT SANG BUT COULDN'T FLY

Next in the sights of Dewey's gun was Louis "Lepke" Buchalter, boss of the New York garment industry and the unions. This time Dewey had the good fortune to find an insider who was willing to talk. The canary, to use the argot of gangland, was Abe "Kid Twist" Reles, general of Murder Incorporated. His evidence solved 59 gangland killings and led to Buchalter taking a one-way trip to the electric chair.

Buchalter wasn't really important to the Mob, but it was known that Reles could have given evidence against bigger fish like Albert Anastasia and Bugsy

Luciano is brought back to New York from Arkansas to face trial.

Siegel. Luciano, who continued to run his rackets from prison, wanted Reles to be silenced. Reles, though, was under police protection at the Half Moon Hotel at Coney Island. Even with six cops to look after him, Reles could not be prevented from finding his way out of his sixth-floor bedroom window and plunging to his death. Later, Frank Costello explained that $50,000 had been paid to the guards to lend Buchalter a hand with his flying lesson. Among those who received a payment was William O'Dwyer, then the District Attorney for Brooklyn and later to become Mayor of New York. In gangland Reles was described as "the canary that sang but couldn't fly".

That was in 1941. The following year America entered World War II and there was the *Normandie* incident in which

Luciano did his deal with the naval authorities. He went even further by contacting the Mafia in Sicily and asking them to help the invading Americans. In later years Luciano claimed that his men

LUCIANO WAS ASKED WHY HE CARRIED A SMALL ARMOURY IN HIS CAR. "TO SHOOT BIRDS WITH," HE REPLIED. "WHAT KIND OF BIRDS?" ASKED DEWEY. "PEASANTS," SAID LUCIANO.

had started the *Normandie* fire. It was all a scam to obtain his release. Scam or not, Luciano didn't get exactly everything he'd wanted. He was released from prison, but he was also deported from the United States.

Throughout his time in prison and later, when forced to live in Italy, Luciano retained control of the National Crime Syndicate and received his share of the proceeds. By 1946, however, Vito Genovese had returned to the United States and was bidding to topple Luciano and seize his crown.

In that year Luciano went to Cuba. Meyer Lansky had been running the casinos in Cuba for Batista, the one-time chief of staff of the Cuban army and for a long time the effective, if not elected, ruler. In 1940 he was elected president and governed for four years. Later, when out of office, he staged a coup, became president and suspended the constitution. He ran a corrupt government that was overthrown on January 1, 1959, by Fidel Castro. But back in 1946 Cuba welcomed the Mob. Luciano held a meeting to beat off Genovese, but also to decide what to do about Bugsy Siegel.

Siegel had been building a city in the desert – Las Vegas. In south-eastern Nevada, Las Vegas – which means "the meadows" and was so named by early Spanish explorers who saw grassland there – was first settled in the 1850s by Mormons. The US Army later built a fort there, Fort Baker, to protect the route through to California and the city began to grow following the arrival of the railroad in 1905. There wasn't a community to speak of until the 1930s. Siegel was in some ways the shaper of Las Vegas. Using the Mob's money, Siegel had transformed sleepy Las Vegas into the gambling capital of the United States.

The reluctant tourist: Luciano was deported to Italy after his release from jail.

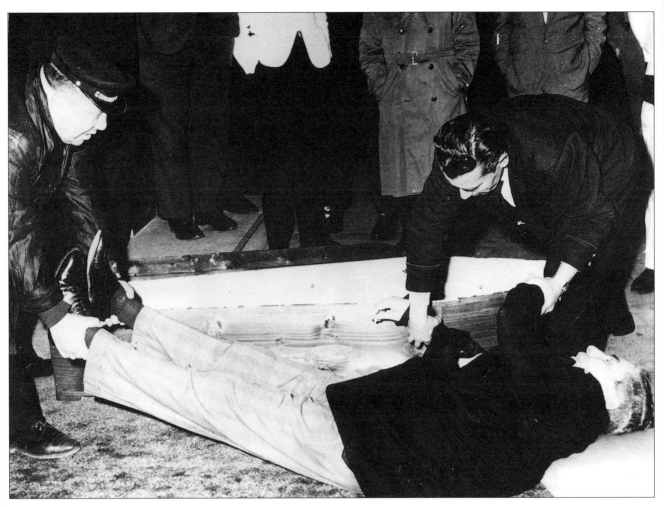

Unlucky at last, claimed by a heart attack at Naples Airport in January 1962.

The trouble with Siegel was his tardiness in repaying the five million dollars he owed the Syndicate for the massive building programme. When Luciano had demanded the money Siegel's reply had been uncompromising and to the point: he'd pay when he was "damned good and ready". He should have known better than to treat Luciano with such contempt. A few months later he was visiting the home of his girlfriend, Virginia Hill, when bullets slammed through the windows. Bugsy had a nice funeral.

The FBI meanwhile learned of Luciano's presence in Cuba and put pressure on Batista to deport him. Luciano tried to get into Brazil and Venezuela, but neither country would accept him. Then he went back to Italy. There he concentrated on creating a drug-smuggling route from the Middle East through Italy to the United States. (The network he set up survives today.) The Italian government tried repeatedly to close down Luciano's operation. First they threw him out of Rome and he was forced to live in Naples; then they banned him from travelling more than 16 miles from Naples. In 1955 he was placed under curfew and had to stay in his house between dusk and dawn.

He opened a couple of legitimate businesses, was well supplied with money by his friends, and lived a comfortable existence with his girlfriend, Igea Lissoni. He matured into a bespectacled, well-groomed man whom you might have mistaken for a regular, law-abiding citizen. His eyes, though, gave him away, for they never lost the impersonal stare of the violent Lower East Side thug.

On January 26, 1962, Lucky Luciano was at Naples Airport. He was working on a projected film of his life and had gone to meet the scriptwriter. Suddenly his features contorted and he collapsed to the ground. He had suffered a fatal heart attack. His body was returned to the United States and buried in his family vault in Queens, New York City.

THE
LINDBERGH
KIDNAPPING

Until the moment he "fried", Bruno Richard Hauptmann protested his innocence of the crimes with which he was charged – the kidnapping and murder, in 1932, of the baby son of America's national hero, aviator Charles Lindbergh. Hauptmann was sent to the electric chair four years later, but from that day until this there have been those who have seen his trial as an insult to the American judicial system – who are convinced he was executed for a crime he did not commit.

■

N **1919** A **PHILANTHROPIST** named Raymond B. Orteig had offered a prize of $25,000 to the first person to complete a solo, non-stop Atlantic crossing between New York and Paris. In 1927 Charles Augustus Lindbergh decided to make the attempt. Born on February 4, 1902, in Detroit, he'd attended the University of Wisconsin, but left after two years and joined a flying school in Lincoln, Nebraska. He'd learned to fly and got a job flying mail between Saint Louis, Missouri, and Chicago. Lindbergh left Roosevelt Field at 7.52am on May 20, 1927, in his single-engine monoplane, Spirit of St. Louis. He landed at Le Bourget Airport near Paris after a flight of 33 hours 32 minutes and walked into the history books. He became a hero in both Europe and America.

Bruno Richard Hauptmann was born in Kamenz, a small town in Germany. As he was too young to enlist in the German army until the latter part of the Great War of 1914–1918, he escaped the very worst of the fighting. When he was discharged in 1919, he found a humbled, wrecked Germany in which crime was common and often a necessity. With a partner he committed a series of serious offences, was caught and sentenced to five years in prison.

Hauptmann then made two illegal attempts to enter the United States, but he was caught both times and deported. Desperate to flee Germany and start a new life, he made a third attempt in 1924. This time he was successful and in the same year he met a fellow German, Anna Schoeffler, whom he married.

An apparently industrious and capable carpenter, Hauptmann was able to build up savings of $2,500 and began lending money to fellow Germans at high rates of interest. This enabled him to buy thousands of dollars of shares at low prices after the stock market crash of 1929. By the time of the kidnapping he was only a part-time carpenter – and the day after the ransom was paid, he gave up carpentry.

ABDUCTION

After dinner on March 1, 1932, Charles Lindbergh was working in the library of his 500-acre hideaway home near the village of Hopewell in New Jersey. It was a stormy night, and raining hard. There was a crack of what Lindbergh thought to be lightning. Upstairs 20-month-old Charles Jr., affec-

tionately nicknamed "Little It", was asleep in his cot. It was unusual for the Lindberghs to be at their Hopewell home in the week. Usually they stayed with Mrs. Lindbergh's family in Englewood, which was closer to New York, and only went to Hopewell at weekends. But "Little It" had caught a cold and the pregnant Mrs. Lindbergh wanted him to get well before journeying to Englewood.

> ## "WHAT TYPE OF MAN WOULD KILL THE CHILD OF COLONEL LINDBERGH? HE WOULDN'T BE AN AMERICAN!"
> ### DAVID WILLENTZ, ATTORNEY GENERAL OF NEW JERSEY

Mrs. Anne Lindbergh was the daughter of banker and diplomat Dwight Morrow, one of the richest men in the eastern United States. Anne was his second daughter and overshadowed by her flamboyant elder sister, Elizabeth. She had a love of literature and would later become a successful writer; her book *Gift from the Sea* was a bestseller in 1955. Another book, *Hour of Gold, Hour of Lead*, published in 1973, consists of extracts from her diaries written at the time of the abduction of her infant son.

At 10.00pm Betty Gow, "Little It's" British nursemaid, found the child missing. She rushed to Mrs. Lindbergh. Had

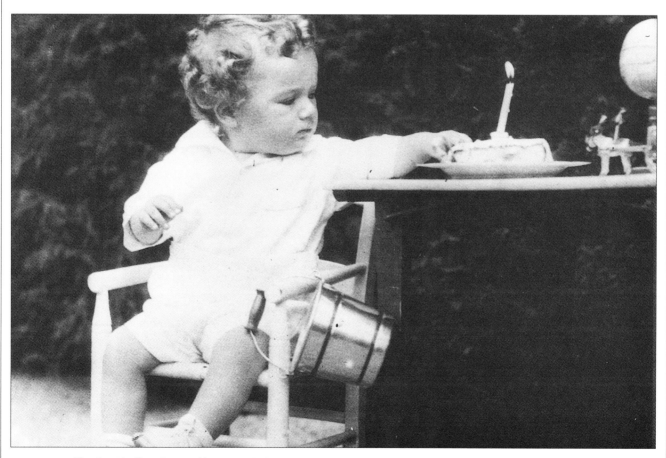

Charles Lindbergh Jr., affectionately known as "Little It", was snatched from his cot on March 1, 1932.

National hero Charles Lindbergh with his family.

she got the child? Mrs. Lindbergh hadn't. Nurse Gow turned to Mr. Lindbergh. In the child's room he found an empty crib. The window was open, the shutters forced, and there was mud on the floor. On the radiator there was a note. Lindbergh called the police.

The note was very nearly unintelligible, written either by a near illiterate or by a foreigner unfamiliar with written English. It read:

'dear Sir!

Have 50 000 $ redy 25 000 $ in 20 $ bills 15 000 $ in 10 $ bills and 10 000 $ in 5 $bills. After 2-4 days we will inform you were to deliver the Mony.

We warn you for making anyding public or for notify the Police

the child is in gute care.

Indication for all letters are

signature

and 3 holds'

The letter ended with two overlapping unfilled circles with a solid black oval where they overlapped. Analysis suggested that the spelling "gute" for "good" and "anyding" for "anything" indicated that the writer was Teutonic.

Police, closely followed by newspaper reporters, descended upon the Lindbergh home. One of the first things they found was a crudely-made ladder, some 60 to 70 feet or more away from the window of the Lindbergh child's room (why the kidnapper should have dragged it so far has remained an unanswered question). In the soil there were two imprints of a person's feet. The top rung of the ladder was split. Charles Lindbergh recalled the cracking sound he'd heard earlier and dismissed as lightning. For the rest of his life he would curse himself for not going to investigate what that sound was.

When Americans opened their newspapers the following day they were horrified. Lindbergh was a national hero, as important as mom, apple pie, the Declaration of Independence and the Statue of Liberty. That somebody had caused him pain, taken his child, was sacrilegious.

The shock reverberated through all sections of society. On the one hand, President Hoover promised: "We will move heaven and earth to find out who is this criminal." On the other, Al Capone offered a reward of $10,000. "I know what Mrs. Capone and I would feel," said Al from jail, who reckoned he'd be able to find the baby if he were released. Maybe he could have done; it has been suggested that Capone had had the child kidnapped in an attempt to bargain for his release from prison.

J. Edgar Hoover, head of the FBI, offered his help, but the New Jersey police wanted to run the investigation themselves and police chief Colonel Norman Schwartzkopf turned Hoover down. Curiously, there is considerable evidence that Lindbergh himself didn't want the services of the FBI either. He was approached several times, but refused to provide the FBI with information – not even the content of the kidnappers' note – and wouldn't even let them check the fingerprints found on the ladder with their records. Ultimately Lindbergh's behaviour caused a law – the so-called "Lindbergh Act" – to be passed which made it a federal offence, punishable by life imprisonment, to kidnap and transport a person across a state line. The passing of this act significantly strengthened the hand of the FBI in future cases.

THE SUSPECTS

Suspicion first fell on the 30 or so staff members at the Lindbergh home and at that of Mrs. Lindbergh's parents. The Lindberghs had never stayed at Hopewell for more than a weekend, yet the kidnapper apparently knew that they were there that Monday night. That information had to have come from a member of the staff.

Betty Gow, the child's nurse, was the obvious first suspect, but she was cleared following the most rigorous questioning. Not so the parlourmaid, another Briton, 28-year-old Violet Sharpe. She first told the police that she had been at the movies on the night of the kidnapping. Later she changed her story and said she'd been with a man. Then she changed her story again.

On June 10, on learning that the police wanted to question her further, Violet Sharpe committed suicide.

Lindbergh did not want to play games with the kidnappers and readily elected to pay the ransom money to get his son back. And, perhaps with Capone's offer in mind, he hired two infamous gangsters, Salmash Vitali and Irving Fritz, to act as go-betweens.

A couple of days later Vitali said his inquiries had produced no information of

The $50,000 ransom, which was deposited in a New York bank in March 1932.

value. "This one was pulled by an independent," he said. Nonetheless, a press announcement that the gangsters had been hired produced a response – two letters, identifiable as genuine by the secret interlocking circles. One said that the kidnappers wouldn't deal with any intermediary nominated by Lindbergh.

Instead, the note-senders nominated their own intermediary, an obscure, retired academic, Dr. John Francis Condon.

A compulsive writer of letters to the newspapers, Dr. Condon had offered a personal reward of $1,000 and himself as a go-between in a letter printed in *Home News*, a local newspaper published in a suburban area of the Bronx district of New York. Lindbergh and Condon then received instructions to advertise when the money was ready. They did so, and signed the advertisement "Jafsie" – a word they coined from the sound made by Dr. Condon's initials, JFC.

Condon was an eccentric, to put it mildly. Ludovic Kennedy, in *The Airman and The Carpenter*, described him as "so great a self-deluder that neither then nor now can one believe without confirmation anything he says".

On the evening of March 11 a man telephoned Dr. Condon, who later said the caller had a Scandinavian or German accent. There were what sounded like

An aerial view of the Lindbergh estate in Hopewell, New Jersey.

Italian voices in the background and suddenly a voice snapped some Italian words that Condon knew meant "shut up". Following this telephone conversation, there came a series of developments that culminated in a rendezvous being arranged at Woodlawn Cemetery in the Bronx. Condon, who would later make personal appearances at music halls telling about his involvement in the Lindbergh case, wrote a book, *Jafsie Tells All*, published in 1936, in which he said that in the cemetery he saw an Italian-looking man with a handkerchief covering his face. He thought this man was a lookout. A short time later he saw a second man standing in the shadows who wore a hat pulled down over his eyes and whose mouth was covered with a handkerchief. When this man spoke his voice was recognized by Jafsie as the voice that had spoken to him over the telephone. The man said his name was John – he became known as Cemetery John – and that there were six gang members, two of them women, and that the baby was safe on a boat. Then, suddenly and dramatically, he asked: "Would I burn if the baby is dead? Would I burn if I did not kill it?"

Condon and the man made further arrangements and several more messages passed between them. Then Condon received a package through the post. It contained a child's sleeping suit. Lindbergh identified it as the one his son had been wearing on the day of his kidnap.

Arrangements were made for Lindbergh to hand over the ransom money. It was put together at the J.P. Morgan bank. Lindbergh didn't want the serial numbers of the bills recorded, but the US Treasury demanded that the ransom be paid in easy-to-trace gold certificate bills. With the money packaged and ready to be handed over, Condon and Lindbergh went to another Bronx cemetery, St. Raymond's. They reported later that they both heard a shout: "Hey, Doc!" Then they handed the money over a hedge and Jafsie heard a voice say that the child was safe on a boat off the coast of Massachusetts.

At this meeting, which was on April 2, Lindbergh also saw a second man and would give testimony about him to a Bronx grand jury. The man walked past the Lindbergh car a couple of times, then dropped a handkerchief which the police found. Lindbergh was convinced that the man was a lookout.

As soon as it was light, Lindbergh took to the skies, flying over the ocean in search of the boat *Nellie* on which he'd been told his son was being held. He didn't find the boat.

BODY FOUND

On May 12, two truck drivers in the woods of Mount Rose, some four and a half miles from the Lindbergh house, found the decomposing remains of a child's body. It lay face down, partly covered by leaves. At the mortuary it was first identified by Nurse Betty Gow as the body of Charles Lindbergh Jr. Lindbergh himself later identified the body and clipped a curl of hair from the child's head. Post-mortem analysis showed that the little boy had been killed within hours of being kidnapped.

The only lead now was the ransom money. It had begun to show up, but it was two years before the police got the break they needed and had been hoping for. On September 16, 1934, on New York's East Side, a man paid for gas

Jamboree at the Hauptmann home as police, journalists and spectators gather.

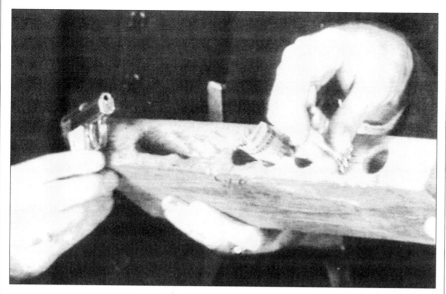

A search of Hauptmann's home revealed a gun and dollar bills.

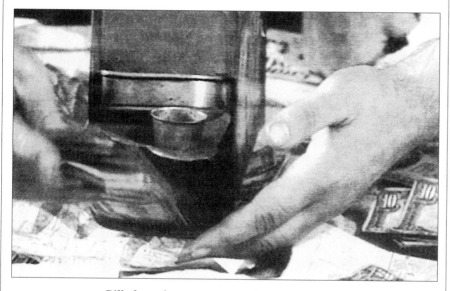

Bills from the ransom were also found in a tin.

with a $10 gold certificate bill. Walter Lyle, the manager of the filling station, was afraid the bank might not cash the bill and made a note of the number of the car. Later, when the police were told about the bill turning up, they discovered the car belonged to 34-year-old Bruno Richard Hauptmann.

When Hauptmann was arrested, he had one of the ransom bills in his pocket. $11,930 were found the following day, then another $830 turned up. More money and a gun were found concealed in a piece of wood. All of it was ransom money. Hauptmann explained that the money was not his, but had belonged to a business partner named Isidor Fisch. Fisch, he said, had gone back to Germany and died there. He'd owed Hauptmann money, so Hauptmann had kept it to spend. He had played no part in the kidnapping, he said.

A Polish Jew raised in Germany, Fisch had arrived in New York in the 1920s and worked as a cutter in the fur trade. But Fisch was a crook. He conned people, including friends, into investing their savings in businesses that were either bankrupt or fake. In Hauptmann, who was a clever and shrewd investor, Fisch recognized someone who would give his own illicit dealings an air of respectability. Interestingly, Fisch, when he went to Germany, paid for his sea voyage with gold certificate bills. Lou Wedemar, a newspaperman, wrote in *Fifty Unanswered Questions in the Hauptmann Case* that the "possibility had to be considered" that "the lookout" seen by Lindbergh at St. Raymond's Cemetery, "was Isidor Fisch".

New Jersey petitioned New York to allow Hauptmann to be extradited. Severely questioned by the Attorney General of New Jersey, David Willentz, Hauptmann strongly denied ever having been near the Lindbergh mansion and said he had never seen the ransom notes before. "That's not my handwriting. That's the first time I've seen those notes," Hauptmann told the court. Despite these denials, the prosecution loudly asserted that the ransom and other notes were "written by Hauptmann as we have proven".

Nothing had in fact been proven, but David Willentz shouted the prosecution's claims loudly and resorted to attacking Hauptmann's character. "What type of man would kill the child of Colonel Lindbergh?" he asked. "He wouldn't be an American!" Willentz loathed the German character and took this opportunity to take out his personal hatred for the German race on one individual. Hauptmann, it seemed, was standing trial for the German nation.

Eight handwriting experts matched Hauptmann's writing to the ransom notes.

Also brought to testify against Hauptmann were a string of witnesses who claimed to have seen him near the Lindbergh home in Hopewell. New York's governor had no choice but to sign the extradition papers.

ON TRIAL

On January 2, 1935, the trial of Bruno Hauptmann began at the County Courthouse in Flemington, New Jersey. The judge was Thomas Trenchard, the prosecution was led by David Willentz and Hauptmann was defended by Edward Reilly, a flamboyant man nicknamed the "Bull of Brooklyn". Hauptmann himself looked and apparently felt confident. He declared his innocence and had total faith that the law would prove it.

He did not appreciate how the prosecution would play upon the emotions of the jury: how Lindbergh would be presented as representing the United States; how patriotism would be invoked so that the tragedy of the hero's only child being taken and brutally murdered would be seen as an insult to the nation by a foreign power; and how the prosecution would appeal to the jury's desire for vengeance. Hauptmann also failed to realize that, in the eyes of many, police included, he was guilty before he even entered the courtroom.

Witnesses, too, were selective in what they remembered. Lindbergh said that the man in the cemetery who had taken the ransom money – the man popularly known as Cemetery John – had called out, "Hey, Doctor!" in a foreign accent. Previously Lindbergh had said the man shouted out, "Hey, Doc!" and he never mentioned a foreign accent. Neither had Dr. Condon, who before the trial had voiced reservations as to whether Hauptmann was Cemetery John, but who during the trial seemed not to doubt it.

The prosecution produced Amandus Hochmuth, who testified that on the day of the kidnap he had seen Hauptmann in Hopewell with a ladder in his car.

Hochmuth, though, was 87-years-old and nearly blind. He also enriched his bank balance with $1,000 reward money for telling this tale. State Troopers, who previously stated that they'd found two sets of footprints in the mud below the baby's window, now swore on oath that they'd found only one set.

Eight handwriting experts matched Hauptmann's handwriting to the ransom letters. In vain did the defence's single graphologist give his evidence. And the defence couldn't even challenge one piece of prosecution evidence: an expert on wood matched one of the rungs in the home-made ladder with a sawn floorboard in Hauptmann's attic, yet the defence had been refused access to the house to check for itself.

Hauptmann's alibi that he had been working in New York at the time of the kidnapping was confirmed by his wife and by his supervisor, but suddenly the vital time-sheets and payroll records disappeared and the supervisor refused to take the stand. Hauptmann, though, could offer no explanation for Dr. Condon's telephone number being found on the door in his home. Years later it was revealed that a reporter for the *Daily News* had written it there prior to fabricating a story.

The prosecution's case was desperately weak, but the defence did not take the many opportunities presented to punch holes in it – for example, Lindbergh's certainty that the voice of Cemetery John was Hauptmann's voice. The defence never challenged Lindbergh's memory by pointing out that he had been some distance away from "John" and that he'd heard the voice only briefly, some two and a half years earlier. But

Edward Reilly's handling of the whole case was hugely inept, so much so that one of his team accused Reilly in open court, saying he was guilty of "conceding Hauptmann to the electric chair". A year later Reilly would enter a mental hospital suffering from tertiary syphilis.

The evidence against Hauptmann was circumstantial. In his closing speech, Reilly observed: "The State has miserably failed to produce any evidence to connect him with the crime. They have not put him in the State of New Jersey on the night of March 1. They have not put him in the nursery. They have not put him in possession of the child."

Hauptmann was found guilty and sentenced to the electric chair. He was held in Trenton State Prison. There he began to prepare his appeal.

APPEALS

Appeals are expensive and Hauptmann desperately needed money to pay for his. He was especially unfortunate in that his defence counsel, the inept Reilly, had billed him for a massive $25,000. The Hauptmanns did all they could to raise sufficient money, with Hauptmann even writing his life story. Interestingly, perhaps significantly, he refused $90,000 from a newspaper to write a confession.

Slowly the public mood began to shift. New Jersey Governor Harold Hoffman spoke with Hauptmann and his wife and emerged convinced of his innocence. The wife of President Roosevelt admitted to having a "question in my mind".

The appeals made no difference, however. Hauptmann was executed on April 3, 1936. He is said to have "died bravely. Walked to the chair by himself."

Questions are still asked about the trial. It has even been suggested that the Lindbergh baby was never killed and that the body found was not that of Charles Lindbergh Jr. Sadly, though, we shall probably never learn the truth.

Bruno Hauptmann (centre) on trial at Huntercon County Court, Flemington, in January 1935.

NEVILLE HEATH

Surprising things sometimes turn up in hotel rooms. Surprising discoveries can occur when the chambermaid comes to clean up and make the bed, after her discreet tap on the door has received no answer. Surprising, and sometimes very nasty. Rarely nastier, however, than the discovery made by Alice Wyatt at the Pembridge Court Hotel in west London on the afternoon of June 21, 1946.

■

OLONEL AND MRS. NEVILLE George Clevely Heath, booked into the room since June 16, had not apparently stirred all day. Nor were they inside when chambermaid Alice Wyatt opened the door. Instead, a dark-haired woman, who had not checked in as Mrs. Heath, lay in the bed.

The bedclothes covering her were stained with blood. The naked woman's ankles were tied together; her nipples had been bitten till they were almost severed from the aureoles. Seventeen lash marks showed where she had been flogged with a diamond-meshed dog-whip, whose pattern was etched on her skin in bruises; two of the strokes had slashed her eyelids. Something solid – possibly a poker – had been forced into her vagina and rotated savagely to cause internal injury.

And the lady had been suffocated.

The alert went out for Lt.-Col. Heath. Would he please come forward to help the police with their enquiries?

The newspaper publication of this request astonished the young woman who actually had registered at the Pembridge Court as Mrs. Heath. For her "husband" had told her all about the body in their room, telling her that he and Superintendent Tom Barratt were actually together when the police answered the hotel's summons. And Yvonne Symonds saw no reason to disbelieve Neville Heath.

Of course they were not husband and wife. They had met less than a week before, on June 15, at a dance in Chelsea, when 19-year-old Yvonne was bowled over by the handsome and dashing ex-officer. He took her out for a drink at his favourite night-time haunt, the Panama

Club in Knightsbridge, and telephoned the next day, asking her to marry him. Yvonne accepted willingly and, on the strength of the engagement, agreed to spend the night with Heath at the Pembridge Court Hotel, a nice family-run establishment in a tree-lined road near the Notting Hill district in west London.

The colonel turned out to be a gentle and considerate lover. On June 17 Yvonne went back home to her parents in the south coast town of Worthing, and told them about her betrothal to this delightful and eligible young gentleman. The Symonds family looked forward to meeting her suitor, who telephoned Yvonne daily, promising to visit her very soon.

On Friday, June 21, he turned up in Worthing and asked Yvonne to join him for lunch. On Saturday they lunched together again, and that afternoon Yvonne took him home. Her parents were charmed, as she had expected. In the evening, the colonel took his fiancée to dinner at the Blue Peter Hotel in Ammering, and casually asked her whether she had seen anything about the death of Margery Gardner in the papers?

Yvonne had not. She was horrified when Neville revealed that he had spent

Thursday night in north London, and that he had lent "their" hotel room to a friend who wanted it for an assignation with Mrs. Gardner. The following day, he said, the police had contacted him and asked him to accompany them to the hotel, where he and Superintendent Tom Barratt had been appalled by the chambermaid's shocking discovery. Something was likely to appear in the papers,

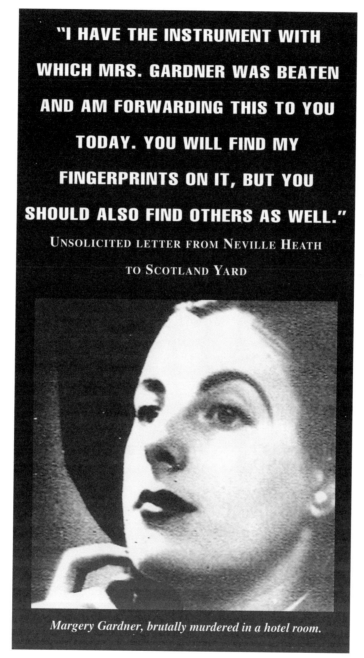

"I HAVE THE INSTRUMENT WITH WHICH MRS. GARDNER WAS BEATEN AND AM FORWARDING THIS TO YOU TODAY. YOU WILL FIND MY FINGERPRINTS ON IT, BUT YOU SHOULD ALSO FIND OTHERS AS WELL."
UNSOLICITED LETTER FROM NEVILLE HEATH TO SCOTLAND YARD

Margery Gardner, brutally murdered in a hotel room.

Heath continued, something that Yvonne should prepare herself for.

Yvonne was not at all prepared for the fact that the police urgently wanted to interview Neville George Clevely Heath in connection with the body discovered in his abandoned bedroom! Her parents were extremely worried by the disparity between Heath's story and the newspaper accounts.

"Yes, I thought they might be," was Heath's disarming response. Boyishly charming as ever, he assured Yvonne that he was going off to London to sort out the confusion.

"What sort of person could commit a brutal crime like that?" Yvonne wondered aloud.

"A sex maniac, I suppose," was her fiancé's measured response.

And that was the last time the Symonds family saw Neville Heath.

THE OCELOT WOMAN AND THE CON MAN

The dead woman in the Pembridge Court Hotel was 32-year-old Margery Gardner. She had no convictions, but was nevertheless known to the police as an associate of pimps and drug dealers. Her good looks found her occasional work as a film extra and her competent draughtsmanship allowed her to describe herself as a commercial artist.

Among the expensively seedy demi-monde of west London she was usually known as "Ocelot Margie" or "the panther lady" because of the ocelot fake-fur coat she sported.

In private she was a masochist, with bondage and beatings central to her enjoyment of sex. But, of course, she expected her partners in the sado-masochistic games she liked to play to allow her to control the situation. An agreed code word or gesture would indicate that the pain was passing her threshold of enjoyment and that they should stop.

N.G.C. Heath, the signatory of the hotel register, was also familiar to the police. Not as a sadist – that was strictly part of his private life, and none of his partners had complained to the law that he went beyond their agreed bounds of mutual pleasure – but as a habitual petty thief and fraudster. Superintendent Barratt and Inspector Reg Spooner knew that Heath was not and never had been a lieutenant-colonel. They knew, too, that Heath's most recent conviction was for claiming military decorations and ranks to which he was not entitled.

Born in 1917, Neville Heath was educated at Rutlish, a good independent south London school, later attended by British Prime Minister John Major. He wasn't an especially popular schoolboy. His nickname was "Smelly", and he was remembered as a bully. He left school at 17 and went to work as an office boy. He also joined the Territorial Army.

He didn't stay long in the office job before enlisting as an air force cadet at Cranwell, Lincolnshire. He was posted to Duxford, Cambridgeshire, and transferred to Mildenhall in Suffolk. It soon became clear that funds were missing from an account he had handled in the Duxford mess. Heath absconded, leaving an IOU and a casual letter of resignation for his Squadron Leader. "I consider I have been a disgrace to a service that will be well rid of me," was his comment. He would always feel that a glib acknowledgement of guilt met all responsibilities.

A court-martial led to Heath's discharge from the service. Then he embarked on his pathetic career as a fraudster. He discovered from *Debrett* that the young Earl of Dudley was about his own age, so he had a chequebook printed in the earl's name, giving Trinity College Cambridge and c/o the House of Lords as his addresses. After he'd carried out a few frauds by this method, he was approached by a burly stranger, who asked him, "Are you Lord Dudley?"

"Yes, I am, old man," he replied smartly.

"Well, I am Detective Inspector Hickman of the CID."

"In that case, I am not Lord Dudley."

He was put on probation after passing off the escapade as a boyish prank. But the burglaries in Brighton and London which next brought him before the courts could not be so lightly dismissed. Convicted of robbing a friend's flat in

Heath (wearing uniform) liked to pass himself off socially as a military man.

Edgware Road, he had another 10 cases taken into consideration, and went to Borstal in Suffolk. He kept his nose clean and passed as a model prisoner, though the staff thought him nasty, sly, superior and snooty.

In October 1939 he was released for war service and drafted into the Royal Army Service Corps. Private Heath was swiftly promoted to NCO, and by May 1940 his accent and public school manner gained him his commission. But he fretted at the social insignificance of the "Galloping Grocers", and told fancy stories about the efforts he made to find action when posted to Palestine.

By his own account he was drummed out of the corps for pluckily going on an unauthorized raid with men from the Arab Legion and a Home Counties regiment. In fact, he was cashiered for buying a general's car with a dud cheque. (The £175 he realized from the sale of the car was the largest amount earned by any of his crimes. Heath's swashbuckling manner concealed the extreme pettiness of his financial criminality.)

He was sent back to England, but en route jumped ship at Durban, South Africa. During the voyage, he told Adjutant Paul Hill improbable stories about his exotic experiences in the flagellant brothels of Cairo and Beirut, and made a half-confession to having *possibly* killed a belly-dancer he had beaten savagely when too drunk to be sure what happened. He also asserted that upper-class girls with a passion for horses made excellent masochistic lovers. He claimed to have flogged dozens.

On his first day ashore in Durban, passing himself off as "Bruce Lockhart", Heath managed to get engaged to a young woman he had just met, borrowed money from her, and then disappeared.

He joined the South African Air Force as James Robert Cadogan Armstrong, and his military career's finest legitimate hour followed. His previous training at Cranwell made him seem a natural flier. His sturdy six-foot build made him a useful rugby forward. And even when the SAAF discovered that Major Armstrong was using a false identity, they kept him on as an excellent pilot instructor.

Heath married 18-year-old Elizabeth Pitt-Rivers, whom he met in Johannesburg in 1942. For Elizabeth, marriage started as a dream. She had a big, handsome, fair-haired, stylish, blue-eyed charmer at her side, and soon a baby boy called Roy. But it deteriorated into a nightmare as debts and other woman intruded on their life together. Eventually her husband disappeared.

Heath was actually seconded to the RAF and returned to Finmere in Oxfordshire, where he was noted as a womanizing partygoer. During his time there, a WAAF at a nearby camp was murdered by an unknown person and her sexual parts horribly mutilated. Heath was not suspected at the time, and in 1946, when he stood trial for murder, the prosecution chose not to raise the question.

Heath flew a few bombing sorties over France, Holland and Belgium, the sum total of his real experience of active service. Despite his mendacious boasting, his contribution to the war effort would seem to be remarkable only in the fact that he twice ordered the premature abandonment of his plane.

During 1944 he refused the chance of a reconciliation with Elizabeth, writing a deliberately offensive rebuff which compelled her to divorce him. Meanwhile, back in South Africa in 1945, he

The builder's ladder that Heath used to re-enter the Tollard Royal Hotel, unseen by the night porter.

Former WRN Doreen Marshall (left) met charming Group-Captain Brooke while convalescing in Bournemouth.

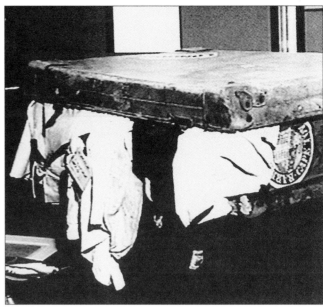

Heath's suitcase: it was found to contain a blood-stained silk square and scarf and a steel-cored, diamond-meshed whip.

used false names and ranks until the SAAF decided that enough was enough and he was thrown out of the air force and the country.

His subsequent life in England was spent perpetrating petty swindles. He showed rare flashes of stylish impudence in these. Once, for example, he claimed to be accompanying players on the South African Springboks' rugby tour, and thus wangled himself a seat in the distinguished visitors' stand at Twickenham. There is said to be a photograph showing him there, alongside eminent politicians Clement Attlee and Ernest Bevin!

More typical, however, was the petty scam engaging him on the night Margery Gardner died. He passed the evening in a Fleet Street pub, making false offers to fly journalists to the continent in a private plane. One gullible hack had turned over £30 to Heath in expectation of a trip to Copenhagen.

> "ARE YOU LORD DUDLEY?"
>
> "YES, I AM, OLD MAN," HE REPLIED SMARTLY.
>
> "WELL, I AM DETECTIVE INSPECTOR HICKMAN OF THE CID."
>
> "IN THAT CASE, I AM NOT LORD DUDLEY."
>
> EXCHANGE BETWEEN HEATH AND AN OFFICER OF THE LAW

By this time Heath's private life was threatening to get him into trouble. On one occasion, an assistant manager of the Strand Palace Hotel had been called by residents to investigate unseemly noises coming from one of the rooms. When the manager let himself into the room with the passkey, he found Heath and a barely conscious Miss M.B. (her name has never been published) naked. The lady's hands were tied behind her back with a handkerchief, and there was visible bruising on her face and neck.

When the woman recovered her composure, she described Heath's idea of lovemaking. No sooner had they entered the room than he twisted her arm up behind her back and told her that he hated women. Then he ripped her coat off and banged her against the wall so that she passed out. She came round to find her clothes removed. Heath tied her hands when she tried to escape, then undressed himself and started to rape her. She struggled away from him and screamed, whereupon his hands went round her throat, and only the manager's arrival saved her from a fate that might have included death. But the police had no record of this incident to compare with the unpleasantness they would uncover later at the Pembridge Court Hotel.

Heath met Margery Gardner through their common friendship with another public schoolboy gone bad: burglar Peter Tilley-Baillie. Around this time Heath discovered a brothel in west London which specialized in flagellation. From this establishment he bought himself a steel-cored, diamond-meshed whip....

GROUP-CAPTAIN RUPERT BROOKE

Doreen Marshall came down with measles shortly after her demob from the WRNS. When her rash receded and her temperature returned to normal, her parents sent her to the south-coast resort of Bournemouth to convalesce. The 21-year-old found the conventional resort rather boring, and was cheered when a big, handsome, fair-haired man warmly greeted her friend Peggy on the promenade, having apparently met her at a dance. But as he walked with them, it became apparent that Doreen interested him more than Peggy. Peggy politely excused herself when Group-Captain Rupert Brooke invited Doreen to tea at his hotel, the Tollard Royal.

How well-read were Doreen and Peggy, one wonders? The alias "Group-Captain Rupert Brooke" should surely have raised an eyebrow, especially as the handsome officer had evidently been born round about the time when the doomed First World War poet was at the height of his fame.

Tea passed pleasantly, and Doreen accepted a further invitation to return to the hotel for dinner. After dinner, over late-night drinks, the "Group-Captain" imbibed a little too freely. Fellow guests at the Tollard Royal noticed that Doreen was finding him a little too ebullient, and by 11.20pm she had clearly had enough. She was tired and tense when she asked a fellow guest to order her a taxi.

Group-Captain Brooke cancelled the order and announced that he would walk Doreen to her hotel, the Norfolk.

"I'll be back in half an hour," he told the porter within the hearing of others.

"He'll be back in a quarter of an hour!" Doreen flashed. But he was not. He didn't appear to come back at all. By 4.00am the night porter was worried for the jovial officer's safety, and checked his room. There was the Group-Captain, sleeping the sleep of the just.

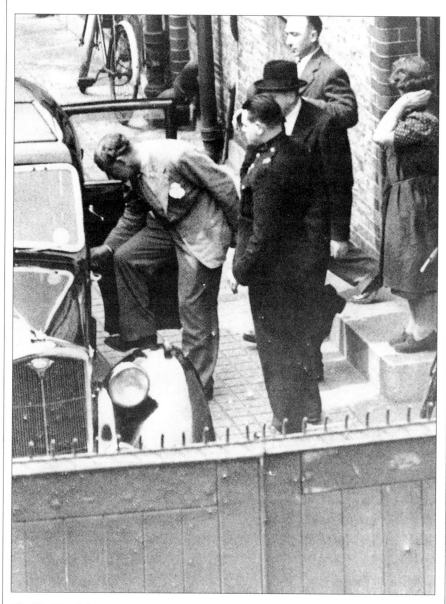

Neville Heath leaving court in west London after being remanded in custody for the murders of Margery Gardner and Doreen Marshall.

The following morning he explained his mysterious reappearance. Some workmen had left a ladder outside the building overnight. He had borrowed it and climbed into his room through the window, to tease the porter. But within 48 hours, other people were wondering about his unorthodox and unsubstantiated re-entry to his room.

Miss Marshall had not returned to the Norfolk Hotel, and the manager there became worried about this young woman, staying on her own. He learned from his staff that she had last been seen taking a taxi to a dinner date at the Tollard Royal. He telephoned to ask whether Group-Captain Brooke's guest had been Miss Marshall from Pinner. The dashing officer denied it. Challenged with the fact that she surely *was* Miss Marshall, he insisted that he had known her a long time, and she most certainly did not come from Pinner.

Then, apparently to confirm his story, he telephoned the police and asked if he could see a photograph of the missing Doreen Marshall. He arranged to meet Doreen's parents at the police station, and walked into his immediate arrest, as he must have anticipated.

MAD OR BAD?

Detective Constable Souter was assigned to interview Group-Captain Brooke. Like every CID man in the land, he had studied the circular and photographs sent out by Scotland Yard describing petty confidence trickster Neville Heath, whose fingerprint had been found on a washstand at the Pembridge Court Hotel, and who had written to Barratt from Worthing, promising to explain about "the acquaintance" who had borrowed his room (a promise he never fulfilled).

Heath's mugshots had never been made public, lest Heath's defence should claim that photographs appearing in the newspapers had corrupted the memories of identification witnesses, who might confirm that Heath really was the self-styled Colonel who booked the room where Margery Gardner died.

The police were to be criticized for this caution. Since some of them knew about the murdered WAAF in Finmere, they had reason to suspect that Heath was the kind of maniac who might strike again, so publicizing his picture might have prevented further murders.

Souter noted that Brooke resembled the pictures of Heath. He also noted the man's distinct unease when confronted with Doreen Marshall's parents and sister. He suggested to the Group-Captain that he looked very like the pictures of the wanted Heath published in the papers, and the Group-Captain affably agreed that friends had commented on the likeness.

He was trapped. There had been no picture in the papers. As though casually doodling or making notes, Souter wrote on a scrap of paper, "THIS MAN IS HEATH", and sent it out to his superiors by messenger.

Soon Heath had admitted his identity and, saying he was cold, asked for his coat to be brought from the Tollard Royal. The police collected it, and found in the pockets a left luggage ticket and a single artificial pearl. The ticket led them to a bag, containing a steel-cored diamond-meshed whip, exactly matching the weals on Margery Gardner's body, and a silk square and a woollen scarf, both of which were bloodstained. It turned out that the square had tied the hands of the so called "ocelot woman" and the scarf had been used to gag her.

Barely three months would pass between Heath's arrest, in July 1946, and his conviction, in October. Neither the jury nor the wider public believed his insanity

The significance of the pearl emerged on Monday July 8, when a girl out walking her dog on Branksome Chine found Doreen Marshall's body hidden among rhododendrons. Dorothy's clothes had been torn off and dropped on top of her body. Her throat had been cut and she had been beaten savagely over the head. One of her ribs had been broken and had punctured her lung. A great gash, like those inflicted by Jack the Ripper, had torn her open from her thigh, through her pudenda and abdomen to her breasts. A transverse wound was cut from one breast to the other, and the nipples were viciously bitten. Scattered around the body lay 27 of the artificial pearls from Doreen's necklace. The 28th was in Heath's pocket.

Heath took the view that he might as well plead guilty to the murders. "After all, I did kill them," he observed. However, Mr. J.D. Caswell, his counsel, urged him to think of his family and at least allow them the relief of believing that mental illness rather than sheer wickedness lay behind his crimes. "All right, old boy. Put me down not guilty," said Heath, contemptibly as shallow and insouciant as ever.

Dr. Henry Hubert was called by the defence to prove that Heath was so mad he did not know that what he was doing was wrong. Nobody seemed likely to dispute that Heath's idea of erotic fun went well beyond the bounds of what is

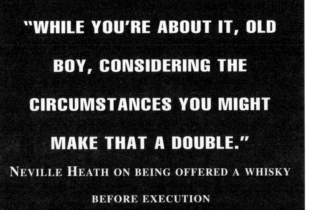

"WHILE YOU'RE ABOUT IT, OLD BOY, CONSIDERING THE CIRCUMSTANCES YOU MIGHT MAKE THAT A DOUBLE."
NEVILLE HEATH ON BEING OFFERED A WHISKY BEFORE EXECUTION

considered normal. Hopelessly demented he might be, but, by the McNaghten Rules then applied in the law courts, if Heath actually knew what he was doing and knew that it was wrong, then he could be found guilty and hanged.

Dr. Hubert's task was made virtually impossible by the fact that Heath so cheerfully acknowledged his own wrongdoing. On the witness stand he displayed the same glib complacency that had accompanied his first attempt to "resign" from the RAF with an easy apology for embezzling mess funds.

The degree of planning in Heath's murders and escapes also went against him at the trial. During both murders he had undressed fully before starting his assaults, so that there was never a trace of blood on his clothes. Doreen Marshall had somehow been forced to walk a mile in the wrong direction from her hotel, indicating that his intention was to kill her in a secluded place. The jury took less than an hour to convict him.

Empty boyish jauntiness stayed with Heath to the very end. When he was offered a tot of whisky to steady his nerves before execution, he held out his glass and said, "While you're about it, old boy, considering the circumstances you might make that a double."

Even as the hangman came to lead him to the scaffold, Heath appeared unconcerned, saying cheerily, "Come on boys, let's get on with it."

Heath remained calm and collected to the last: the ultimate confidence trickster, he could make believable the unbelievable.

JOHN GEORGE HAIGH

The drab austerity of Britain in 1949 was sensationally interrupted by the arrest and trial of John George Haigh. The "Acid Bath Murderer" had disposed of his victims' bodies quite unspeakably. By his own account he was also a vampire, tapping his victims' jugular veins for a routine glass of blood before dissolving them into unrecognizable sludge. He was something new, something different, and something quite horrible in the world of rationing and identity cards and utility suits.

■

LIKE THE SPIVS of the black market, Haigh found the resigned idealism of the Second World War an irrelevance: the slow recovery from a bankrupting victory a petty absurdity. As deliberately as any sharp-suited, pencil-moustachioed purveyor of nylons smuggled away from the export drive, Haigh used the disturbed times for his own selfish ends. As firmly as any forger of counterfeit petrol coupons, he was dedicated to "good old-fashioned greed". But though he was classier and more intelligent than the "wide boys" who flourished in the 1940s, Haigh far surpassed them in his avaricious evil-doing.

Hints of Haigh's murders first reached the press when he and Mrs. Constance Lane went to London's Chelsea police station to report the disappearance of Mrs. Olive Durand-Deacon. All three were residents at the respectable Onslow Court Hotel in South Kensington. (In those days the cost of accommodation was still reasonable enough for residence in a hotel to be common among the retired middle classes.)

Mrs. Lane and Mrs. Durand-Deacon were both elderly widows. Haigh, at 39 years of age, was one of the younger hotel residents. He described himself as an engineer and entrepreneur; he might have added gigolo, as his dapper good looks and attentive charm made him an acceptable companion to some of the ladies at the Onslow Court Hotel.

Mrs. Durand-Deacon's table faced Haigh's in the hotel dining room. She had been impressed by a government directive urging the rich to invest their money in exportable enterprises, so she approached the young engineer with an idea for a business venture.

She felt there should be a market for artificial fingernails, and she asked Haigh whether he would be able to help her in manufacturing them. She showed him models she had cut out of thick paper, and he agreed that it should be possible for him to find some appropriate material by experimenting at his factory in Crawley, Sussex. Mrs. Durand-Deacon made an appointment to travel down to the factory with him on February 18, 1949, to inspect the premises and consider possible sample materials.

Unknown to her, Haigh was in desperate need of money. He was in debt to the hotel and in danger of being summonsed or thrown out. Far from being a go-ahead entrepreneur, he was hopeless at business and had no means of support. His "factory" was a little workshop where he stored a few tools and chemicals, and his engineering enterprises were completely imaginary.

Also quite unknown to anyone was the fact that Haigh, a convicted fraud and forger in pre-war years, had lived since 1944 off the proceeds from the murders of two families, whose property he had acquired by forging legal documents.

INQUIRIES BEGIN

On February 19, Haigh over-reached himself, proving too clever by half. Mrs. Durand-Deacon did not appear in the dining room, and Haigh approached her friend Mrs. Lane wondering where she was, and whether the old lady was ill. He was discomfited to learn that Mrs. Lane assumed he of all people must know Mrs. Durand-Deacon's whereabouts, as

Olive had told her friend she was going with Haigh to Crawley to discuss the fingernail venture the previous day.

Haigh retained his composure, and claimed that Mrs. Durand-Deacon had failed to keep the appointment: hence his inquiry. When the hotel management discovered that Mrs. Durand-Deacon's bed had not been occupied the previous night, Haigh heartily endorsed Mrs. Lane's opinion that the police should be informed, and the following morning thrust himself into the proceedings by driving her to the police station in his shiny Alvis car. He also made his own lengthy statement to the police back at the hotel.

The police were disinclined to worry unduly about a 69-year-old lady who might have taken herself off about her

Haigh's murder victim: well-meaning 69-year-old widow, Mrs. Olive Durand-Deacon.

Mrs. Lane (left), friend of Mrs. Durand-Deacon, arriving at court with the manageress of the hotel where they both lived.

own business without informing fellow-residents who were neither relatives nor close friends. But an agency reporter picked up the story and an account of it appeared in an evening newspaper. Soon the police were under pressure to investigate the disappearance of the respectable London widow.

Routinely checking out Haigh's story, they discovered that his "factory" was hardly suitable for serious engineering work or manufacturing experiments. They also found that he had been seen in Crawley on the afternoon of February 18, at one point accompanying an old lady who matched a description of Mrs. Durand-Deacon. And he had been back there on his own the following afternoon. On neither ocasion had there been any-

thing suspicious about his appearance, and he had made no attempt to conceal his movements. Still, it seemed necessary to confirm all the details of his story once more, and woman police sergeant

> # "YOU CAN'T PROVE MURDER WITHOUT A BODY!"
> #### JOHN GEORGE HAIGH

Alexandra Lambourne was sent to interview him for a third time. Sergeant Lambourne took an instant dislike to Haigh. Some women did: others took a bit longer to reach the conclusion that John

Haigh was a phoney. Only Barbara Stephens remained friendly with him after a few dates, maintaining a relationship that would last six years. Subsequently, she would refuse to comment on the character of Haigh.

Sergeant Lambourne found Haigh's ingratiating eagerness to please distinctly off-putting and, although there were no suspicious discrepancies in his story, she decided that Mr. Haigh warranted further investigation. In her report she recommended that his background should be thoroughly examined.

And so it was that the police uncovered his previous form: a short prison sentence for fraud in 1934; subsequent convictions for theft and forgery; and a four-year sentence for obtaining money

Smooth poisoner John George Haigh is still all smiles as he leaves court in police custody.

by false pretences in 1937. Since his release from prison in 1940, he appeared to have gone straight. But how? There was no evidence of the engineering contracts and patented inventions that were supposed to support his reasonably affluent lifestyle at the Onslow Court Hotel.

NO BODY

Haigh was pulled in for serious interrogation on February 28, 1949. He repeatedly denied knowing anything about Mrs. Durand-Deacon's movements 10 days previously, but at last the pressure told, and he blurted out, "Mrs. Durand-Deacon no longer exists. I've destroyed her with acid. You can't prove murder without a body."

This was his first cardinal error. Like many people, he was vaguely aware that for a murder charge to be brought, the prosecution must produce what the law calls the *corpus delicti* – Latin for "body of the crime". Like many people, he wrongly believed that if there is no body, there can be no murder.

In fact, *corpus delicti* really means a body or sufficiency of evidence to prove that a murder has been committed (as opposed to natural death or sudden accidental death). And for this, no body need be recovered – as, for example, would be the case in a deliberately murderous drowning at sea in front of witnesses, whose testimony would provide the *corpus delicti*.

Haigh was taken back to Crawley by the detectives, and the contents of the shed proved sufficiently that his weird confession was substantially true. Rubber gloves and a rubber apron, a World War II gas mask, a stirrup pump, a 40-gallon drum, and several empty carboys

Barbara Stephens, the one woman who did not consider Haigh to be a phoney.

– the large glass containers in which acid is supplied in industrial quantities – indicated that the wretched little workshop was well equipped for dissolving a human body. And when it was reduced to a sort of acid gravy, what did Haigh do with it?

Outside on the path was a fatty sludge. This was all that remained of poor Mrs. Olive Durand-Deacon. And the distasteful task of sifting through it to see if any identifiable trace of the murdered woman could be found fell to pathologist Keith Simpson.

He did very well. First he found a gallstone which, being covered with fat in the body, would have taken some weeks to dissolve. Mrs. Durand-Deacon was known to have suffered from gallstones. Then he found the remains of a plastic handbag which could be identified as similar to one owned by Mrs. Durand-Deacon. Finally, and damningly

for the confident Haigh, her false teeth emerged, indestructable and absolutely identifiable.

MAD, MAD, MAD

With conclusive physical evidence mounting against him, Haigh asked a curiously revealing question. "What are the chances," he wondered, "of getting out of Broadmoor?" His cunning mind was already planning to cheat the gallows with a defence of insanity.

With this intention he made a full – a more than full – confession. He had taken Mrs. Durand-Deacon down to Crawley where they had, indeed, been seen together, making their way to the workshop. Inside the building he shot her. (The police found his revolver there.) Then he stripped the body and placed it in the 40-gallon drum.

To fortify himself before the really heavy labour, he took a break, went into

Police search for clues in the yard of the factory at Crawley.

town, and had a poached egg on toast at the Ye Olde Ancient Prior's Restaurant (which, even by the tasteless standards of the early twentieth century, seems to have gone way over the top in its anachronistic romantic nomenclature).

Returning to work, he donned apron, gloves and gas mask; stirrup-pumped his carboys of acid into the drum until the body was completely covered, and gave it all a good stir. Then he went out and ate a hearty dinner.

It took several days for the body to dissolve completely, and on one of his return visits Haigh had to empty the drum and refill it with fresh acid. He also collected Mrs. Durand-Deacon's jewellery, which he pawned for a few hundred pounds, and her Persian lamb coat. This he took to the cleaners, preparatory to selling it. The frighteningly calculated and brutal murder realized very little profit for the perpetrator – and indeed, it was a mark of his desperation to pay off

his hotel bill that he should have chosen as his victim a woman so intimately linked to him.

But with this crime definitely attributed to him, Haigh set about "proving" his madness by confessing to others. His first murder, it transpired, was of a young man named Donald McSwann. In 1936 Haigh had been employed by McSwann's father, William, as secretary-cum-chauffeur. William McSwann was the wealthy proprietor of an amusement arcade.

Haigh's compulsory incarceration at His Majesty's expense the following year for fraud and forgery terminated that association. But McSwann was not one of the victims of his frauds, despite forger Haigh's ample opportunity to master his handwriting. When the two men met again, in 1944 after Haigh's release, McSwann was delighted to learn that Haigh was in a position to service and repair his pinball machines. For this

was wartime – spare parts and equipment were virtually unobtainable. A bit of a rogue, like John George Haigh, who could lay dishonest hands on the nuts and bolts that should have been going into tanks and aeroplanes, was a godsend to a businessman whose income was grinding to a halt for lack of mainte-nance. McSwann turned his machines over to Haigh, who took them to a base-ment workshop he was renting opposite Gloucester Road underground station.

Young Donald dropped by from time to time to see how the work was going, and to chat to Haigh, whose knowledge-able worldly charm was highly impres-sive to a man in his early 20s.

In September 1944, Donald disap-peared. But his parents did not inform the police. For Haigh told them that call-up papers had at last reached the young man and, rather than risk his life for his country, he had gone into hiding. Haigh was in touch with him, but Donald expressly didn't want his parents to know just where he was, as the Military Police would be bound to question them as soon as they came looking for the run-away, and they might accidentally give something away.

The elder McSwanns would appear to have been almost as selfishly unpatri-otic as Donald – or perhaps they were just foolishly devoted to their son. In any case, they accepted Haigh's story with-out question, and were overjoyed when, early in 1945, Haigh told them that Don-ald was temporarily hiding in his Gloucester Road basement. The couple were invited to visit their son before he moved on. Mr. and Mrs. McSwann went to Gloucester Road and they were never seen again.

Haigh would later explain the McSwanns' demise. He had asked Donald to come to the basement workshop to take a look at the pinball machines. In the backroom of the basement, out of sight of the window visible from Gloucester Road, he had coshed Donald. Then he had dissolved the young man's body in a drum of acid. A few months later, his plans carefully prepared, he did the same to Donald's parents.

The plans were simple, but daring. With Donald's identification papers and his own knowledge of William McSwann's handwriting and business affairs, he had perfectly legal power of attorney documents drawn up in Donald's favour. Haigh forged William's signature on the documents and identified himself to the lawyers as Donald. Haigh took over and promptly cashed all of William McSwann's property.

This was a very large and successful fraud. Haigh obtained properties in Raynes Park, Wimbledon and Beckenham, in addition to £4,000 in cash and securities. Yet within two-and-a-half years it had all disappeared, gambled away at the dog track, where Haigh believed he had an infallible "system" for doubling his money.

Broke again, he turned once more to murder. Dr. Archibald Henderson and his wife Rosalie, a middle-aged couple with no occupation since the doctor's retirement, other than the running of a small doll's hospital and toyshop in Fulham, advertised the sale of a house in Ladbroke Grove. Haigh met them on the pretext of wanting to buy the house, and cultivated their friendship over the next few months when he learned they were contemplating going to South Africa.

In February 1948, it seemed they did so – leaving their friend "Johnny" Haigh as trustee of their affairs in England. Letters forged by Haigh in Dr. Henderson's handwriting told relatives and friends of their plans to emigrate, and attempts to

> ## "IF YOU EVER SIN, SATAN WILL MARK YOU WITH A BLUE PENCIL ALSO."
> ### HAIGH'S FATHER, ACCORDING TO HAIGH

trace them in South Africa were still going on when Mrs. Durand-Deacon's disappearance was noticed. However, by that time, their "trustee" had cashed in all their property. This time he realized even more than he had from the

McSwann murders, and again he poured it straight into the satchels of the bookmakers. For the Hendersons, too, had been killed and dissolved in acid.

There really didn't seem to be anything irrational or insane about the murders of the McSwann and Henderson families. All too clearly Haigh had realized that huge amounts of money could be made by a smooth-talking con artist with a gift for forgery. All he had to do was to pick a prosperous victim, eliminate all traces of them and then come forward with documents which appeared to transfer control of their affairs quite legitimately to himself. So Haigh added new victims – and a new motive.

COMPULSIVE BLOOD-DRINKING

In addition to the five known victims, Haigh claimed to have killed three others – two men and a woman; all strangers picked up from streets or pubs; all totally

The workshop of Hurstlea Products where Haigh murdered Mrs. Durand-Deacon.

dissolved in acid and completely unidentifiable. And his motive, he said, was to drink their blood.

After every killing, and before throwing the body into the drum for conversion to sludge, Haigh claimed to have cut the victim's throat with a pen-knife, and held a tumbler to the flowing vein. It was really this lust for a glass of blood that drove him to kill: the money was just an accidental afterthought.

To support this ghastly story, he told horror tales of his dreadful childhood. His parents were Plymouth Brethren – strict nonconformists, who carried the principles of self-denial to the extent of avoiding cinemas, theatres, novel-reading, recreational music, sports and even children's parties.

Haigh claimed that his father had suffered an accident while working as an electrician. This had caused a blue scar to run down his forehead. Haigh claimed that his father explained this was a mark placed on him by Satan as a punishment for sin, and warned the boy, "If you ever sin, Satan will mark you with a blue pencil also." This dreadful threat terrified Haigh, who checked his face in mirrors for years to come to see whether the mark of Satan had yet appeared.

After a car accident in 1944, when blood ran down his forehead and into his mouth, giving rise to the vampiric appetite he satisfied through murder, he suffered a recurring nightmare: "I saw before me a forest of crucifixes which gradually turned into trees. At first there

appeared to be dew or rain dripping from the branches, but as I approached I realized it was blood."

The *Daily Mirror* newspaper picked up these sensational stories and reported them to its readership. The then editor, Silvester Bolam, was given a three-month jail sentence for contempt of court when he published a prejudicial lead story about Haigh's arrest, which read: "The Vampire killer will never strike again. He is safely behind bars, power-

> **"I SAW BEFORE ME A FOREST OF CRUCIFIXES WHICH GRADUALLY TURNED INTO TREES. AT FIRST THERE APPEARED TO BE DEW OR RAIN DRIPPING FROM THE BRANCHES, BUT AS I APPROACHED I REALIZED IT WAS BLOOD."**
> JOHN GEORGE HAIGH

less to lure his victims to a hideous death." Ironically, he found himself imprisoned in the same jail as Haigh.

While on remand Haigh charmed his guards, several of whom later described him as the most pleasant murderer they had ever met. He also indulged a habit intended to demonstrate madness: daily drinking a glass of his own urine.

TRIAL AND CONVICTION

Haigh's trial brought Attorney-General Sir Hartley Shawcross down to Lewes Assizes in Sussex to prosecute, so impor-

tant was this sensationally headlined case. Only one of Haigh's murders could be listed on the indictment, that of Olive Durand-Deacon, and so Sir Hartley guided the court through Detective Inspector Shelley Symes' interrogation of Haigh and Keith Simpson's careful analysis of the fatty sludge outside his workshop.

Haigh seemed entirely uninterested in the proceedings, and passed the time doing crossword puzzles while the prosecution case unfolded.

His defence was in the hands of David Maxwell Fyfe, who would later, as Home Secretary, refuse a last minute reprieve from the gallows for the unfortunate Derek Bentley. Fyfe called only one witness, Dr. Henry Yellowlees, who offered the professional opinion that Haigh's was a rare case of pure paranoia. This, he explained, would mean delusions of grandeur, coupled with the erroneous belief that other people were constantly plotting against him.

In support of these delusions of grandeur, Haigh's self-confident fraudster's manner and persistently smart appearance could be adduced.

The fear of outsiders was attributed to Haigh's rigid upbringing by his Plymouth Brethren parents – but the fact that they were among the more liberal members of the sect, and allowed their son to sing in Wakefield Cathedral choir – an association with outsiders that many of the Brethren would not have tolerated – was completely disregarded by his defence counsel.

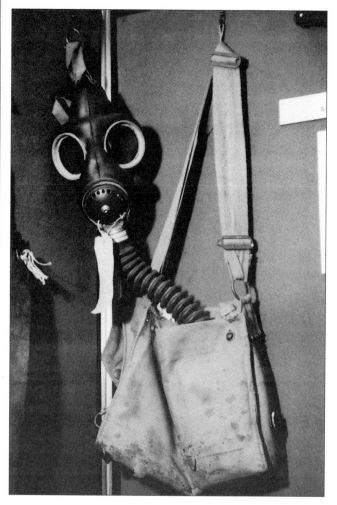

The gas mask which Haigh wore as protection while he disposed of his victims in acid.

Another exhibit from Haigh's gruesome wardrobe of murder-wear: his apron.

Ultimately the judge, Mr. Travers Humphreys, who had been a junior member of Oscar Wilde's defence team in his younger days, could stand no more of this extravagant special pleading which centred on damning the Brethren. He snapped that he wished to hear no further denigration of a religious body whose reputation for integrity stood virtually as high as that of the Quakers.

In any case, Dr. Yellowlees was bound to confess, under Sir Hartley's shrewd cross-examination, that Haigh would have been aware that his actions were wrong. And that, under the McNaghten Rules, was that. If a lunatic's lunacy permitted him to know what he was doing and know that it was wrong, the law in 1949 did not admit that his mental illness provided any defence against any criminal charge brought against him.

Haigh himself went through his account of the recurrent nightmare of bleeding crucifix trees and a man who forced him to drink the blood. But Dr. Yellowlees was unwilling to commit himself to more than a belief that Haigh *might* have had such dreams and *might* have felt impelled to drink blood. It wouldn't seem to have much to do with classic paranoia, in any case.

Mr. Justice Humphreys summed up with a scrupulously fair account of the defence's paranoia theory. It made little difference to the jury, though. They took a mere 13 minutes to find Haigh guilty, and he was sentenced to death.

The man's vanity was only slightly less than his greed. While charming his warders in the death cell, he made arrangements to leave his favourite suit and tie to Madame Tussaud's so that his effigy in the Chamber of Horrors should convey the proper smartness on which he prided himself. And in the Chamber of Horrors, where he so rightly belongs, Haigh still stands in wax.

JOHN CHRISTIE

November 30, 1949. A little Welshman in a new camel-hair overcoat and a garish tie went into the tiny police station at Merthyr Vale and asked to see a sergeant or an inspector. Only a detective constable was available to speak to 25-year-old Timothy John Evans – a Detective Constable Evans, coincidentally . Timothy had a startling confession to make: "I have disposed of my wife." He had, indeed. Down the drain outside his house at 10 Rillington Place, London.

■

DETECTIVE CONSTABLE EVANS sighed and took a full statement. The little man told a sad story of pinched purses and cramped lodgings leading to marital strife.

He was a van driver. His young wife Beryl, once a telephonist at the swanky Grosvenor House Hotel, had proved a dreadful housekeeper. Their top-floor flat at the end of a row of tiny houses in Rillington Place was always a mess, and Beryl couldn't manage her housekeeping money. Tim handed over the lion's share of his wages to her, keeping back only pocket money for cigarettes and beer at the "KPH", a back-street pub in Notting Hill which went under the grand title of the Kensington Park Hotel.

But Beryl slid quietly into debt, falling behind with the instalment payments on their furniture and owing rent. This situation made Tim angry and provoked serious arguments.

There was one child, baby Geraldine, whom they both adored. Then Beryl found herself pregnant again. Knowing she couldn't cope with more responsibilities, she was determined to have an abortion. Tim, raised a Catholic, disapproved, but she insisted.

One day, in a transport café near Chelmsford, Tim continued, he got chatting to a stranger who bummed a cigarette off him. He told the stranger about Beryl's problems. With a wink, the stranger slipped him a bottle of white liquid. When Beryl found it in his pocket and learned it was an abortifacient, she determined to use it, while Tim was safely out of the way. One day Tim came home from work to find her dead.

Not knowing what to do, he put her down the drain outside the house, sold his furniture to a secondhand dealer, and headed back to his birthplace, Merthyr, to stay with his uncle and aunt, Mr. and Mrs. Probert. But it preyed on his mind to think of Beryl down the drain. So here he was, making a clean breast of things.

That was *his* story. D.C. Evans didn't believe much of it. The man in the transport café was obvious fiction. It seemed likely that this little man had poisoned his wife. But she would have to be fished up from the drain. D.C. Evans kept Timothy John in the interview room while he telephoned London.

ENTER CHRISTIE

A couple of hours later the detective came back with a few more questions. Evans said he'd put his wife down the drain outside Rillington Place? By himself? Well, how did he raise the manhole cover? It had taken four strong policemen with a special key to move the cast-iron disc. Evans was a short man, and not at all robust. He still limped from the effects of the tubercular verrucca which had kept him in hospital for much of his childhood and left him so badly schooled he was still illiterate.

"Well, I did it," Evans asserted.

The police assumed he was off his head. There was no body in the drain. Nobody had made Evans come in and confess. They informed Mr. and Mrs. Probert that their nephew was in the police station, as near as dammit confessing to a murder he hadn't committed. They learned from his uncle and aunt that Tim had always been a fantasist, making up incredible stories that hadn't a shred of truth in them.

Timothy Evans now gave a second statement to the police. His first, he claimed, had been made to protect a man called Reg Christie.

It was all true about the money and the pregnancy and Beryl wanting an abortion. But, of course, he'd made up the man in the Chelmsford transport café and his little bottle. In fact, Reg Christie, the ground-floor tenant at 10 Rillington Place, had some medical experience, and he had offered to abort Beryl while Tim was out at work. But it went wrong, and Tim came home to find Beryl dead. He helped Christie hide the body in the empty first-floor flat overnight, after

The house of murder in London's Notting Hill, scene of eight murders. Rillington Place was later renamed Rushton Place.

which Christie told him he had disposed of it down the drain.

Furthermore, Christie had arranged for baby Geraldine to be looked after by a childless couple in East Acton. Evans had never met them, and didn't know their name and address. He was most anxious that his mother (who lived nearby) should find out where Geraldine was and go and see that she was all right.

The message went back to Evans' deeply puzzled mother, who could not understand why her son had suddenly left his job and fled to Wales, leaving a trail of debts. Nor could Christie, a middle-aged Post Office clerk, cast much light on the subject. He hadn't seen Beryl since the first week of the month, he said. Like everyone else Evans had spoken to, he believed Beryl had gone either to Bristol, where Evans said he had a new job, or to stay with her father in Sussex. But he could confirm that the Evanses had often quarrelled, and that Tim used to knock Beryl about.

Christie had been a special constable during the war and knew the ins and outs of police investigation. Ladbroke Grove CID found him easy to deal with, and his motherly wife, Ethel, backed up his story.

When the police thoroughly searched 10 Rillington Place, they found Beryl

and Geraldine in the tiny wash-house beside the outside lavatory. Both had been strangled and wrapped in blankets.

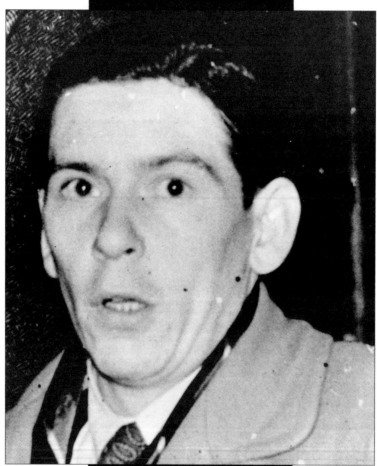

"CHRISTIE DONE IT. HE'S THE ONLY ONE THAT CAN HELP ME NOW."
TIMOTHY JOHN EVANS

Timothy Evans, a fantasist with the mental age of an 11-year-old.

Brought back to London under arrest, Evans soon confessed to killing Beryl in a quarrel over money, and to killing Geraldine a day later. He repeated his

confession to the prison doctor, and only changed his story when his mother came and asked why he did it. "I didn't, mam," he replied. "Christie done it. He's the only that can help me now."

At his trial Evans still blamed Christie for Beryl's death – but not even his counsel believed him. Christie, on the other hand, presented a most sympathetic figure in the witness-box: he was an old soldier whose voice had been reduced to a whisper by gas in the First World War.

It seemed a sad recompense for his attempts to be kind to a young neighbour that he should be accused of murder, and during the course of the trial have a criminal record for minor acts of petty dishonesty brought out, even though he had gone straight for 13 years and had served as a wartime policeman, despite his obvious health problems.

Evans was found guilty of both murders and sent to the gallows in 1950. Only his family and his priest had any doubts about the justice of his sentence.

CHRISTIE THE KILLER

What nobody knew was that John Reginald Halliday Christie had killed two women during the war, and their bodies still lay buried in the tiny garden at 10 Rillington Place. Police searching the house had completely overlooked the

The washroom in the yard where a discarded tobacco tin was found to contain several tufts of pubic hair.

A dig in the garden at 10 Rillington Place revealed the skeletons of Ruth Fuerst and Muriel Eady.

stick-like piece of fencing that was actually a human thighbone which had been put to good use by the thrifty Christie.

Ruth Fuerst was his first victim. A young Austrian girl who had come to England to train as a nurse, she was working in a munitions factory when the war broke out, and supplemented her wages with casual prostitution. While Mrs. Christie was away visiting relatives in the north, Christie brought her back to the house. The pair were making love when a telegram arrived, warning them of Mrs. Christie's imminent early return. Ruth asked Christie to run away with her, and he responded by strangling her and hiding her body under the living room floorboards until the opportunity came to bury her in the garden at night. But first he raped her lifeless body, an experience he enjoyed so much that he was to repeat it five times.

In 1944, he invited fellow-worker Muriel Eady to come to Rillington Place and try a cure he had for her chronic catarrh. Mrs Christie was again away,

and Muriel unsuspectingly inhaled from the bubbling jar with tubes emerging from it that Christie gave her. The principal aroma was Friar's Balsam, which effectively masked the household gas Christie was letting into the container. When Muriel had passed out, Christie raped her, strangled her, and buried her in the garden by night.

Just before Christmas 1952, Christie wrote to his wife's relatives telling them that arthritis in her hand had prevented Ethel from signing the usual Christmas card, and jauntily remarking that he would cook Christmas dinner that year. In fact, nobody had seen Mrs. Christie since late November.

In March 1953, Christie's landlord was shocked to find that Christie had sold his furniture and done a moonlight flit, leaving a young couple in the flat who had paid him three months' rent in advance, under the impression that Christie was entitled to sublet to them. Landlord Ernest Brown relet Christie's kitchen to Jamaican Beresford Brown.

One day Brown was tapping the walls to find a secure place to put up a bracket for a radio. At one point the wall seemed hollow – indeed, mere paper. Beresford Brown tore a little hole in the wallpaper, and found himself gazing at the naked back of a dead woman. She was seated on a pile of rubbish and held upright by her bra strap which was tied to a bundle in front of her.

When the police came to the house, they discovered that the bundle contained another naked female body, propped up against the wall. And beneath her was yet a third woman, also wrapped in a blanket.

For a week 10 Rillington Place was taken apart, with bodies, it seemed, emerging from every corner. Under the living room floorboards lay Ethel Christie – the only one of his victims who had not been stripped and raped.

To this day, no one really knows why Christie killed his wife. But it is certain that her death released him on a dreadful spree of picking up, gassing, raping and strangling prostitutes from the seedy Notting Hill neighbourhood.

In addition, from the garden came the skeletons of Ruth Fuerst and Muriel Eady. In the yard, a discarded tobacco tin contained Christie's collection of four tufts of women's pubic hair – forensic revealed that none of these had been taken from the victims in Christie's private morgue.

ON THE RUN

The police issued Christie's photograph to the press in 1953 with the announcement that they wanted to interview John Reginald Halliday Christie in connection with the Notting Hill murders. For a week he was on the run, drifting around London and sleeping rough after he left the hostel for men near King's Cross Station to which he had originally fled.

On March 29 he telephoned the *News of the World* newspaper, complaining, "They're hunting me like a dog and I'm tired out. I'm cold and wet and I've nothing to change into." The reporter arranged a rendezvous, though warning Christie he would have to inform the police as soon as the interview was completed. Christie was willing to take the risk in return for a decent meal. But the meeting never took place. Two policemen on beat duty came by, frightening off Christie who slipped away without speaking to the reporter.

While he was on the run, Christie continued to haunt backstreet pubs and cafés and chat up women, even suggesting to one that he might arrange an abortion for her.

Finally, P.C. Thomas Ledger noticed him staring moodily into the River Thames beside Putney Bridge. Ledger asked the vagrant his business. As Christie was giving the constable fictitious personal details, Ledger recognized the bespectacled face. He made Christie take his hat off – one glimpse at the bald pate, and the policeman was certain. It was Christie, and he was under arrest.

Back at the police station Christie seemed almost glad it was all over, and in his ingratiating whisper he confessed to murdering the women found in his house. Not that he volunteered damning information without prompting: although he talked about Mrs. Christie and the three bodies papered into the kitchen alcove, he said nothing about the two in the garden until he was told that the police had found their remains. Nor did he ever give a truthful account of the sources of his pubic hair collection.

The three dead women in the kitchen alcove, Hectorina MacLennan, Kathleen Maloney and Rita Nelson, were all prostitutes picked up in the backstreets of Notting Hill. Christie had taken them home and given each a nice cup of tea which they drank, seated in the filthy string mesh deckchair in his kitchen. (He had little other furniture left, having sold most of his things immediately after killing Ethel.) Then he stood with his head by the open window while he held a tube from the gas tap under the chair until they were overcome by fumes.

Typically, Christie did not admit that his motive was sex with their inanimate bodies until his interrogators revealed that his semen had been found inside them. The creepy killer wanted it to be supposed that he had strangled them in a rage at their immoral propositions – and he had made a similar suggestion about his first victim, Ruth Fuerst.

While strangling Ruth, he had discovered that this form of killing caused spontaneous ejaculation. With subsequent victims he always tied a diaper round them after they were unconscious.

The sight that confronted lodger Beresford Brown when he tore the wallpaper from the wall in his room: the naked back of a dead woman.

Of his two "respectable" victims, Muriel Eady and his wife, he claimed that their deaths had been the unfortunate outcome of his attempts to relieve them from the pain of illness.

TRIALS AND OFFICIAL INQUIRIES

Reg Christie was a Yorkshireman, born in Halifax, and brought up severely by a martinet of a father. He showed an early love of uniforms, joining the scouts and becoming a scoutmaster. When he was 16, he suffered the humiliation of impotence when an experienced girl took him to the local lovers' lane. Afterwards, she told her friends, who taunted him with the name "Reggie No-Dick".

He served with the Sherwood Foresters during the First World War: a meticulous signalman, who kept his nose as clean as his exemplary notebooks. But in his short period of active service he was gassed, suffered hysterical blindness for a short time, hysterical dumbness for a few months, and disabling difficulty in speaking for several years.

Shortly after the war he married Ethel, but swiftly became the black sheep of his very respectable family.

> ## "THE MORE THE MERRIER."
> ### CHRISTIE, CONFESSING TO THE MURDER OF BERYL EVANS

Christie was known to use the services of Halifax prostitutes, and he was convicted of several acts of petty dishonesty. He left Ethel and came to London where he built up a small criminal record for theft and (once) violence, when he battered the head of a prostitute with whom he was living. (He claimed that practice strokes with a cricket bat had misfired!) In 1938 Ethel rejoined him, and, thanks to her influence, he appeared to be back on the straight and narrow.

During the Second World War he was an officious but effective special constable for three years, but it seems that he was blackmailing the prostitutes on his beat into sleeping with him. He left the police force after a soldier on leave found Christie with his wife, and beat him up. Christie then became a Post Office clerk.

His criminal record should have made it impossible for him to work for the Post Office – as it should have prevented him from joining the police. But Christie was a fluent and habitual liar and he got away with the deception.

Though the Crown could only charge him with one offence at a time, and had chosen the murder of Ethel Christie as the charge, Mr. Derek Curtis-Bennett, defending him, decided to bring out in

Bodies seemed to grow out of the woodwork of Rillington Place. Ethel Christie was found under the floorboards.

Two more bodies, wrapped in blankets, were found blocked up in the wall.

court the whole chain of murders. The defence of insanity could best be established by demonstrating Christie's extraordinary fetish for raping dead or unconscious women.

As this defence was prepared, Christie was asked about the death of Beryl Evans. "The more the merrier!" Christie said to the prison chaplain, and admitted that Timothy Evans' second statement, implicating him, was true. He denied knowing anything about the death of baby Geraldine, however.

At his trial, the judge, Mr. Justice Finnemore, pressed him on the question of Geraldine's death. However, his counsel, Mr Curtis-Bennett did not want to

follow up that line: the self-interested murder of a baby whose untended presence could have led to the discovery of her mother's death had no place in an insanity plea. Nor did Attorney-General

> ## "I MUST HAVE GONE HAYWIRE."
> ### CHRISTIE, CONFESSING TO THE MURDER OF HECTORINA MACLENNAN

Sir Lionel Heald wish to press the point for, as it would emerge later, the authorities desperately wanted to suppress the fact that, three years earlier, they had hanged an innocent man.

Christie's insanity plea fell on deaf ears. The jury took half an hour to find

him guilty, and Mr. Justice Finnemore donned the black cap to pass the sentenced of death on him.

Most people found Christie a creepy and repellent character, with his insinuating, self-exculpatory manner. He purported to feel he had a good reason for helping each of his victims to a merciful exit, and shiftily played down his malign sexual designs on them. He desperately wanted people to think well of him, and always hoped he might be reprieved from the gallows on the grounds of his insanity. Prison doctors and warders considered him loathsome, even by the standards of murderers, and were irritated by his half-educated pretensions to knowledge and

John Christie, charged with the murder of his wife, on his way to court, April 29, 1953.

fastidiousness. A very few people were impressed by his superior intelligence, and he became known by some inmates as "Chris the chess champion".

The contrast with Evans, who had a mental age of 11 and, apart from scrawling his signature, could neither read not write, was marked. It was easy to believe that the little van driver had been putty in Christie's hands.

Common sense persuaded huge numbers of people that it was too much of a coincidence that two stranglers of women should have been living in the same house at the same time. Nobody could doubt for a moment that Christie's evidence at Evans' trial would have been severely tarnished had anyone known that two victims of his lust already lay buried in the garden.

Before Christie's execution, the Home Secretary had to give way to public and parliamentary pressure, and set up a new inquiry into the murder of Beryl Evans. This proved to be a whitewash job, in which a distinguished barrister made the presumption that Evans (a known fantasizing liar) had consistently lied throughout his trial, whereas Christie had only lied in claiming to kill Beryl. Christie, always obsequious to authority, willingly went along with this. But it did not save him from being hanged in 1953. On his last night on earth, he refused to answer questions about baby Geraldine's death.

Many people remained uneasy, however, even though Christie had gone to the gallows. Solicitor Michael Eddowes published a book called *The Man on Your Conscience*, which took as its theme the miscarriage of justice that had befallen Timothy Evans.

The Christie murder trial attracted a great deal of public and media attention.

Successive Conservative Home Secretaries, however, took the view that no good could be done by raking over old coals. It was not until Harold Wilson's Labour government was elected in 1964 that fresh steps were taken to reopen the case and look at the evidence against Timothy Evans anew.

The new inquiry was helped by Ludovic Kennedy's masterly book *10 Rillington Place*, which clearly established the impossibility of Evans' confession to having placed the bodies of Beryl and Geraldine in the wash-house. Workmen carrying out repairs for the landlord had been in and out of the house until Evans left London for Wales, and they could not possibly have missed the two sinister bundles, barely concealed by old timber and the back of the door. At the time of Evans' trial they had accepted the police view that they must have been mistaken about the day when they cleaned and swept the room. And, indeed, since Evans had spontaneously confessed to something he had not done,

there was every reason to imagine that he was likely to be right in recalling the traumatic murders, and the workmen wrong in trying to account for their mundane movements.

Now all that had changed. Yet the government's new inquiry came up with an even more extraordinary conclusion. It reported that Evans had been wrongly convicted, since he had been tried for Geraldine's murder and he had not killed her. But that he had been rightly executed, since he must have killed Beryl, just as he had confessed in his statement to the police at the time.

This conclusion was staggering. No reason at all was offered to explain Christie's murder of baby Geraldine – a completely unnecessary crime if he had had nothing to do with killing Beryl. Home Secretary Roy Jenkins swept this attempt of a whitewash aside, granting Evans a posthumous free pardon and accepting the unpalatable fact that a completely innocent man had been executed in the name of justice.

CRAIG AND BENTLEY

Two men embark on a robbery. One has a gun and murders a policeman. The other is unarmed. The first robber is sent to prison for 10 years. The other robber, arguably in the custody of the police at the time of the murder, is hanged for the crime. Doesn't seem possible? This is exactly what happened in the notorious case of Christopher Craig and Derek Bentley.

■

MANY PEOPLE BELIEVE that the authorities made an example of Derek Bentley because of rising juvenile crime. Others have gone further and suggested that he was set up by the police. For over 40 years this case has been argued, with supporters of Derek Bentley regularly petitioning the Home Secretary that he be granted a posthumous pardon.

Increase in crime, it seems, is an inevitable post-war reaction and in post-World War II Britain, with rationing still in force, black marketeering was widespread. There was a flourishing trade in forged ration coupons, house break-ins were common and lorries carrying rationed goods were frequently hijacked. London was home to many small but well organized and ruthless gangs. Shootings in the street are thought of as a modern-day phenomenon, but at this time London experienced an unprecedented increase in the use of firearms.

The Metropolitan Police could barely cope with the increase in crime, especially the gangs, and responded by creating a small team of detectives who were assigned the task of going undercover to obtain information. These operatives were never to visit Scotland Yard, and never to appear in court to give evidence. As far as the Yard was concerned they did not exist. These men became known as the Ghost Squad.

The Ghost Squad was conceived by Chief Constable Percy Worth and its chief wraith was one John Capstick who, in his autobiography, attributed the origin of the idea to a policeman known as "Squibs" Dance. According to Capstick, "Squibs" worked "under cover" almost permanently.

At this time a popular television series with a loosely factual basis was *Fabian of the Yard*. In April 1947, Chief Superintendent Tom Barratt, who ran what was called No. 1 District within the Metropolitan Police, took his annual holiday. Robert Fabian took temporary charge and so had responsibility for the Alec de Antiquis case, a minor *cause célèbre* of the day.

Off London's Tottenham Court Road runs Charlotte Street and it was here, on April 29, 1947, that three men held up a jewellery shop. As they were armed, the staff were able to prevent the robbery and the men escaped into the street. Here they discovered that a lorry was blocking their getaway car, so they fled on foot. Alec de Antiquis was at this moment manoeuvring his motorcycle around the parked lorry and, on seeing the robbers, he threw his bike into a skid and rode into their path. One then aimed his gun and shot de Antiquis in the head.

It fell to Robert Fabian to investigate the case, but all his efforts seemed to draw a blank until a cab driver volunteered some information that led to the discovery of a raincoat, unquestionably worn by one of de Antiquis' killers, which was traced to 23-year-old Harry Jenkins. Jenkins was tight-lipped and admitted nothing, but Fabian was convinced by his behaviour of the young man's involvement in the de Antiquis killing. Further spadework uncovered two more likely suspects: 21-year-old Christopher Geraghty and 17-year-old Terence Rolt. They were friends of Jenkins, and Fabian reckoned that they were involved in the attempted robbery. They were charged, Christopher Geraghty specifically with having shot and killed Alec de Antiquis. All three were tried and found guilty. Jenkins and Geraghty were hanged at Pentonville Prison on September 19, 1947. Rolt escaped the noose, being below the age when the death penalty could be carried out. He served a prison sentence instead.

The hangings of these two thugs, one of whom had killed without compunction and deprived a family of a husband and father, caused a public outcry which overshadowed the death of the brave if perhaps foolhardy de Antiquis. One element of concern was the execution of Jenkins, who had merely participated in a foiled robbery. His was not a hanging offence, so why was he executed? A few years later the same question would be asked in the case of Craig and Bentley.

In February 1948, the 13th to be precise, a plain-clothes policeman named Nathaniel Edgar saw, stopped and began questioning a petty criminal and army deserter named Donald George Thomas. Thomas, 23-years-old, was suspected of having committed or participated in several burglaries. Without warning, Thomas produced a gun and fired three shots. P.C. Edgar did not take long to die, but he lasted long enough to tell colleagues that he'd written the name of his murderer in his notebook. Policemen

Barlow and Parker in Tamworth Road, Croydon, the scene of one of the most controversial cases in English legal history.

P.C. Sidney Miles pursued Craig with fatal consequences.

found Thomas's name and soon traced his whereabouts. Knowing him to be armed and a murderer, the police did not mess about. Surprising him at his lodging, they grabbed him before he could reach for his gun. "You were lucky, I might just as well be hung for a sheep as a lamb," said Thomas.

Thomas was tried, convicted and sentenced to death, but was saved from hanging by a temporary suspension of the death penalty pending a Parliamentary vote on whether or not the death penalty should be abolished. The vote went against abolition and on June 10, 1948, hanging was reintroduced. By that time two more policemen, P.C. Harris at Forest Gate and P.C. Kay at Acton, had been shot dead.

Overall, though, the death penalty seemed to have little, if any, effect on criminals. As has repeatedly been observed, but almost always ignored, criminals weigh the potential benefits of a crime against the risks of getting caught, not against the punishment if they are caught. Perhaps crime figures could be reduced by increasing the probability of capture rather than the severity of the punishment. However, with the reintroduction of hanging, some people thought an example was needed to drive the message home – and that example may have been Derek Bentley.

In his book *Scotland Yard*, former Commissioner Sir Harold Scott

described the Craig and Bentley case as "an affray such as had not been seen in London since the Battle of Sidney Street in 1910..." This is a gross overstatement.

In 1910 a gang had attempted to rob a jeweller's shop in Houndsditch, on the border of the City of London. The police gave chase to the criminals. Three officers were killed, two more crippled, and

"LET HIM HAVE IT, CHRIS."

DEREK BENTLEY, ALLEGEDLY

The revolver used by Craig in the shooting of P.C. Miles.

a little boy who happened to be in the way was also killed. The robbers fled into London's East End, but a tip-off told the police that the wanted men were hiding in a house in Sidney Street. Armed policemen and troops surrounded and lay siege to the house. The scene was visited by several notable people, among them the Home Secretary, a young Winston Churchill. The outcome of the affair was that the house in which the men were holed up was burnt down with the robbers inside.

Next to this event the Craig and

Bentley case was almost petty, but Sir Harold Scott's exaggerated comments serve to show that in the 1950s outrages against the police (and the public) by juvenile criminals was a matter of very serious concern.

CRAIG AND BENTLEY

Barlow and Parker's warehouse was in Tamworth Road, Croydon, six miles to the south of London. On Sunday, November 2, 1952, at 9.25, a telephone call to Croydon police station stated that two men had been seen climbing over the tall gates into the warehouse yard. The police arrived in two vehicles about 10 minutes later. In a van were Detective Constable Frederick Fairfax and Police Constables Norman Harrison, Claude Pain and Allan Beecher-Brigden. D.C. Fairfax examined the ground-floor doors and windows, without finding any sign of a forced entry, and told Harrison, Pain and Beecher-Brigden to separate, position themselves around the warehouse and see what they could.

The second police vehicle, a wireless car, now arrived, bringing P.C. Leslie Miles and P.C. James McDonald. They learned over the radio from someone who'd called the station that the criminals had reached the roof of the warehouse. McDonald immediately told D.C. Fairfax, who climbed up a drainpipe to the roof.

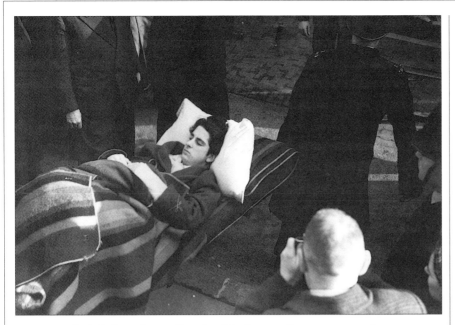

Craig being taken to Croydon Magistrates Court on a stretcher.

The would-be robbers were 16-year-old Christopher Craig and 19-year-old Derek Bentley. Fairfax approached them and from a distance of within six feet said: "I'm a police officer. Come out from behind that stack." Drawing nearer, Fairfax grabbed Derek Bentley, who was nearest, but Bentley pulled away and allegedly called out: "Let him have it, Chris!" There was a gunshot. Fortunately, Fairfax was only hit in the shoulder and was able to take cover. Remarkably, he did not release his grip on Bentley and managed to drag him behind a roof light. There Fairfax rapidly searched Bentley, and found that he was armed with a knife and a knuckle-duster.

Bentley, who had made no attempt to escape, said, "That is all I have got – I have not got a gun." Fairfax began to work his way from the roof light to a doorway, which provided better cover in case Craig should begin shooting again. Bentley went with the policeman without resistance, even allowing the wounded policeman to use him as a shield.

Arguably, through this action, Bentley saved Fairfax's life.

Meanwhile, P.C. McDonald had followed Fairfax up the drainpipe, but could not quite manage to haul himself onto the flat roof of the warehouse. He gave a shout to Fairfax, who went over to help his colleague, leaving Bentley alone. Bentley could have rejoined Christopher Craig, but he made no attempt and showed no inclination to do so. Instead he waited until the two policemen rejoined him, then volunteered the information that Craig's gun was a .45 and that there was plenty of ammunition. "I told the silly b— not to use it," he's reported to have said.

By this time P.C. Harrison had also reached the roof, but Craig fired at him, at least once and possibly twice, forcing him to retreat the way he had come. About quarter of an hour had passed and more policemen were arriving at the scene. One had managed to obtain the key of a door to the stairway to the roof. Several policemen went up, but the first to reach the roof was P.C. Sidney Miles. He pushed open the door leading onto the roof and stepped out. There was a shot and P.C. Miles fell to the ground. Christopher Craig had killed him.

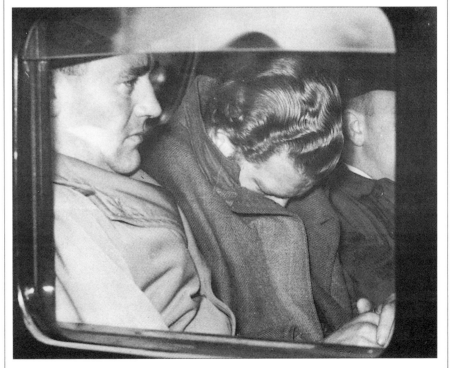

Bentley, his head bowed, shortly after being charged with murder.

Using Bentley as a shield again, D.C. Fairfax tried to manoeuvre to the stairway. Bentley helped by yelling out, "Look out, Chris. They're taking me down." Craig didn't shoot and Fairfax safely reached the stairs. He took Bentley down. Guns had now been issued to the police and Fairfax managed to get one. He returned to the roof and fired several shots at Craig, who was now out of ammunition. Recognizing that he couldn't hold out much longer and not wanting to be taken by the police, Christopher Craig threw himself from the roof, badly hurting his back. He was lucky the fall didn't kill him.

Christopher Craig and Derek Bentley were tried for murder.

"LET HIM HAVE IT, CHRIS"

The case against Bentley rested on a fine point of law. The law states that if two or more people commit a crime, the action of one is regarded as the action of all. As we have seen, it was Geraghty who shot and killed Alec de Antiquis, but Jenkins was also deemed guilty and hanged with him at Pentonville in September, 1947. In this case the law decreed that Derek Bentley was as guilty of shooting P.C. Miles as if he had pulled the trigger himself. Moreover, it was believed Craig was incited to begin shooting by Bentley allegedly shouting "Let him have it, Chris". Bentley was therefore seen as beginning the sequence of events which led to the murder of P.C. Miles.

Those words, "Let him have it, Chris", were to prove to be crucial at the trial. In the course of his summing up the Judge said that of the police testimony: "...if their evidence is untrue that Bentley called out, 'Let him have it, Chris,' those

three officers are doing their best to swear away the life of that boy. If it is true it is, of course, the most deadly piece of evidence against him. Do you believe those officers have come into the box and sworn what is deliberately untrue...?"

Bentley denied yelling these words and Craig claimed that he never heard them. Unfortunately, Derek Bentley was

mentally subnormal. He contradicted himself in statements to the police and denied almost everything that could be denied. He said he did not know Craig was armed, however there was police testimony to the effect that he did know Craig had a gun, that he had seen it, knew it to be a .45, and that he'd warned Craig not to shoot. Worst of all for Bentley, he denied being in police custody

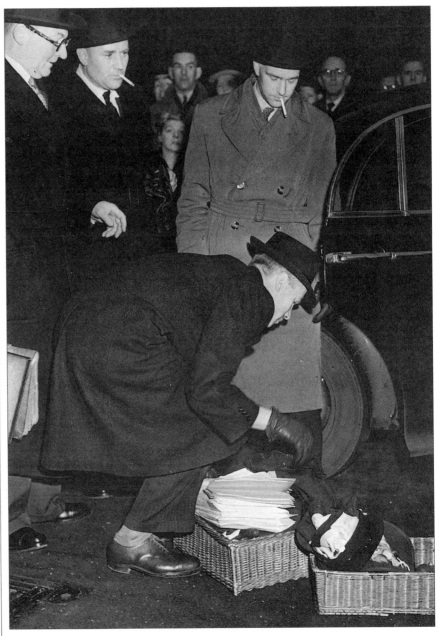

Detective Inspectors Smith, Sheppard and Fairfax watch as exhibits presented at the trial of Craig and Bentley are loaded into a police car.

when P.C. Miles was shot dead. Since then, of course, people have pointed out the ambiguity in the words "Let him have it, Chris". Was Bentley telling Craig to shoot D.C. Fairfax or to hand the gun over to him? Unfortunately, what he meant by these words was never discovered because Bentley repeatedly denied shouting them.

Derek Bentley was convicted of murder and executed at Wandsworth Prison in January 1953. Christopher Craig was too young to hang and was sent to prison instead. He was released 10 years later. Ever since the execution controversy has raged over whether or not Bentley was the victim of a miscarriage of justice.

On the one hand, Craig and Bentley were hardened criminals. They had gone to the warehouse to commit a crime and both were armed, Craig with a gun, of course, and Bentley with the knife and knuckle-duster. It is assumed in law that carrying a weapon infers a probable willingness to use it in resisting arrest. Both men were therefore engaged in the commission of a crime and were equally guilty of the outcome of the endeavour. It was only by mere chance that Craig was too young to hang and Bentley therefore legitimately went to the gallows.

However, lawyers have asked whether or not Bentley had by word or action severed his partnership with Craig. If he had, from the moment of severance he would not have been responsible for Craig's actions. What, they argued, would be the legal position if P.C. Miles had been killed *after* Bentley had been taken down from

Smiles all round for the policemen on the case. Sergeant Fairfax (left) received the George Cross, P.C. McDonald the George Medal and P.C. Jaggs the B.E.M.

the roof? What if Christopher Craig had managed to escape from the roof and maybe shot a policeman a month later? Would Bentley have still been responsible for Craig's actions?

The fact is, from Bentley allegedly

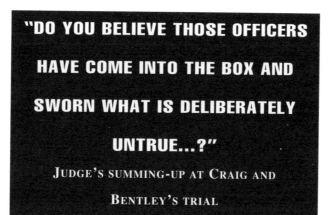

"DO YOU BELIEVE THOSE OFFICERS HAVE COME INTO THE BOX AND SWORN WHAT IS DELIBERATELY UNTRUE...?"

JUDGE'S SUMMING-UP AT CRAIG AND BENTLEY'S TRIAL

shouting "Let him have it, Chris" to Craig shooting P.C. Miles was separated by 15 minutes. According to undisputed evidence, evidence accepted even by the prosecution, for all of that time Bentley had been held by the police. He'd offered no resistance and made no

attempt to rejoin Craig. He had supplied the police with information and risked his life by letting Fairfax use him as a shield. Arguably Bentley's actions could be seen as a cessation of support for Craig. However, if by shouting "Let him have it, Chris" he incited Craig to start firing, beginning the sequence of events leading to P.C. Miles' death, Bentley could not have easily escaped responsibility for the outcome of what he'd begun.

The problem here, though, is not whether the words were shouted or not – and there are those who deny that they were – but the fact that Craig consistently denied hearing them. If Craig did not hear them then he was not incited by them and if he was not incited by them then Bentley could not be held responsible for starting the sequence of events resulting in the murder of P.C. Miles. The arguments surrounding the words are therefore irrelevant and the question of whether or not Bentley was rightfully hanged would seem to revolve around whether or not Bentley's actions when in police custody abrogated his shared responsibility for Craig's actions.

That Bentley had withdrawn his support of Craig seems clear from police testimony about his behaviour during that quarter of an hour. Additional information was given by Craig in an interview with David Yallop, author of a book on the Craig and Bentley case, *To Encourage the Others*:

"To me one of the most terrible things that happened was Bentley turning against me. Helping the police like that. They got him to come over to me to persuade me to give myself up. Bentley walked towards me and called out, 'For Christ's sake Chris, what's got into you?' I realised what he was up to and I told him to stop or he'd get it too. Bentley stopped for a moment, then he started to move towards me again, not in a straight line, but as if he was trying to work his way behind me. I told him that I knew what he was up to, and that he was trying to get behind me to get at the gun. Again he asked me, 'What's got into you Chris?' I told him to 'get back or I'll shoot you. Get back or I'll shoot you.' For a moment I thought he was still going to come on. Then he turned and walked back to the police."

This incident appears to have taken place *after* P.C. Miles was shot and if Christopher Craig's story is true, and there seems no particular reason for dis-

An angry crowd outside Wandsworth Prison as the execution notice is posted.

believing it, Bentley unquestionably had stopped supporting Craig; had, indeed, not merely ceased to support Craig, but had risked his own life to persuade Craig to surrender to the police.

To the lay observer it would seem from every angle that Derek Bentley should not have been hanged. The words "Let him have it, Chris" are ambiguous and what he meant by them was never ascertained. The words were uttered, if they were uttered at all, 15 minutes before the fatal shooting, a time during which Bentley had manifestly ceased to support or condone Craig's actions. Also, as Craig denied having heard them, he could not possibly have been incited by them.

Today it is widely held that Derek Bentley was the victim of a gross miscarriage of justice, or, in the argot of the underworld, that he was "stitched up" by the police. A recent book has even suggested that Bentley was condemned by a judge who derived sexual satisfaction from passing the death sentence. Whatever the truth of such claims, there is probably little doubt that Derek Bentley should not have been hanged.

Bentley's sister, Iris, who was 21 at the time of the shooting, has spent the last 40 years campaigning for a posthumous pardon for her brother and the case

> "TO ME ONE OF THE MOST TERRIBLE THINGS THAT HAPPENED WAS BENTLEY TURNING AGAINST ME. HELPING THE POLICE LIKE THAT."
> CHRISTOPHER CRAIG

has been reviewed several times.

This case did much to foster the belief in Britain that hanging should be abolished. Added fuel was given to the anti-capital-punishment campaign by the execution in 1953 of John Christie – he of 10 Rillington Place – for a series of murders, possibly even the murder of the baby Geraldine Evans for which Timothy Evans had already been hanged. In 1966, Evans was given a posthumous pardon. He was not absolved of guilt, but it was acknowledged that he may have been tried and hanged for the wrong crime, being guilty of having murdered his wife, not his daughter. Nevertheless,

in 1953 the revelation that 10 Rillington Place had harboured a multiple murderer at the time when Evans' wife and child were murdered was sufficient to throw doubt on Evans' guilt and lend weight to the anti-death-penalty campaign.

Hangings continued to take place, against a backdrop of mounting concern. In July 1955, Ruth Ellis was executed at Holloway Prison. She had cold-bloodedly shot dead her lover in the street outside a pub. There was no doubt of her guilt, but mitigating evidence – that a couple of days earlier her lover had punched her so hard in the stomach that he caused a miscarriage, for example –

was never heard at her trial. Although such information was not widely known at the time, considerable disquiet was expressed publicly and the Ruth Ellis case was instrumental in bringing about the end of capital punishment. She was the last woman to be hanged in Britain.

Further concern was generated by subsequent cases, one of the most famous being that of James Hanratty, hanged for murder and rape in 1962 although he produced witnesses who swore that he was nowhere near the scene of the crime.

Capital punishment in the United Kingdom was finally abolished in 1966.

Bentley's mother and sister, Iris, are consumed by grief after a final visit. Bentley was hanged shortly afterwards.

SAM
SHEPPARD

Bay View City, Ohio, was quiet on July 3, 1954.

The township overlooking Lake Erie, close to

Cleveland, was gearing itself up for the usual

parades and celebrations the following day. The

newspapers expected no big stories. So news-

hungry reporters flocked to the lakeside residence

of 30-year-old Dr. Sam Sheppard when a daybreak

call from the mayor to the police department

indicated that something was wrong.

■

ESTHER AND SPENCER HOOK were the first to know that violence had stained the small, quiet residential area where they lived. It was a generally affluent community. The houses fronted lakeside jetties where the residents' yachts and cabin cruisers lay moored. Dr. Sam Sheppard, the good-looking, stocky and slightly balding osteopath, was the Hooks' neighbour. When they received a call from him at dawn and heard the ominous cry, "I think they got Marilyn", the couple were alerted to an unnamed danger that threatened to destroy the good life they enjoyed in their idyllic retreat.

Indeed, someone had got her. Upstairs in a bloodsoaked bed, Sam's pregnant wife had been savagely battered to death with a blunt instrument. There was also a stab mark in her pillow, made by some sharp weapon. And the room had been ransacked.

Sam Sheppard's tale was simple in its esentials. The previous night, he and Marilyn had entertained guests to dinner. The socializing had lasted until 12.30am, but Sam said that he had fallen asleep on the couch long before the guests left. Marilyn had gone quietly upstairs to bed without disturbing him. He was sleeping soundly until roused by the sound of his wife screaming. Intermingling with her screams were noises consistent with a ferocious struggle.

Sam rushed upstairs to help her, but was knocked unconscious as soon as he entered the bedroom. When he came to, Sam found Marilyn beaten to death on the bed beside him. He heard noises from downstairs, but hurried to check that his child was all right before rushing down to investigate.

In the living room he saw a bushy-haired intruder, who ran away toward the lake as Sam approached. Sam chased after him across the yard, but was again felled by a stunning blow. When he regained consciousness this time, he went to the phone and summoned help through his good neighbours, the Hooks.

When details of the murder became public, everyone in the local community sympathized with the popular doctor, who came across as a somewhat passive character, despite his burly build.

Sam's successful career in the surgical ward of Bay View Osteopathic Hospital had been decreed by his father, who had insisted that all three of his sons work for him. Sam had been employed there since qualifying in 1949.

Sam's wife Marilyn was two months older than he, and dictated, to a considerable extent, the way the marriage was to work. After a difficult childbirth, she became extremely unwilling to indulge in marital sex. Despite this she was again four months pregnant at the time of her death. Sam swore at the inquest that their marriage had been very happy.

SUSPICIONS

The inquest was not a pleasant experience for Sam Sheppard. Dr. Sam Gerber, the coroner, took against him, and quickly revealed that he shared the suspicions of detectives Robert Sharkey and Patrick Barrow. These two instantly picked up a couple of features of Sam Sheppard's

> ## "I THINK THEY GOT MARILYN."
> SAM SHEPPARD

tale that sounded like familiar fictions. Firstly, the "bushy-haired stranger" is one of the favourite imaginary assailants invented by guilty murderers, if they decide to pass off their own deeds onto a sinister marauder. For some reason, shaggy or bushy hair comes quickly to mind when a murderous spouse wants a plausible yarn to tell the investigating officers. Sam told just such a story.

Secondly, he talked of being struck over the head, knocked out, and coming round soon enough and fit enough to go out and chase the intruder before being knocked out again. Surely, as a doctor, Sam ought to have known that the hearty uppercut from John Wayne that leaves the villain reeling, but ready to go on fighting at once, is a myth. He should have known that concussion, jarring the brain against the skull, is potentially a very serious form of injury, and the victim does not pick himself up in a daze, shake his head, and get straight on with his life. Even the padded fisticuff blows exchanged in the boxing ring have more serious effect than the imaginary "knockout blows" seen in the movies.

A skilled doctor should have been far more worried about the long-term possibility of brain damage if he had actually been hit on the head twice, in fairly quick succession, each time hard enough to induce unconsciousness. Sam Sheppard was just too fit and well and uninjured to be the victim he described so graphically when questioned by police.

Given the state of Marilyn's room and bed, her murderer must have been covered with blood. Sam's clothing

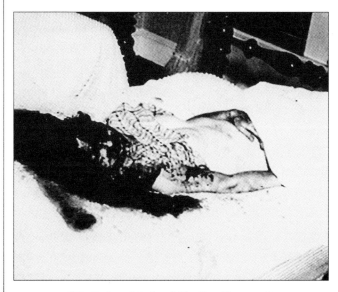

The battered body of Marilyn Sheppard.

Susan Hayes, one-time lover of Sam Sheppard.

Sam Sheppard with Arianne, the pen-pal who became his wife.

would also have been splattered with blood. The clothes he wore when the investigators arrived showed no more bloodmarks than were consistent with his story of going into the bedroom and seeing the carnage.

But why was he bare-chested? What had become of the T-shirt he was wearing when he fell asleep on the couch? Sam could not say. And the detectives inevitably concluded that he had himself disposed of the garment which absorbed the major blood splashes as he leaned over Marilyn and killed her. No one could imagine a murderous robber stopping to strip an ordinary T-shirt off his unconscious victim!

Finally, Coroner Gerber made a substantial point regarding the stab thrust in Marilyn's pillow. This, he declared, was obviously made by a surgical instrument. And Sam Sheppard, it was well known, was the surgeon of the Bay View Osteopathic Hospital.

TRIALS BY PRESS, CORONER AND JURY

Gerber refused to let a lawyer represent Dr. Sheppard at the inquest. Apart from Sam's own impassioned denials, no serious defence was mounted against the detectives' and coroner's belief that he had killed his wife. So the case of Sam Sheppard went forward for trial.

The fickle press, which had started by sympathizing with the traumatically widowed doctor, changed its mind, and started to write sensational stories pointing to his guilt. Sam's case was also immensely damaged when he had to confess that he had lied at the inquest about the state of his marriage. Far from being happy and faithful, he was, in fact, having an affair with pretty young Susan Hayes, a lab technician in the practice.

Then, as now, the press enjoyed a good case of furtive adultery as much as a murder. Both Sam and Susan had to admit their guilt on the witness stand,

and public opinion mercilessly refused to allow any mitigation of their sin by reason of Marilyn's unilateral decision to cut down on marital sex.

Sam Sheppard was found guilty of second degree murder. The jury believed he had killed Marilyn during a quarrel, and not after premeditation. He was sentenced to life imprisonment.

There were further tragic experiences awaiting the once successful osteopath. His elderly mother had supported him staunchly in his plea of innocence, and never believed him guilty of murder. But she was so horrified by the news of her son's sexual infidelity that she shot herself. And a few days later, Sam's father died of grief. Truly, Sam Sheppard was paying a heavy price for a casual liaison.

Yet there was important evidence that had not been brought out at the trial: evidence strongly in favour of Sam's claim that an intruder had entered the house that night. A fragment of tooth was found in the bedroom. Now, Sam suffered broken teeth as a consequence of his coshing, and had to go to the dentist immediately after the murder. But this piece of tooth was not his. Nor was it Marilyn's. Nor, indeed, had it come from any known person with legitimate business in the house.

There was a tiny scrap of red leather in the sitting room which could not be connected with any possession of the Sheppards, nor with any of their friends.

As is standard in violent murder cases, scrapings from under Marilyn's fingernails were routinely taken for laboratory examination. A victim who fights off her killer will scratch up microscopic cells of skin and maybe blood, and will remove tiny sections of thread from the fabric of her killer's clothes. These things can be used to link him to the crime. Nothing under Marilyn Sheppard's nails, not a single microscopically examined molecule, could be traced back to her husband, Sam.

This was all strong positive evidence in his favour. And there was more. There was a spot of blood on the wardrobe that came from neither Marilyn, nor Sam, nor anyone else known to have been in the bedroom. Taken in conjunction with the fragment of tooth, this should surely have permitted the possibility that Sam might have seen that "bushy-haired stranger". A criminologist called Dr. Paul Kirkwood picked up another point: Marilyn's injuries showed that her killer was left-handed. Sam Sheppard was not.

Surely with all this, there was enough to take the case to appeal? But the authorities had no wish to see the case re-opened. Sam Sheppard could stay in jail for the rest of his natural life, as far as they were concerned.

But then this bizarre case took a strange twist A former cab-driver in Florida, already in jail for other crimes, confessed to the murder of Marilyn Sheppard. Sam excitedly hoped this development really would lead to his freedom, but the man withdrew his confession, and nothing further came of it.

Erle Stanley Gardner, the creator of Perry Mason, was dragged into the case. Like Sir Arthur Conan Doyle, creator of Sherlock Holmes, Gardner quietly revelled in the fact that many people thought he must have the astute detective mind of his fictional creation. Cashing in on this reputation, Gardner had formed

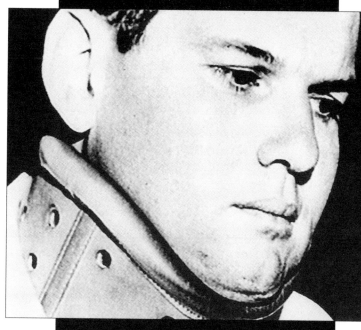

"TEN POUNDS OF HOGWASH IN A FIVE POUND BAG."

F. LEE BAILEY, ON THE CASE AGAINST SAM SHEPPARD

Sam was injured by the alleged intruder.

what he called "the Court of Last Resort". After the law of the land had failed you in every way, you could turn to the detective might of Erle Stanley Gardner himself, and trust that he would pull victory out of the jaws of defeat in true Perry Mason style, leaving the prosecution snarling like Hamilton Berger as yet another suspect got away.

In Sheppard's case, Gardner had a simple procedure to recommend: let Sam take a lie-detector test. The doctor was willing. But the authorities, who had power over his physical movements, refused to permit it.

BAILEY AND ARIANNE

Not until two glamorous younger figures came to his aid did Sheppard's case start to look hopeful. Arianne Teban-Johannz, a dazzling German blonde, read about Sam and wrote to him in prison. The two started a correspondence which became a romance. In 1964, Arianne came to America to see whether her pen-friend was as attractive in the flesh as he was on paper, and to throw her considerable wealth into the struggle to secure justice for him.

She came just at the time when Sam had engaged the services of controversial lawyer F. Lee Bailey. The Sam Sheppard case was to make the name of the then 29-year-old advocate. He and Arianne immediately started making headlines. Arianne's were favourable at first but turned sour (and sold just as many papers) when it emerged that she was the sister-in-law of Hitler's evil propaganda minister, Dr. Josef Goebbels, and had herself been an active member of the Hitler Youth.

Bailey opened sensational proceedings with a writ of *habeas corpus*. He claimed that Sam had been improperly locked up by the authorities ever since he came forward with new evidence that should have prompted a fresh trial. There was little hope of securing Sheppard's immediate release, but the proceedings enabled Bailey to get some pretty unsavoury doings of Ohio State penologists into the open. Sam Sheppard testified that he had been slapped into solitary confinement, battered against doors, and once left without food and water for six days, all to compel him to relinquish his ties to the embarrassing publicity machines of Arianne Teban-Johannz and F. Lee Bailey. Whether Sam Sheppard suffered quite such indignities or not we may never be certain, but the allegations enabled Bailey to take the case on to appeal.

With a retrial looking possible, the authorities paroled Sam on bail. The doctor took the opportunity to marry Arianne. The authorities then declared that it had been a mistake to let him out and promptly locked him up again.

Bailey focused his appeal on the faults he found in Sam's original trial. Although the case had been a media sensation, the jury had not been sequestered, and were able to read all the hostile press coverage Sam received. The defence had never raised the questions of the strange blood spot, tooth fragment and scrap of leather in the house. Neither prosecution nor defence had considered the question of whether Sam's injuries could or could not have been self-inflicted. A lack-adaisical defence had led to the erroneous opinion that Sam Sheppard had suffered no serious harm from twice being knocked unconscious.

Coroner Gerber's bias was plain for all to see in his insistence that Marilyn's pillow had been stabbed by a surgical instrument, when no such instrument to fit the rents had been discovered.

RETRIAL

The Supreme Court was strongly disapproving of the sensational press coverage and its availability to the unsequestered jury. Bailey won his appeal on the grounds that the original hearing had been tarnished by the "prejudicial publicity" of the news media's "carnival atmosphere". A retrial was ordered.

So, after 12 years, the osteopath stood trial once again for the murder of his wife. This time all the evidence was placed before the jury, and qualified practitioners were brought in to testify to the nature of Sam's injuries. A dentist had repaired four of his teeth damaged in the struggle. There was, he reported, no way in which Sam could have broken his own teeth.

Bailey produced a photograph of Sam entering the inquest proceedings in a wheelchair, with his neck braced by a surgical collar. The doctor who had treated Sam was called. He reported that the surgical collar was essential because Sam had cracked a vertebra – had broken his neck, in effect. Was there any way he could have done this to himself, F. Lee Bailey wondered?

"Only if he had dived out of a second floor window," was the response.

Coroner Gerber was compelled to confess that in 12 years of searching he had been quite unable to come up with a surgical instrument matching the rip in Marilyn's pillow.

Sam's missing T-shirt was also explained. A T-shirt with a small amount of bloodstaining had been picked up on the lakeshore. Evidently this was the one Sam had worn. And equally evidently, like his other clothes, it supported his story of having entered the bedroom after Marilyn's death. But it could not have been worn by Marilyn's murderer, who, without doubt, would have splashed blood all over himself.

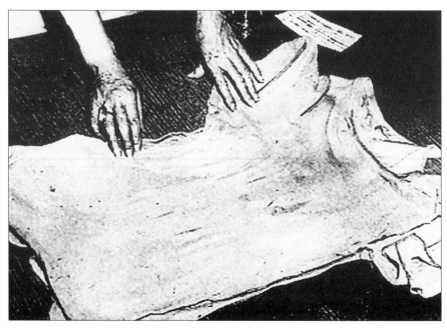

Sam's blood-stained T-shirt was an important piece of evidence in the defence case.

Bailey summed up the prosecution case in a ringing derogatory phrase. It was "ten pounds of hogwash in a five pound bag", he declared. And with his stunning courtroom oratory and the weighty additional defence evidence, Sam Sheppard was found not guilty.

But hindsight shows up one small chink in the defence case. The doctor was never put on the witness stand to testify in his own defence. This is really surprising. Juries are strictly prohibited from meditating on a defendant's unwillingness to explain his innocence, and in America are supposed to listen to pleas of "the Fifth Amendment" without letting it influence them.

It seems peculiar, today, that the man who had loudly protested his innocence for 12 years, and who was sufficiently articulate to make effective presentations at hearings considering his outrageous sequestration, when the Ohio State Penitentiary wanted him to dismiss Bailey and abandon Arianne, was unable or unwilling to explain the events leading up to Marilyn's death.

True, the prosecution at his first trial had made hay with his affair with Susan Hayes and the lies he told about it at the inquest. But that was back in the square and puritanical days of the Eisenhower era in the 1950s. Surely Sam's story might have found a more sympathetic audience in the swinging 60s?

Questions might also be raised regarding the competence of the prosecution. An astute team of prosecutors would surely have asked Sam questions about the possibility that the murderer had entered the house with his full approval; that Marilyn might not have been battered to death by him but by a

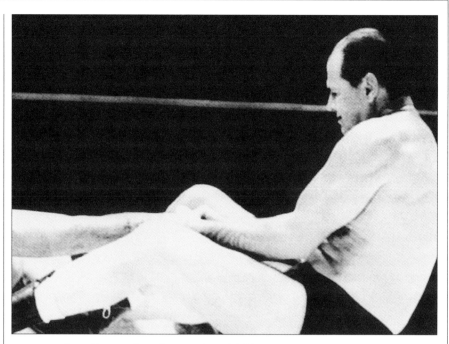

Sam Sheppard getting to grips with his new career as a wrestler.

co-conspirator paid by Sam to eliminate her; that Sam's injuries were inflicted by this confederate, by prearrangement, to demonstrate his innocence; that Sam must surely remember just when and how his T-shirt came to be stripped off as he chased the villain with the bushy hair toward Lake Erie? It is not suggested that Sam Sheppard did hire an assassin to kill Marilyn; merely noted that his exclusion from the witness box meant that this possibility was never tested.

Who killed Marilyn Sheppard remains one of the great mysteries of true crime.

AFTERMATH

Sam's freedom was not to be the occasion of his living happily ever after, however. The stress was telling on him, and he was becoming increasingly dependent on excessive use of alcohol and tranquillizers. Arianne accompanied him on a promotional tour for the book he wrote about his experiences, entitled *Endure and Conquer*. Their public image remained one of the happy and united couple but privately the marriage was undergoing strain, and within two years Arianne had returned to Germany and started divorce proceedings. She declared, ominously, that Sam's violence made her fear for her life.

Nor did Sam's renewed medical career prosper. His licence to practice was restored after his acquittal, but a medical malpractice suit that he lost caused it to be withdrawn again. Sam took up a new profession, one so far removed from his original calling as to seem ridiculous. He became a professional wrestler, with a fanfare of public declarations that this was not a sad come-down for a former doctor in his 40s, but a triumphant full-time entry to a sport that had always been one of his favourite hobbies.

In 1969 he married his trainer's 19-year-old daughter. Two weeks later Dr. Sam Sheppard died.

ADOLF
EICHMANN

On October 18, 1945, 24 men were charged with

crimes ranging from starting a war to murder.

Some were also charged with having committed,

sanctioned, or otherwise been involved in the

commission of crimes against humanity, the most

shocking and unbelievable being genocide – the

extermination of a racial or religious group – and

the deportation to slave labour camps of hundreds

of thousands of inhabitants of countries occupied

by Nazi Germany.

■

THERE WERE SEVERAL PEOPLE missing from the dock: the whereabouts of Martin Bormann, tried and convicted *in absentia*, were unknown. He may have been killed when fleeing Nazi Germany, or he may have reached, and vanished in, South America. It was long suspected and then confirmed that Dr. Josef Mengele had gone there. But in 1961, Israeli agents brought from Argentina Adolf Eichmann, architect of the devastating so-called "final solution".

When the Third Reich collapsed, few people realized Adolf Eichmann's full role in the horror that would be Nazi Germany's legacy. Nobody looked for him as he joined the hundreds of thousands of returning German troops, losing himself, vanishing in his own obscurity. For four years he hid on a farm in Germany before being spirited away to Argentina by the Odessa network, organized by former SS colleagues. There he took a new identity as Ricardo Klement. His wife joined him and together they began a new life.

On November 20, 1945, at Nuremberg, the trial began of the 24 men and seven organizations – including the Schutzstaffel (otherwise known as the SS), the Geheime Staatspolizei (Gestapo – the secret police), the Sturmabteilung (SA), the Sicherheitsdienst (SD) and the General Staff and High Command of the German armed forces – accused of committing war crimes. The judgement of the International Military Tribunal was handed down on September 30 and October 1, 1946. Twelve defendants were sentenced to death: Goering, von Ribbentrop, Keitel, Kaltenbrunner, Rosenberg, Frank, Frick, Streicher,

Sanckel, Jodl, Seyss-Inquart and Martin Bormann (*in absentia*).

All except Bormann and Goering, who committed suicide before the sentence could be carried out, were hanged on October 16, 1946, in the gymnasium of Nuremberg Prison, The execution was badly carried out and several died from slow strangulation – the writer Rebecca West said that "Ribbentrop struggled in the air for 20 minutes". The bodies were cremated in the death ovens at the Dachau concentration camp.

Seven received prison terms ranging from 10 years to life and were sent to Spandau Prison. They were Rudolf Hess, Dr. Walther Emmanuel Funk (released 1957, died 1960), Admiral Erich von Reader (released 1955, died 1960), Albert Speer (released 1966, died 1981), Baldur von Schirach (released 1966, died 1974), Baron Konstantin von Neurath (released 1954, died 1956) and Karl Doenitz (released 1965).

Three, including the German politician and diplomat Franz von Papen and the president of the German Central Bank, Hjalmar Horace Greeley Schacht, were acquitted.

Twelve further trials were held, 185 people being indicted, including doctors, judges, industrialists, SS officials and high military and civilian officials. 35 people were acquitted, over 30 were executed and about 120 were imprisoned.

The defence contended – and in some quarters the validity of the trials has been attacked on these grounds – that those charged were tried for and convicted of *ex post facto* crimes, meaning that their conduct was retrospectively deemed to be criminal. The judges rejected this argument, which has since received little support, since there was

> **"THE TRUE TEST... IS NOT THE EXISTENCE OF THE ORDER BUT WHETHER MORAL CHOICE (IN EXECUTING IT) WAS IN FACT POSSIBLE."**
>
> STATEMENT OF THE INTERNATIONAL MILITARY TRIBUNAL AT NUREMBURG 1945

overwhelming evidence of large-scale and systematic atrocities being committed as a matter of official policy. At least five million persons were forcibly deported, many dying through inhuman and openly sadistic treatment, and mil-lions of people belonging to ethnic and religious minority groups, including Jews and Gypsies, were condemned to concentration camps, where huge numbers were murdered in gas chambers.

There was and is little doubt that Nazi policy was inherently criminal. The Tribunal, with the statement "the true test... is not the existence of the order but whether moral choice (in executing it) was in fact possible" also rejected the contention of several defendants that they did what they did because they were ordered to do so.

Adolf Hitler was not tried. He had committed suicide, probably in anticipation of what the alternative fate would be; Martin Bormann had vanished, possibly killed when fleeing Nazi Germany or maybe escaped to a new life in South America, probably to join Dr. Josef Mengele, who performed experiments with Jewish inmates of concentration

Eichmann listening to the proceedings at his trial in Nuremberg with fellow Nazis.

camps. Another notorious Nazi thought to be in South America was Karl Adolf Eichmann, widely believed to have been the architect of the "final solution", the extermination of the Jews.

ANTI-SEMITISM

Every child knows the story of Noah and his Ark. Noah's eldest son was named Shem and originally his descendants (or supposed descendants) were called Semites. Semitic was later used as an adjective for a wide range of peoples, Arabs as well as Jews, but by the late 1800s was used to define Jews alone. In or about 1879 the term anti-Semite or anti-Semitism was coined to denote hostility toward Jews.

The Jews, of course, had been discriminated against for several thousand years, even before Christianity became one of the world's dominant religions. But in the late 1870s and early 1880s in Germany there developed a theory, wholly rejected by responsible ethnologists, that Jews were inferior to the Aryan race.

Proving that one can be both intelligent and incredibly stupid at the same time, the French diplomat and social philosopher Comte Joseph Arthur de Gobineau and the German philosopher and economist Karl Dühring, among others, wrote books endorsing this hypothesis. Probably, but by no means certainly, the political and social instability in Germany and Eastern Europe engendered widespread support for this anti-Jewish propaganda, the Jews being used as the scapegoats for economic instability and other frustrations requiring an outlet.

Anti-Semitism did not take hold in the same way in Britain, which allowed thousands of Jews to settle in the country, many of them living in the East End of London. In France, a flirtation with anti-Semitism culminated between 1894 and 1906 in the affair of Alfred Dreyfus (1859–1935), a Jewish officer in the French Army who was imprisoned for treason – and thereafter almost disappeared as a political issue.

But in Eastern Europe thousands of

Eichmann the family man, with his son, Horst.

Jews were slaughtered in organized massacres known as pogroms. There were pogroms in the 1880s and again in 1906. They were organized by governments and were designed to direct widespread public discontent away from those in power. Much of the bigotry was fostered by a document called the *Protocols of the Elders of Zion*, published as a book in Russia in 1905. It revealed the existence of a supposed international Jewish conspiracy aimed at world domination, but was a manifest forgery, a piece of fiction that would indirectly lead to the deaths of hundreds of thousands of Jews.

Anti-Semitism in Germany was illegal, but the National Socialist (Nazi) Party under Adolf Hitler was openly anti-Semitic and when the party succeeded to government in 1933 it introduced a series of laws that deprived Jews of legal protection and allowed their property to be seized. Jews were sent to concentration camps. In 1938 there was a nationwide pogrom and from the outbreak of war in 1939 anti-Semitic activities increased. Hitler barely concealed the slaughter of the Jews, which became known as the "final solution of the Jewish problem" – approximately six million Jews were exterminated. The organizer of the "final solution" was a small, almost insignificant little man named Adolf Eichmann.

Since the end of World War II, small groups of neo-Nazis and white supremacists have been responsible for anti-Semitic propaganda and violence against individual Jews. In South America, where many Nazi leaders fled following the collapse of the Third Reich, some of the most serious anti-Semitic behaviour was triggered by the Israeli seizure of Adolf Eichmann in Argentina in 1960.

BROUGHT TO TRIAL

Ricardo Klement, who lived in Buenos Aires, the capital of Argentina, seemed an insignificant little man who caught the bus to and from work each morning and evening. But he'd attracted the attention of the *Mossad Le Aliyah Beth*, the Israeli secret service, who believed him

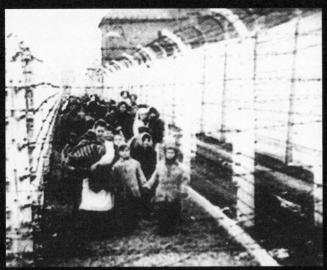

Eichmann's "final solution" took no account of sex or age.

Political opponents of Nazism were also sent to death camps.

"IN ONE CAMP ALONE, AUSCHWITZ-BIRKENAU, 9,000 PEOPLE WERE KILLED EVERY 24 HOURS."

Inmates of Belsen, using the boots of the dead as fuel for those still alive.

to be Karl Adolf Eichmann, organizer of the "final solution", who had disappeared after the war. For weeks a special squad of agents watched "Klement's" house in the suburbs of Buenos Aires and had noted every detail of his daily routine. On May 11, 1956, "Klement" caught his bus home from the office. Followed by Israeli agents, he was snatched by four men as he waited for his bus connection, hustled into a waiting car and taken to a hideout.

Not surprisingly, the captive protested about being held against his will and denied being Eichmann. The Israeli agents had little doubt, but they checked medical details and compared their captive with photographs of Eichmann in his SS uniform. There was no question about it, they had Eichmann.

Argentina would not have extradited Eichmann and, unless he agreed to leave the country voluntarily, an international court would have no alternative but to demand Eichmann's return to Argentina and the arrest of those responsible for his kidnapping. The agents presented Eichmann with a simple choice: they could murder him there and then, or he could sign a document testifying to his identity and to having left South America of his own free will.

Argentinians were preparing for the country's Independence Day celebrations and little attention was paid to the disguised Eichmann as he was taken to the airport and smuggled aboard an El Al airliner flying the newly opened route between Buenos Aires and Tel Aviv. Once he was safely in Israel, Eichmann's arrest was announced to the world and caused an immediate sensation. The response in Israel was incredible. Many Nazi leaders had escaped at the end of the war, but not even the much-reviled Dr. Josef Mengele was wanted as badly as Adolf Eichmann, the architect of attempted genocide.

However, when it was discovered how the Israelis had captured Eichmann, there was widespread disquiet. Eichmann had virtually been kidnapped from Argentinian soil by foreign agents. Whatever the merits of bringing Eichmann to justice, international law had been flouted and a diplomatic incident blew up. At the United Nations, though, Israeli spokeswoman Golda Meir poured scorn on the concerns: "Is this a problem for the Security Council to deal with?" she asked. "This is an organization which deals with threats to peace. Is this a threat to peace? Eichmann brought to trial by the very people to whose total physical annihilation he dedicated all his energies?" There was little that could be said. Almost everyone recognized that, whatever the strict letter of the law might be, Israel clearly had a moral right to abduct and try Adolf Eichmann.

A community centre in Jerusalem was converted into a courtroom. A specially prepared bullet-proof glass booth was made ready for Eichmann, it being feared that a benefactor would attempt to save the government the cost of the trial. Eichmann asked to be defended by Dr. Robert Servatius, who had been the defence counsel at the Nuremberg Trials. Israel agreed and paid Servatius' $25,000 fee, also making all case papers available to him.

On April 11, 1961, the trial began. Eichmann, who to his captors had variously claimed for himself high rank, importance and privilege, or pleaded that he was only a minor bureaucrat who'd carried out the orders of superiors, was brought under a heavy escort to the "court" and, surrounded by a human shield of policemen, conveyed into the glass booth.

Dr. Servatius immediately lodged with the three judges who were to try the case a complaint that the judges, being

The courtroom specially prepared for Eichmann's trial in 1961.

Eichmann in the bullet-proof glass dock constructed for his trial.

died. There was a specific charge against him, namely that he had deported 100 children from the Czech village of Lidice to be murdered in Poland. In 1961, Adolf Eichmann seemed to be living testimony that for some people civilized human behaviour was only skin deep.

Like Martin Bormann, Adolf Eichmann had avoided the limelight as much as possible. His name and activities had only become widely known as a result of the Nuremberg trials. But over the next six weeks of his trial a steady stream of witnesses testified to their experiences in the concentration camps. Few had any direct evidence against or, indeed, had had any contact with Eichmann, but their stories were appalling testimony to the barbaric and sadistic treatment suffered in the concentration camps.

One women told how she was part of a crowd of people herded together, then gunned down. Somehow she wasn't shot, she said, but fell with those who were and was thrown into a mass grave. There

Jews, were liable to be prejudiced. It was a valid point, but the judges ruled that they were no more likely to be biased against the defendant than they would be prejudiced against a thief. Eichmann, who looked isolated and vulnerable in his glass booth in a court and in a country openly filled with hatred against him, then heard the indictment against him: "The criminal code ordinance 1936. Particulars of offense, the accused together with others during the period of 1939–1945 caused the killing of millions of Jews in his capacity as the person responsible for the execution of the Nazi plan for the physical extermination of the Jews, known as the final solution of the Jewish problem."

The charges against Adolf Eichmann were shocking, even in 1961 when few were unaware of what had gone on in concentration camps. What made this event shocking was that it was filmed. People could see the insignificant, balding little man in his glass booth and

know that he was a monster who not only condemned millions of people to death, but spent his days organizing the details of their destruction; who set up the concentration camps, worked out the transportation logistics, helped develop the huge gas chambers in which millions

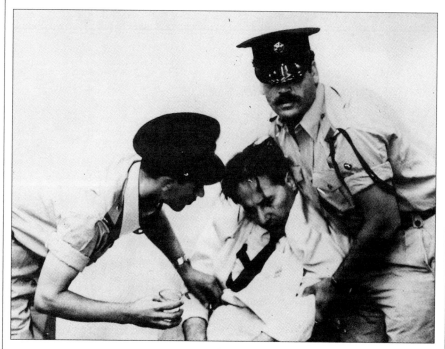

An ex-inmate of Auschwitz collapses while giving evidence against Eichmann.

she lay, on top of and underneath layers of corpses, until she was certain the guards had gone. Then she pushed her way through the bodies, climbed from the pit and made her escape.

Nevertheless, against Eichmann's claims that he was a minor official carrying out orders he barely understood, the prosecution was able to construct a massive case showing that he had been a senior official and organizer in the Nazi killing machine, well aware of what he was doing.

ADOLF EICHMANN

Karl Adolf Eichmann had been born in Germany in 1906 into a strict Evangelical family. Shortly before the outbreak of World War I, the family had moved to Linz in Austria. By the early 1920s young Eichmann had embraced the anti-Semitic arguments and beliefs being promoted in Germany and elsewhere. Later, Eichmann joined Hitler's Nazi Party, which was rapidly gaining support in the chaos of Weimar Germany. As a fervent supporter of Hitler's anti-Jewish doctrine, Eichmann came to the attention of, and was invited to join, those who had been given the task of ridding Germany of its Jewish population,

In 1933 Adolf Hitler became Chancellor of Germany and his anti-Jewish intentions were more openly displayed. First he deprived Jews of their German citizenship, then made marriage of Jews to non-Jews illegal. Hitler also had another plan, entrusted to Eichmann's care and made a reality on November 9, 1938. This has since become known as *Kristallnacht*, "night of the broken glass". On that night more than 7,000 Jewish shops and homes were broken

Eichmann used some of the time he spent in jail in Israel writing his memoirs.

into and looted; synagogues were defiled; some 20,000 Jews were arrested and many were killed. Hitler told insurance companies that they were not liable to recompense those who had suffered.

In December of that year, Jews were deprived of businesses – it was made illegal for them to run a business – and were forbidden to deal in jewellery, property and securities. Eichmann's success on Kristallnacht resulted in him being given an order: to make Germany "Jew free". He attempted to do so. There were two concentration camps already,

one at Dachau and the other at Buchenwald, but these were soon full, so Eichmann ordered a third to be built at Mauthausen. It was at this time, according to one witness at his trial, that Eichmann coined a chilling phrase. On a file in his Berlin headquarters Eichmann wrote the words, "final solution".

Adolf Hitler gave the order to attack Poland and on September 30, 1939, the Second World War began. Eichmann was put in charge of a new department, called Department IV B 4 of the Reich Security Head Office. He was made responsible for the deportation and disposal of Polish Jews. He accordingly deprived them of their property, set up death camps at places such as Auschwitz and Sachsenhausen, and set about the logistics of moving Jews, gypsies, communists, socialists, homosexuals, resistance fighters and dissidents of any persuasion into them. All Polish Jews, said Eichmann, should henceforth wear a yellow star as identification.

Eichmann's next evil deed was to force all Jews to live in a restricted area in Warsaw, the penalty for leaving being death. Before anyone entered the ghetto they were searched for food. Tens of thousands of people died from disease and starvation. People who caused any trouble were taken away, never to be seen again.

There was some murmuring of disquiet within the senior ranks, particularly against the now open policy of extermination of the Jews. Some were concerned that the obvious slaughter was demoralizing to the troops, others were awed by the sheer scale of the problem. There were lots of Jews to be killed. In January 1942, a meeting was held at a villa in Wannsee, outside Berlin, Eichmann presented a detailed plan to implement and

make more extensive use of the gas chambers used so successfully in Poland. Eichmann's superior Reinhardt Heydrich sanctioned the plan, the greatest mass murder the world has ever known. In one

ON A FILE IN HIS BERLIN HEADQUARTERS EICHMANN WROTE THE WORDS, 'FINAL SOLUTION'.

Eichmann covers his eyes as he hears the damning evidence against him.

camp alone, Auschwitz-Birkenau, 9,000 people were killed *every 24 hours*.

In Israel in 1961 survivors of the horror described what had happened within the concentration camps, while prosecu-

tors repeatedly produced documents that proved Eichmann's role in the nightmare. The prosecution even produced a witness, Abraham Gordon, who was able to testify that he'd witnessed Eichmann personally shoot and kill a child who had stolen some of his cherries.

Dr. Servatius tried to dodge and weave the mounting evidence, but Eichmann's plea of being a minor functionary collapsed as the prosecution produced incriminating document after incriminating document, each bearing Eichmann's signature. One such document was a letter signed by Eichmann to Heinrich Himmler confirming that six million Jews had been killed. Under relentless pressure, Eichmann was forced to admit that his main activity in Nazi Germany was to handle the Jewish "problem".

On December 16, 1961, the judges pronounced their verdict. Nobody doubted Eichmann's guilt. Nobody doubted that the verdict would be guilty. Nobody doubted that the punishment would be death.

Karl Adolf Eichmann was hanged at Rammle Prison on May 31, 1962. He was cremated and his ashes flown out to sea, where they were scattered beyond Israel's territorial waters.

THE BOSTON
STRANGLER

In the early 1960s 13 women were murdered by a

serial killer known as the Boston Strangler. Terror

gripped Boston as the police failed to catch the

killer. Not since Jack the Ripper stalked London's

East End had a murder investigation attracted

such worldwide attention. Eventually a mental

patient named Albert DeSalvo admitted to the

murders. He gave details which only the police

knew. But some people have questioned

whether DeSalvo really was the

notorious Boston Strangler.

■

ANNA SLESERS WAS BORN in Latvia. In 1950 she brought her two children to the United States. By the 1960s she was living in Boston. Her daughter had married in 1960 and gone to live in Maryland. Anna had then lived with her son Juris, but at the beginning of June 1962 had taken a third-floor apartment in Gainsborough Street, near the Symphony Hall, where she was able to indulge her love of classical music.

On June 14, 1962, Juris Slesers went to visit his mother at her new apartment. He knocked on the door. As he later told television reporters, "I was very surprised not to receive a reply, so I waited around there, walked up and down the street for a while, and after about half an hour or 40 minutes I decided that something may be wrong, and I was looking for the janitor in order to be admitted into the apartment."

Juris Slesers could not find the janitor, so he broke down the apartment door. It wasn't difficult. It almost gave with a light blow of the shoulder. A slightly heavier blow and the door flew open. He checked a couple of rooms, but there was no sign of his mother. Then he went into the kitchen. She was on the floor on her back, lying on her open housecoat. Apart from the housecoat, she was naked. Her legs had been forced apart. The blue cord from her housecoat had been tied around her neck and fastened in a bow.

Juris Slesers called the police. At first he suspected suicide, but Inspector James Mellon thought murder more likely. He had noted the bath one-third full of water and postulated that Anna Slesers had been about to take a bath when

...THERE WAS NO SIGN OF HIS MOTHER. THEN HE WENT INTO THE KITCHEN. SHE WAS ON THE FLOOR ON HER BACK, LYING ON HER OPEN HOUSECOAT. APART FROM THE HOUSECOAT, SHE WAS NAKED. HER LEGS HAD BEEN FORCED APART. THE BLUE CORD FROM HER HOUSECOAT HAD BEEN TIED AROUND HER NECK AND FASTENED IN A BOW.

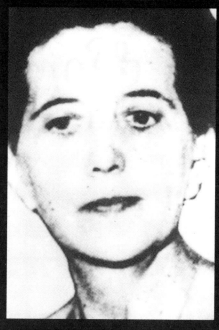

Anne Slesers

Ida Irga

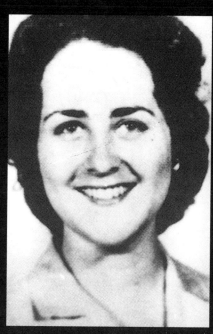

Patricia Bissette

Mary Sullivan

Sophie Clark

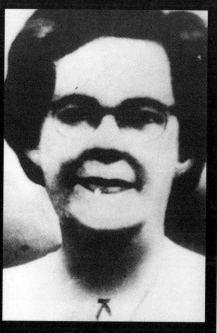

Helen E. Brake

she was interrupted. His suspicions were confirmed by an autopsy report which showed Anna Slesers had been sexually assaulted and strangled.

The police first thought that somebody had broken into the apartment intending to rob it, had discovered Anna Slesers preparing for a bath and had assaulted her, later becoming frightened and killing her. This hypothesis seemed to fit some of the facts, but not all of them. There was no sign of a break-in and nothing seemed to have been taken. On the other hand, Anna Slesers was known to be shy and not to have any men friends. It was thought unlikely that, naked but for her bathrobe and

without her dentures in, she would have answered the door and let someone into her apartment. The murder was a real puzzle for the police.

> **"THERE WAS ME — STRANGLING SOMEBODY! 'OH GOD, WHAT AM I DOING? I'M A MARRIED MAN. I'M THE FATHER OF TWO CHILDREN. OH GOD, HELP ME!"**
>
> ALBERT DeSALVO

It was partly answered on June 30, 1962, only two weeks later, when the body of 68-year-old Nina Nichols was found. She, too, had been strangled – with two of her own nylon stockings,

tied in the tell-tale bow. Her housecoat and slip had been pulled up to her waist. Her belongings had been rifled, but nothing seemed to have been taken, not even an expensive camera, which indicated that robbery was not the motive for the crime. Also, she had broken off a telephone conversation with her sister to answer the door. When she didn't return to the phone, her sister had telephoned the janitor of Nina Nichols' apartment block. He had gone to investigate and found the lifeless body.

Unknown to the authorities, because her body would remain undiscovered for several days, a woman named Helen Brake was also murdered on that same day, June 30, 1962, in Lynn, a small town some miles from Boston. An ex-nurse, she was 65 years old and had been strangled with nylon stockings and a bra. The bra straps had been knotted beneath her chin.

Also in June, though it would only be accepted as a Strangler murder after the arrest of a man named Albert DeSalvo, 80-year-old Mary Mullen was murdered.

There were several similarities between the murder victims. Anna Slesers, in her mid-fifties, was divorced, had no known men friends and enjoyed classical music. Nina Nichols, 12 years older, was a widow of 20 years, outgoing, with no known men friends. Helen Brake had been married but only briefly (the marriage was annulled in 1927), had no known men friends and was said to enjoy listening to classical music.

Juris Slesers, son of the Strangler's first victim. He called at his mother's apartment and found that she had been assaulted and then strangled.

"WE'VE GOT A MADMAN LOOSE"

Whoever the killer was, his motive for killing was killing. He was what we would now term a serial killer, a phenomenon not widely recognized in the United States in the early 60s. The newly-appointed Boston Police Commissioner, Edward McNamara, maybe expressed the feelings of both Boston police and public when he commented, "My God, we've got a madman loose."

Panic suddenly gripped Boston as the newspapers reported and speculated on the killings, giving the killer an assortment of names: "The Mad Strangler", "The Phantom Strangler" and "The Sunset Killer". Door-to-door salesmen, meter readers and researchers suddenly found doors barred against them. People bought fierce dogs as protection. Stores found they simply couldn't get enough security locks and devices to satisfy customer demand. As one locksmith told a TV interviewer, "We have never sold so many (types of lock) in such quantities. The factories have run out...."

On August 21, nearly a month after the murder of Helen Brake and Nina Nichols, came a fourth shocking murder. In Boston's quiet West End a retired nurse named Ida Irga was found strangled in her locked, fifth-floor apartment (police worked out that it could have been reached from the roofs of neighbouring buildings). The body was naked – left so that it would be the first thing anyone entering the apartment would see – and bore the hallmarks now associated with the Strangler. Ida Irga had been dead for about two days.

On August 30 67-year-old retired nurse Jane Sullivan was found murdered.

Public fear of the Strangler reached panic proportions. People bought locks and security devices by the score as protection against the maniac in their midst.

Forensic examination revealed that this latest victim had been murdered within 24 hours of Ida Irga.

BOSTON

Boston was a fine city, noted for its world-famous Boston Symphony Orchestra, Red Sox baseball team, and long history stretching back to colonists who settled the area. It was known to the Indians as Shawmut, and was declared a town in 1630. Named after Boston, England, it became the capital of and largest city in Massachusetts and New England. With a magnificent natural harbour opening onto Massachusetts Bay, it became an excellent port and consequently a major manufacturing area. During the 1950s, however, the textile and leather industries went into a steep and inexorable decline and nearly half

the manufacturing jobs were lost, which in turn hit the port and the commerce of the city, and the population began to move away. Dramatic steps in urban renewal were undertaken by the authorities and had succeeded in reversing the city's economic decline – until, that is, the Strangler phenomenon.

This new menace hurt Boston's recovery programme, causing every murder to be spotlighted, while police and press investigations revealed an unPuritan underbelly. All leave within the Boston Police Department was cancelled and plans were laid for what would be the greatest manhunt in the history of the city. Commissioner McNamara formed a Special Tactical Squad which was assigned the sole duty of investigating the stranglings and catching the Strangler. They checked on recently released

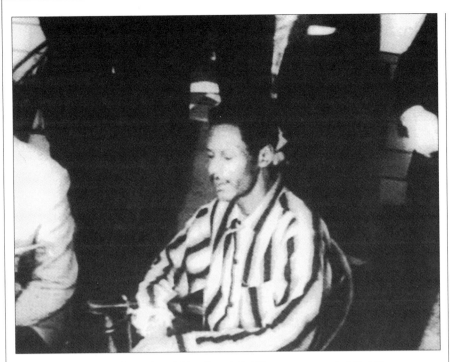

The handyman of murdered Mrs. Israel Goldberg was arrested, but there was insufficient evidence to charge him with the crime.

mental patients and known sex offenders and psychiatrists were consulted in an effort to construct a portrait – what we would describe today as a psychological profile – of the probable killer. The psychiatrists targeted young men – aged between 18 and 40 – who felt persecuted and had a mother-hatred complex, hence the attacks on older women.

The Strangler's next victim destroyed this neat theory: she was 20 years old. The police were forced to cast aside the carefully constructed psychological profile and start again. Murdered on December 5, 1962, the victim was named Sophie Clarke, a student hospital technician. She was the first black victim of the Strangler and lived in the Back Bay area of Boston. Unlike the other victims, she had been raped.

On December 31, 1962, 23-year-old Patricia Bissette was found murdered. She also lived in the Back Bay area and,

oddly, her body was covered. She was also one month pregnant.

Five months went by apparently without a murder by the Strangler, though Albert DeSalvo later claimed the murder in March 1963 of 69-year-old Mary Brown. Her death wasn't attributed to the Strangler at the time. The next murder officially "credited" to him was that of 23-year-old Beverly Samans. On May 6, 1963, she was found raped and strangled. She had also been stabbed in the throat. A student and would-be opera singer, she also had nursing connections, being a music therapist in hospitals.

The case seemed more baffling than ever: the murderer's psychiatric profile had been destroyed by the sudden change from elderly to young women; the change from sexual molestation to full rape was odd; and the sudden flurries of murder followed by long gaps also seemed inexplicable.

On September 8, 1963, the pattern changed again, the victim this time being aged 58. A divorcee, attractive, looking much younger than her age, Evelyn Corbin was a factory worker (no hospital connection) and lived alone.

On November 23, 1963, the pattern reverted again to youthful victims. The victim this time was Joann Graff, a 23-year-old designer and Sunday School teacher. She had been strangled with a leotard, which was tied with the Strangler's tell-tale bow. Her death was a further blow to an already grieving and shocked city: the previous day in Dallas, Texas, President John F. Kennedy had been assassinated. Joann Graff had been watching TV coverage of the assassination when murdered.

A month passed, then a 19-year-old secretary, Mary Sullivan, was found murdered. The details of her murder were horrific. Her body had been viciously abused and with a horrible gesture the killer had placed a Happy New Year card between her toes.

The problem with these murders – as is so often the case with American crimes – is that their wide distribution brought several police departments into the investigation and this inevitably caused communication and co-ordination problems (as well as rivalry). At its simplest, the problem was that one hand often didn't know what the other hand was doing and neither hand – and in this case there were five hands, because five police departments were involved – felt fully informed. Two weeks after the murder of Mary Sullivan, Edward W. Brooke, Jr., the Attorney General, announced that the investigation would in future be co-ordinated by the Attorney

General's Office under the charge of Assistant Attorney General John S. Bottomly. Bottomly's first act was to create a central clearing office and request all law enforcement agencies to deliver copies of every investigative document relating to the case. He received 37,500 pages of documentation and had it computerized for analysis.

The investigation didn't stop with established investigative methods. On January 29, 1963, the authorities brought the famous Dutch psychic, Peter Hurkos, to Boston. Hurkos both excited and baffled police experts with his knowledge of the case – knowledge they were certain he could not have come by through normal channels – and by his description of the killer. Eventually the police requestioned one of their suspects. He fitted everything Hurkos had described about the killer, but proved to have a cast-iron alibi. Hurkos returned home.

THE GREEN MAN

Next another series of crimes began to take place. Across a great swathe of New England, encompassing Connecticut, Massachusetts, New Hampshire and Rhode Island, there occurred over nine months a series of about 300 sexual assaults. The attacker, who was known as the Green Man because of green work trousers he always wore, would quietly break into women's rooms, then physically abuse and sometimes rape them. Eventually one of his victims was able to identify the Green Man as a sexual offender known to the police as the "Measuring Man".

An episode of a TV series starring Robert Cummings had featured a photographer who auditioned would-be models and took their measurements. This gave a man named Albert DeSalvo the idea of hanging around student bars and housing areas. Posing as a representative of a model agency, he would then talk his way into the homes of young women. Sometimes his charm and flattery led him into their beds, sometimes they merely stripped to be measured, sometimes they remained clothed while he took their vital statistics. The police began to get calls about the "Measuring Man" when he didn't return with the promised contracts. They eventually arrested DeSalvo and charged him with being the "Measuring Man". He was imprisoned for eleven months, and then released, in 1962.

Now the police picked up DeSalvo and charged him with the "Green Man" assaults. He was sent to the State Correctional Institute at Bridgewater. It was February 1965, and DeSalvo's cellmate was 33-year-old George Nasser, who was under observation while awaiting trial for the particularly brutal murder of a garage attendant. According to Nasser, during conversation DeSalvo told him about his crimes, enough to convince him that the man sharing his cell was the Boston Strangler. It should be stated that the exact content of their discussions is not known.

It may have been an altruism wholly unconnected with the $110,000 reward for information leading to the arrest of the Strangler that caused Nasser to contact his lawyer, F. Lee Bailey. To Bailey, DeSalvo calmly confessed to the crimes, including two murders the police had not associated with the Strangler, and gave details that had not been made public. Bailey taped his interviews with DeSalvo and later played them to the police. The authorities were convinced: the Strangler was caught.

The Strangler killings involved the Boston Police Department in the biggest manhunt in the city's history.

Albert DeSalvo was born on September 3, 1931, to Frank DeSalvo, a plumber, and his wife Charlotte, a fireman's daughter. Frank DeSalvo was a violent, wife- and child-beating alcoholic. Albert DeSalvo witnessed and experienced much during his childhood. He saw his father beat his mother, knock out her teeth and break her fingers. DeSalvo Senior also brought prostitutes back to the apartment and made his young son watch as he had sex with them, and he introduced young Albert to shoplifting. This was all before 1939, when Frank DeSalvo left home and never again made any attempt to support his family. Charlotte DeSalvo finally divorced Frank in 1944 and remarried a year later.

Albert DeSalvo was cursed with an excessive sex drive. By the age of six or seven he was experiencing sex, and in adult life he apparently had to have release several times a day. In 1948 he joined the army and was sent to Germany, where he met and fell in love with a girl called Irmgard. The couple married and DeSalvo brought her back with him to the States when he returned in 1954. Two years later he was charged with sexual misconduct against a nine-year-old girl, but the charges were dropped and DeSalvo was honourably discharged.

The problem faced by the authorities was that there existed no evidence aside from DeSalvo's confession. This, plus the determination of F. Lee Bailey – who had taken DeSalvo as a client – to keep him from the execution chamber, meant that proceedings could not be taken against him for the Strangler murders. The question, as is so often the case, rested on DeSalvo's mental health. After examination by psychiatrists, if De Salvo were found insane then he would admit his guilt and be sent to a mental institution. If found sane, DeSalvo would withdraw his plea of guilty and, without evidence against him, he would probably walk away a free man.

The legal twists and turns were executed adroitly by Bailey, who produced a brilliant side-step. He had DeSalvo tried for the "Green Man" assaults and rapes. The psychiatrists were then called and testified to DeSalvo's insanity. The result was that Albert DeSalvo was "put away" without ever standing trial for the Boston stranglings.

In his closing speech to the court, Bailey declared: "This man, Albert DeSalvo, is a phenomenon... a unique opportunity for study... We've never had

> "THIS MAN, ALBERT DESALVO, IS A PHENOMENON... A UNIQUE OPPORTUNITY FOR STUDY... WE'VE NEVER HAD SUCH A SPECIMEN IN CAPTIVITY. HE SHOULD BE THE SUBJECT OF A RESEARCH GRANT FROM THE FORD FOUNDATION..."
>
> F. LEE BAILEY

such a specimen in captivity. He should be the subject of a research grant from the Ford Foundation or a similar institution. What I am stating here is not a defense. It's a sociological imperative. Aside from the moral, religious, ethical or other objections to capital punishment, to execute DeSalvo is just as wasteful, barbaric and ignorant an act as burning the witches of Salem."

DeSalvo was sent back to the State Correctional Institute at Bridgewater. Many people associated with the case were unhappy with this as Bridgewater was more a prison than a hospital and it was deemed unlikely that DeSalvo would receive the required treatment.

On February 24, 1967, Albert DeSalvo escaped from Bridgewater. On his pillow in his cell he left a note saying he wanted help and wasn't getting any. Boston was immediately gripped by hysteria, but DeSalvo gave himself up within 48 hours. He explained to reporters that he needed psychiatric help, that he wanted psychiatric help, and had a lawyer who had petitioned for psychiatric help – but that he was not getting psychiatric help. The authorities responded by sending DeSalvo to the maximum security Walpole Prison in Massachusetts. It was a very serious mishandling of the case.

Six years later, on November 25, 1973, Albert DeSalvo was found stabbed to death in his cell. DeSalvo's murderer was never identified and few mourned his death.

WHY?

It is generally agreed that Albert DeSalvo is one of the least understood serial killers. He seems to contradict many of the expected traits of a serial killer, which may be why some people have argued that he was not the Boston Strangler. Notably, he went from molestation to rape, then, suddenly, without any discernible reason, began to kill. There were also gaps between killings: four months between the murder of Beverly Samans and Evelyn Corbin, then three months before the murder of Joann Graff. Then, just as suddenly, DeSalvo stopped and went back to molestation and occasional rape.

According to DeSalvo, his first attempt at murder was a failure. He attempted to strangle a Scandinavian woman, but she fought him and during the struggle he caught sight of himself in a mirror. He later spoke of the experience and the thoughts that rushed through his head. "There was me – strangling somebody! Oh God, what am I doing? I'm a married man. I'm the father of two children. Oh God, help me!" He could not continue to kill and fled the scene. That was in very early June 1962. By the 14th of that month he'd killed Anna Slesers.

This time he went out with the conscious intention of killing. He told his wife he was going fishing, but instead selected an apartment block, wandered its corridors and picked on one of the doors at random.

It was a theme throughout DeSalvo's discussions about the murders that he didn't know why he had committed them. He felt compelled to kill. He didn't want to kill and fought the desire to kill,

he said, but was never able to master the overwhelming urge that possessed him. DeSalvo also said he didn't know why he ransacked the apartments of his victims. He felt as if he was looking for something, but didn't know what.

As near as anyone can make out, DeSalvo considered his wife, Irmgard, to be the cause of his killing spree. Their child, Judy, was born with a deformity. Fearing that more children would be

born deformed, Irmgard stopped having sex with DeSalvo. This decision triggered him into becoming the "Measuring Man". After he came out of prison for the "Measuring Man" crimes, Irmgard still denied him sex, saying he'd have to prove himself to her. This denial of sex, according to DeSalvo, caused him to kill. Some commentators have dismissed DeSalvo's explanation and some, as already stated, have even questioned whether he was the Boston Strangler.

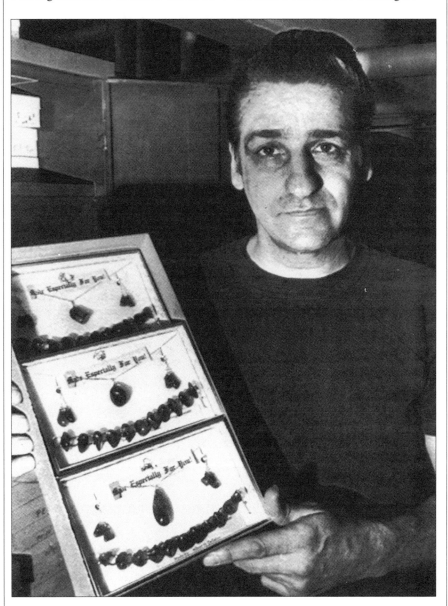

Albert DeSalvo showing the choker necklaces he made in Walpole Prison. Eight months later he was found stabbed to death in his cell.

THE GREAT TRAIN
ROBBERY

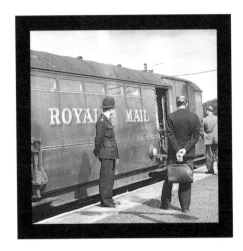

Train robbery has a history almost as long as that of the locomotive train in America. Even before that, 16th, 17th and 18th-century highwaymen held up private carriages, carters' wagons, and, if the opportunity arose, mail coaches and stage coaches from which a goodly haul of marketable paper – be it banknotes or bonds and securities – might sometimes be obtained. But by the time the railways were introduced to England, proper policing had cut the mounted highwayman down to size.

■

IN THE WILDER PARTS of the world, good old-fashioned mail-coach highway robbery continued, however. In the American West, hell-raising outlaws ordered drivers to "stick 'em up". In Australia, the bushwhackers' command was "Bail 'em up". In both places, as railway trains replaced horse-drawn coaches in carrying the mail, masked bandits learned to bring trains to a halt with false signals or derailments, and then at their leisure took travellers' valuables and the contents of the freight cars' safes.

The Reno brothers of Indiana invented the crime in 1866 and Jesse James perfected it over the next decade. The Wild Bunch of Wyoming were the last serious practitioners, at the turn of the century, but, like highway robbery, it died when proper policing was established. Pinkerton's Detective Agency placed efficient guards on the trains and electric telegraphy called out sheriff's officers to pursue and capture would-be robbers. The Great Train Robbery was one of the most famous early silent films, but it celebrated a crime that was, to all intents and purposes, dead.

It was revived once, in 1935, when Public Enemy Number One, Alvin Karpis, robbed a train in Garrettsville, Ohio. He had heard that the train would be carrying a payroll of $220,000 – in fact, he only took $34,000. "Creepy" Karpis didn't care. His real motive was impudence. He wanted to show publicity-hungry J. Edgar Hoover that the crime could still be committed, for all the FBI's boasted establishment of law and order nationwide.

Nobody imagined for one moment, though, that this type of crime would be spectacularly revived in 1960s England: an England of the Beatles and mods and rockers; an England of mini-skirted, kinky-booted fashion; an England, which had never experienced serious train robbery at the time when it really was one of the mainstays of the theft industry.

ROBBERY AT BRIDEGO BRIDGE

Word of this staggering coup reached the news media early in the morning of August 3, 1963. The night mail from Glasgow to London, the "Up Special" (since all trains go "up" to London, be they from north, south, east or west) was carrying a quantity of used banknotes in the High Value Coach. They were being despatched to the Royal Mint for official destruction. This was perfectly normal

procedure, just as it was perfectly normal for the Up Special to consist of a diesel and about a dozen coaches, nearly all of which were mobile GPO sorting offices. As the train hurtled south, Post Office workers diligently sorted letters and cards into pigeon-holes for instant distribution once the train reached King's Cross station in London.

What was unusual was the presence of 128 bags of used notes on the train. This abnormally high number resulted from the August Bank Holiday. The train robbers had excellent inside information from someone who knew the ropes of Post Office and banking practice.

Near the end of the journey, when the train had passed Leighton Buzzard and about half an hour would bring it in

to London, a red signal brought it to a halt. Jack Whitby, the fireman, jumped out of the cab and went back along the line to find out why they had been stopped. He had not gone many yards before a man in a balaclava helmet pushed him down the embankment, and threatened him with a cosh, saying, "If you shout I'll kill you."

Back in the cab, driver Jack Mills had been seized by two more men in balaclavas. He struggled with them, and was rewarded with a crippling blow across the head. This, the only violent action of the entire operation, was to be bitterly regretted by the robbers. It put their "big tickle" into the category of robbery with violence. Without doubt they had committed Actual Bodily Harm

The scene at Bridego Bridge after the robbery. The thieves transferred their haul to vehicles parked on the road below.

and thereby lost a great deal of potential public sympathy for their daring raid.

Driver Mills had assumed that the two men who attacked him were the only thieves on the train. He was astonished when he realized that a gang of 20 or more men were swarming over it. And they were almost silent. They had no intention of alerting the Post Office sorters and bringing them rushing to the aid of the train crew before they could be quietly locked in their coaches. An experienced railwayman among the gang (so driver Mills estimated) uncoupled some of the sorting carriages and put the backing pipe on the stopper again. Then he tried to start the engine to make off with the High Value Coach, but this proved beyond his skill. Jack Whitby was returned to the cab, and Jack Mills was made to take the front of the train, very slowly, to a gentle halt at Bridego Bridge.

More masked men in army uniforms were waiting there. They smashed the windows of the High Value Coach and overpowered the sorters. With drilled precision, they went straight to the bags of used notes and passed them out along a human chain. They worked to a rigid time scheme, allowing themselves 15 minutes and 15 minutes only. When time was up,

there were still eight bags to go. Rather than break their perfectly planned schedule, the thieves left the bags behind, handcuffed Mills and Whitby, and warned them not to try to escape for at least half an hour, or else.

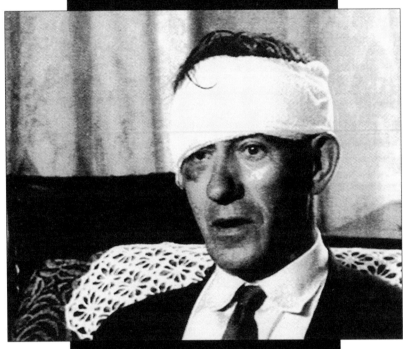

"IF YOU HADN'T HAVE GRAPPLED WITH ME I WOULDN'T HAVE HIT YOU."
UNIDENTIFIED TRAIN ROBBER TO INJURED DRIVER MILLS

Train driver Jack Mills, who was hit over the head by one of the thieves during the robbery.

And with a noise of car and truck engines revving up, the small, irregular army of robbers disappeared into the night. With them they took 120 mailbags containing £2.5 million pounds in used notes: at the time, the biggest haul ever from a robbery.

THE HUNT FOR THE ROBBERS

By 6.00am the train's guard had telephoned an alarm, and investigators had come to find out how this daring crime had been committed. The first mystery for British Railways was the altered signal. How had this been switched from Go to Stop without blowing a fuse or showing up on the warning system as faulty? Astonishingly easily, it transpired. The signal was not the old-fashioned semaphore post, but a modern red or green electric light. The robbers had covered the green bulb with a leather glove to obscure it without damaging it. And it required no great electrical skill to bring along their own red bulb and power it by means of a car battery.

Scotland Yard's team was soon on the spot, but unable to get a firm lead. Local children had clambered aboard the abandoned train, spoiling most of the chances to pick up forensic evidence. But in any case, the thieves seemed to have been perfect professionals who wore gloves and left no fingerprints. Nor were there any signs where they had gone from Bridego Bridge. They had totally and mysteriously disappeared.

The only clue was the warning to Mills and Whitby to keep quiet for half an hour. This seemed a precise length of time, perhaps indicating the distance within which the gang had a base or hideout. Scotland Yard announced that every building within a 30-mile radius of Bridego Bridge was to be searched.

This was a bluff. Warrants would never have been issued for such a widespread trawl, and any householder could refuse the police entry. But there was always the chance that the threat would flush out the thieves, and cause them to break cover. It worked. While there was no panic flight leading to an instant pursuit, the Great Train Robbers left their hideaway earlier than they had planned, taking their loot to London – and the hurried change of plan made them leave incriminating clues behind.

Buckinghamshire police fanned out from Aylesbury, checking remote buildings in the vicinity of the bridge. The outbuildings of Lord Roseberry's country house, Mentmore Park, were searched. Haystacks were combed for bundles of secreted loot.

In London, experienced detectives were gathering whatever information

Leatherslade Farm, the remote hideout 17 miles from Bridego Bridge where the gang intended to lie low until it was safe for them to go their separate ways.

John Morris tipped off police to the gang's presence at the farm.

they could from their "narks". It seemed the word had been out in the underworld that a "big tickle" was planned. Two south London mobs, those of Tommy Wisbey and Bruce Reynolds, were combining forces for some really lucrative robbery, but the precise plans had been kept well away from the ears of the habitual informers.

At last on Monday August 12 there was a breakthrough. Farm labourer John Morris reported that a farm near the village of Oakley had been suddenly abandoned, and there was an army truck in its shed. Since the police were hearing of 400 suspicious sightings a day at this time, the report was tucked away in the files at first. But when Morris urgently repeated his call, a constable was sent to take a look at Leatherslade Farm.

He found a building whose windows had been blacked out. He found a heap of Post Office mailbags and torn up

wrappers with the names of banks printed on them in the cellar. He had found the gang's hideout.

A team of detectives raced to the scene. In the garage were two Land Rovers – both with the same number plates! Outside was the ash of a bonfire and a half-dug hole. It looked as though these professionals might have destroyed all incriminating evidence.

But luck was with the authorities. Although the villains had worn gloves for much of their time in the farm, they had still left finger and palm prints that identified many of them. It later transpired that when the gang made their hurried exit, two men were delegated to clean up the farm and wipe away all the fingerprints. Somehow, these two had failed to do the job properly.

The police were careful not to make the same mistake as with the train. "This place is one big clue," said CID head

Malcolm Fewtrell, warning his men to observe without touching anything. They found abandoned stores, showing that the original intention had been for the gang to lie low until the heat was off around Buckinghamshire. They found board games, indicating that they had prepared to while away the long boring days of waiting. This was to be a careful, patient operation, from which everyone would escape rich and safe from arrest.

CAPTURED MEN AND RECOVERED MONEY

In just two days, such hopes were dashed for the first of the robbers, Roger Cordrey and Bill Boal, who went down to Bournemouth. They tried to rent a lock-up garage, and produced such a large pile of notes in payment that the lessor, a policeman's widow, was suspicious. While they were putting their van away, she telephoned the police.

Cordrey and Boal panicked when detectives approached them, and ran away. They were collared and taken to the station for questioning – and the discovery of a staggering £78,892 in their van made them look very unlike seaside trippers. Cordrey was a known thief who pilfered from mailbags on the Brighton to London line. He had been employed by the gang to fix the signal, and had come up with the ingenious idea of the leather glove and the car battery.

Boal was not one of the original robbers. He was just a friend of Cordrey's, helping him stash the cash. When he realized that his involvement was likely to lead to his wife, Rene, being charged with receiving stolen goods, along with Cordrey's sister Maisie and brother-in-law Alfred Pilgrim, he rapidly admitted

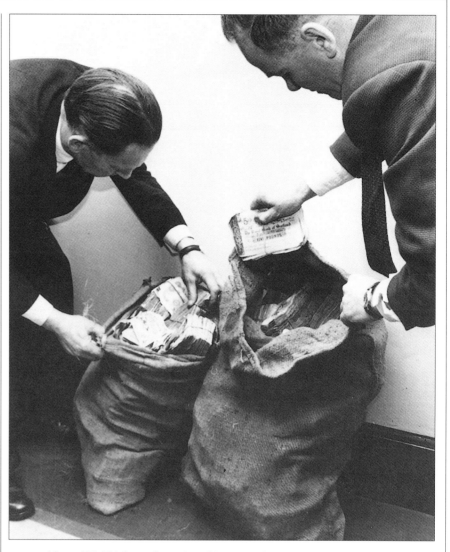

About £50,000 from the train robbery was found in a telephone kiosk.

his own involvement. It was one of the attractive features of the train robbers that they were never happy to see innocent people tagged with their crime.

On August 16, more of the money turned up – £100,000 in four suitcases was found in a wood in Surrey. More important than the cash, however, was a receipt in the cases. This led police to a solicitor's clerk who, it transpired, had handled the conveyancing of Leatherslade Farm to the gang.

Back at the farm the forensic teams were active. Yellow paint had been found on the pedals of the abandoned

vehicles. This would prove useful. The fingerprint men were successfully identifying well known "faces" from the London underworld who had left their dabs behind. Buster Edwards was wanted. So was Charlie Wilson, who had suddenly left his normal haunts, accompanied by his girlfriend Mary Manson, and who was quickly traced and arrested at his Clapham home. Bruce Reynolds, the suspected leader of the gang, had also left fingerprints at Leatherslade Farm.

Jimmy White was wanted, too. His fingerprints had been found in a caravan parked near the point where the money had been found in the Surrey wood. The caravan itself contained a further £30,000, hidden above the ceiling.

There was discord among the police over the release of these names to the public. Some officers believed it would help produce information. Others thought it only alerted the thieves as to which of them had been identified, and would ensure that the most wanted men went into hiding or skipped abroad. They believed that the main reason for giving information to the press was a wish to tell the world that the police were active.

The publicity led Mary Manson to give herself up. The police believed she had been at Leatherslade Farm, but had no evidence to prove it. In the end, they could only charge her with receiving the £820 she had paid for a car on the robbers' behalf, and she was released on bail.

Superintendent Tommy Butler was the man in charge of the case. A hugely experienced detective, he knew the form of all the major crooks in London, and

believed he could pinpoint the men with the experience and skill to handle a job like this. He wanted to talk to a young silversmith and amateur racing driver called Roy John James. The press was delighted to learn that his nickname was "the Weasel", and the satirical television programme *That Was the Week That Was* highlighted the investigation with the refrain, "Pop goes the Weasel!"

Butler was also after Bruce Reynolds' brother-in-law, an Irish antique dealer called John Daly. On December 3, a tip-off from an underworld informer led to Daly's arrest at his hideout in Eaton Square.

Putney hairdresser Gordon Goody was taken in, his link to Leatherslade Farm established by yellow paint on his shoe soles matching that on the abandoned vehicles. Ronnie Biggs, James Hussey, Leonard Field, Thomas Wisbey, Brian Field and John Wheater all found themselves under lock and key, helping the police with their enquiries.

The capture of "the Weasel" made

news headlines. Roy James was traced to a hideout in Ryders Terrace, St. John's Wood, North London. When 40 policeman surrounded the place, James grabbed a leather bag containing £12,000, and raced up to the roof. He made an agile run along the terrace roofs, and jumped lightly to the ground at the end – but a detective was waiting for him. With true professional aplomb, James denied knowing anything about the bag full of money! John Daly was arrested on the same day.

TRIAL AND PUNISHMENT

More of the loot kept turning up. Nearly £50,000 was planted in a telephone box in Great Dover Street, South London. It had been entrusted to an associate by Buster Edwards, who had done a deal with the police to get the hot notes back into the authorities' hands without associating himself with them.

On January 20, 1964, the trial of those gang members arrested started in Aylesbury. With such a large number of

Bruce Reynolds, known villain and suspected leader of the gang.

Charlie Wilson was soon arrested by police at his home in London.

Jimmy White: £30,000 and his fingerprints were found in a caravan.

topnotch villains appearing together, elaborate security arrangements were made. It was decided to hold the trial in Aylesbury, even though so vast a case merited the Old Bailey. The rural setting was preferred by police, who feared that the powerful London villains might well have used contacts to bribe or intimidate jurors in the capital. Empty Black Maria vans left the prisons as decoys. The huge trial brought the world's press to the little market town, and the prosecution brought in 1,700 exhibits and 2,350 written statements from witnesses. Forty barristers found gainful employment from this crime. The prisoners were represented by nine eminent QCs and 18 juniors. They were tried together, on the joint charge of conspiring to rob the Royal Mail. Only Cordrey pleaded guilty. The rest all affirmed their total innocence of any implication in the plot.

The villains were good-humoured and matey in the dock. There was much ribald mirth among them, especially when it seemed that the police wanted to try and match a pubic hair found at the farm. Mary Manson was cheerfully warned not to do herself an injury if a wardress took her away with a pair of nail scissors.

The prosecution case took three weeks to present. There were 200 witnesses, each adding their piece to the picture of the immense criminal conspiracy which unfolded.

The defence case took months to present rather than the anticipated few weeks. No eyewitnesses could place any of the defendants at the farm or on the train. Whitby and Mills were quite

Detectives put together an irrefutable batch of evidence with which the prosecution was able to persuade the jury of the train robbers' guilt.

unable to identify men who had only been eyes, peering out of the sinister balaclavas. Mills' case evoked great public sympathy. The blow he suffered had left him permanently injured, and led to his early retirement.

WITH SUCH A LARGE NUMBER OF TOP NOTCH VILLAINS APPEARING TOGETHER, ELABORATE SECURITY ARRANGEMENTS WERE MADE.

In the end, the fingerprint evidence, the yellow paint, and the paperwork by which the farm had been purchased all added up to an irrefutable tale of a brilliantly planned robbery. It was a matter of concern to the authorities that the Post Office insider who must have tipped the

gang off to rob that particular train for a really big haul was never identified, nor the railwayman whom driver Mills believed must have assisted with the uncoupling.

John Daly was acquitted, however. His fingerprints had been found on certain movable objects in the farm, but the jury decided that it was not proved beyond a reasonable doubt that they had been made there. He might have touched the things before they arrived at Leatherslade.

The remaining male defendants were all found guilty. And very long sentences were handed down. Bill Boal's 24 years (later reduced to 14) was much resented by the robbers. They knew that Boal – at 50, the oldest man in the dock – had not been involved in the conspiracy, but had tried to help his friend Cordrey get rid of his share of the loot. Charlie Wilson, Tommy Wisbey, Jim Hussey, Gordon Goody, Bob Welch, Roy James and Ronnie Biggs all got 30 years. They were all professionals: Wisbey the leader of a gang of railway thieves brought in for their expertise; Wilson, a plotter who raised the needed capital to get the enterprise off the ground; Goody, a thief who led the assault on the engine; James, an assistant to Cordrey in fixing the signals and cutting telephone wires by the track; Hussey, a strong-arm man who organized getting the money out of the coach; Welch, a heavy; and Biggs the minder who recruited the gang's unidentified driver. John Wheater, the solicitor who arranged the conveyancing of Leatherslade Farm, got a mere three years, since his fine war record was taken into account. His clerk, Brian Field, got 24 years, as did Lennie Field, who fronted the purchase. Cordrey's guilty plea won him a mere 14-year sentence (later paroled to seven).

The police were still looking for Bruce Reynolds, the mastermind; Buster Edwards, one of his co-plotters; and Jimmy White, the quartermaster, who took charge of the supplies and the truck.

Within 18 months, Ronnie Biggs had escaped from Wandsworth Prison and Charlie Wilson from Winson Green Prison. Wilson was retaken in Canada three years later, after travelling through France and Mexico. Buster Edwards gave himself up after three years on the run, and was given a 15-year sentence for his pains. Jimmy White was taken in Dover and given 18 years. And finally, in 1968, the gang's suspected leader, Bruce Reynolds, came back to England

in disguise, after following the same route as Wilson. He was arrested in Torquay and given 25 years.

THE ONE THAT GOT AWAY

Ronnie Biggs is the man on the run the police still long to catch. He escaped though Australia to Brazil. He cannot be extradited, though, since his Brazilian girlfriend Raimunda Castro has borne a child for him, and Brazilian law insists that he remain there. Chief Superinten-

dent Slipper of Scotland Yard was appalled when Biggs was released after he had arrested him in Rio.

When bounty hunters kidnapped Biggs, they too were foiled. They put in at Barbados for supplies, and the laid-back Barbadian lawyer Fred "Sleepy" Smith easily persuaded the courts to prohibit such a vigilante exercise. Biggs still lives in Rio with his wife and son, and Scotland Yard still hope to put him behind bars in England one day.

The one that stayed away: Ronnie Biggs, seen here in 1979, still enjoying life in the Brazilian sunshine on his share of the haul from the Great Train Robbery.

MURPH THE SURF
JACK MURPHY

You would expect a glamorous, handsome, headline-catching young cat burglar to have a glamorous, handsome name. You would expect a gentleman jewel-thief, whose hauls included a world-famous sapphire as big as a golf ball, and actress Eva Gabor's jewels, taken at gunpoint from her hotel room, to be known by some distinguished title or nickname. You would expect a ruthless murderer, once picked up on vagrancy charges, to have a sinister-sounding sobriquet.

■

YOU WOULD NOT EXPECT all three to be the same man. And you would not expect him to sound like a cartoon character: "Murph the Surf". But in Jack Murphy's case, the nickname came first, and the headlines and glamour followed it. And the nickname itself was glamorous, because Murph the Surf was a product of the heady, youth-worshipping 1960s.

Probably the young in all generations feel that the particular decade in which they came to maturity was the one in which splendid youth triumphed over stuffy old age. D.H. Lawrence remarked for all of us, "I like the men and women of my generation." But the 60s, more than any other, secured a lasting reputation as the decade of change; the new styles and new happenings set then would have a profound impact on culture and morality well into the future.

The astonishing papacy of John XXIII signalled that (for a few years at least) the largest religious institution in the world would offer the West moral and spiritual guidance in new and generous directions, rather than sitting four-square on doctrines worked out by eremites of the North African deserts 1,600 years ago, and resolutely protecting its own vested interests.

The election of John F. Kennedy suggested that America was throwing off the bigoted, xenophobic anti-Catholicism that marred its politics for generations. His short-lived presidency suggested that youth, charm, liberalism, and the good taste promoted by the First Lady might replace the perceived small-town mediocrity represented by presidents like Harding, Coolidge, Hoover, Truman and Eisenhower. Even Kennedy's tragic death allowed that magnificent emblem of hugely flawed grandeur, Lyndon Johnson, to put through the best parts of JFK's liberal domestic programme, using the subtle legislative skills that always eluded the more glamorous elder Kennedy brothers.

Lyndon Johnson had just won election as president in his own right when Murph the Surf came to public attention. But Murph's temporary appropriateness owed less to the politics than the youth Kennedy had superficially represented. Murph's wave of opportunity was more recognizable in another event of 1964: the first American tour of the singing sensation of the period, the Beatles.

Almost as influential as the Beatles were the Beach Boys (with capital letters) – and Murph the Surf was a beach boy with small letters.

SURFERS

Surfing rose to its cultural apogee in southern California. The big, ugly anonymous sprawl of Los Angeles is bounded on the west by the beaches of the Pacific Ocean; Long Beach, Venice Beach, and Malibu Beach; names suggesting the wealth and glamour of Hollywood at play. In fact, Venice was more of a funfair centre and in the 50s it became the headquarters of the "Beat Generation"; intellectual drop-outs who

set an agenda of pot-smoking, free love and radical politics which would influence the hippies of the next decade.

By the time the hippies were emerging, Venice was best known for its bevvies of narcissistic body-builders who exercised and showed off their gleaming oiled biceps and wasp waists on a section of the shoreline that become known as Muscle Beach. The rest of the beachline was a paradise for surfers. More attractive than the meaty males of Muscle Beach, the surfers had natural muscle promoted by hard physical exercise, not by the weight-lifting excesses that could make a man look like a prize bullock fattened for the market.

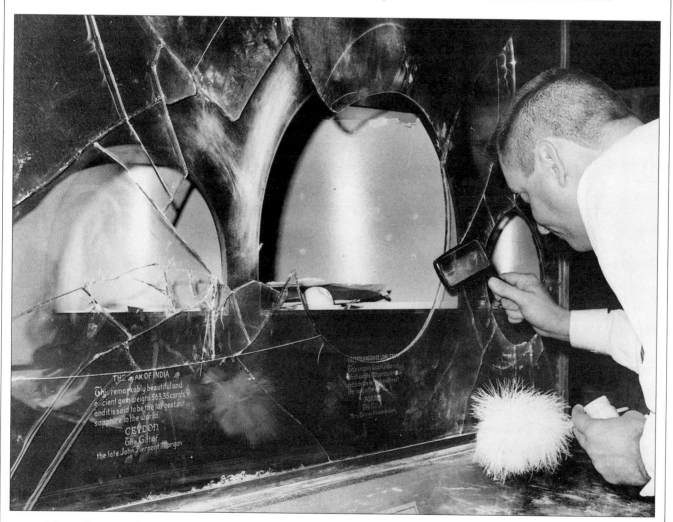

A forensic expert dusts for fingerprints following the daring jewel heist at New York's Museum of Natural History.

The surfers lived a healthy open-air life; yet their dedication to the beaches suggested that it was entirely leisured. And, since surfing demands real fitness, the surfers were, by definition, young.

THE FIRST SURFER

Jack Roland Murphy was not a Californian. He came from Florida: the other sun, sand 'n' sea paradise of the USA. He had won surfing championships in his hometown of Miami. He claimed to be the true and original promoter of surfing in America, having discovered the sport in Hawaii and brought it back to Miami Beach.

If you believed Jack, the Californian surfers were all Johnny-come-latelies, riding their own personal wave to celebrity and success. Back home in Miami, civic pride allowed a good many people to believe "Murph the Surf's" claim to have introduced this new leisure activity and its back-up industry of boards and fashionable beachwear, which injected new life into the American holiday trade. But it was not until he was 27 that the handsome tide-rider made a name for himself in metropolitan New York. And he achieved that not by capitalizing on his surfing talent but through crime.

In the autumn of 1964, Murph, accompanied by two fellow-surfers from Florida, went to stay in the Big Apple. Roger Clarke was the oldest at 29. He was quiet in manner and angelic in appearance. Alan Kuhn was younger than Murph and Roger, but materially more successful. At 26, he was a sought-after diving instructor and the proud owner of a two-masted schooner and a 50-ft speedboat, but he wanted more. Like his companions, he wanted the leisured lifestyle to last forever, and it didn't seem that hiring out boats and entertaining tourists with their skills in the water was going to bring the sun-bronzed young men the kind of wealth they wanted. So they hit the big city, intent on making their fortunes.

> ## "WELL, WE HAVE SOME THEORY WHICH IS BEING EXPLORED AND EXPLOITED AT THE PRESENT MOMENT, AND – ER – AT THIS PARTICULAR TIME I WOULD RATHER REFRAIN FROM ANSWERING THAT QUESTION."
>
> POLICE SPOKESMAN, TRYING TO EXPLAIN HOW SECURITY HAD ALLOWED THE MUSEUM JEWEL ROBBERY

They checked into the best suite of a very expensive hotel, about ten blocks away from the Museum of Natural History, overlooking Central Park. They passed themselves off as an underwater salvage team; an occupation which certainly could make fortunes for those lucky enough to trace or stumble upon really valuable wrecks. These particular submariners spent much of their city vacation making repeated visits to the geological section of the Museum of Natural History.

THE GREAT BREAK-IN

For most people other than mineralogists, a geology museum is one of the most boring entertainments imaginable. Case after case of motionless, inanimate rocks do little to stimulate the imagination. However, the Museum of Natural History contained some rocks that were spectacular by any standards: the De Long Star ruby was a gigantic gem of 100 carats; the Midnight Star sapphire was even bigger, at 161 carats; and the astonishing Star of India, at 563.35 carats, was the largest sapphire in the world, and one of the world's largest precious stones of any kind. All these three treasures lay temptingly in one case.

Murphy, Clarke and Kuhn went back again and again to the museum, identifying the position of the most valuable stones, and buying plans and guides to the building from the museum shop. They surreptitiously examined the galleries for any alarms that might impede their caper. Unknown to them, this was a futile exercise – the whole alarm system had been turned off two years earlier as an economy measure!

On October 29 the three thieves struck. They had watched a number of exciting films about top-notch jewel robbers, and were determined to emulate Hollywood's ideal of the glamorous criminal. One kept watch, while the other two scaled a 10-foot wall and forced open a door. Using their knowledge of the building's layout, the pair

Jack Murphy (centre right) and Alan Kuhn (centre left) under arrest as suspects in the great museum jewel heist.

made their way to an office on the fifth floor. They opened its window, and embarked on the genuinely athletic, daredevil part of their crime.

From a height of 100 feet above Central Park, they lowered themselves to the windows of the J.P. Morgan Hall of Gems and Minerals, using Venetian blind tape. The hall's windows were routinely left two inches open, and they were not alarmed, so the rest of the robbery was a cinch. The thieves went straight to the case containing the richest gems. Following the example of so many Hollywood films, they scored a circle on the glass with a glass-cutter, stuck masking tape over the circle to stop it from

shattering, and then used a metal window washing squeegee taken from a porter's locker to remove it. With that, they thrust gloved hands in to scoop out the most valuable gemstones, and away they went, out of the building, as fast as possible.

In the morning, embarrassed police and security men had to explain to New York's press how thieves had managed to get into a building containing such valuables that it would have been assumed there were excellent locks, bolts and alarms. A police spokesman, asked outright whether the thieves were professionals and had come in by the window, produced a classic awkward and evasive reply that fooled no one: "Well, we have

some theory which is being explored and exploited at the present moment, and – er – at this particular time I would rather refrain from answering that question."

In fact, the police had privately concluded that the robbers were certainly not professional jewel thieves. Their removal of world-famous named stones proved their amateurism. These would be almost impossible to sell as they stood, because of the certainty of their being recognized if they came on the market. It would be vital to recut them: an expensive process in its own right if the stones were to appear in good enough shapes to command a reasonable price. But that price would be immensely lower than the market value of the originals, and could far more easily be realized by stealing smaller and less valuable stones that would not need disguise. The police realized they were hunting thieves who knew what they were looking for – the best stones; but did not know their business in choosing them.

While the police fended off reporters' questions, the three surfers and their jewels were heading for cover. Roger Clarke headed north to stay with his parents at their home in Connecticut. Murphy and Kuhn went for a celebratory night out at their New York Hotel, where Kuhn "chatted up" a 19-year-old girl called Janet Florkiewicz who was going to Miami the following day. Exercising the charm of fit and sun-tanned surfers, Kuhn and Murphy persuaded Janet to take a locked briefcase with her on their behalf. They then made the mistake of travelling on the same flight and pretending not to recognize her.

Janet Florkiewicz was an honest young lady with no aspirations to be a gangster's moll. She could not understand what Jack and Alan were up to, and telephoned a girlfriend back in New York to say, "Something fishy's going on." The girlfriend mentioned it to another hotel resident, who remembered that the three salvage divers had kept a book called *The Story of the Gems* in their suite: a book published by the Museum of Natural History.

By the time Roger Clarke returned to Manhattan to collect property he had left there, the FBI were waiting to meet him. They wanted him to explain why his belongings included burglary tools and photographs of parts of the museum. Meanwhile down in Florida, FBI agents raided the apartment shared by Jack Murphy and Alan Kuhn. They found Murphy sitting around in a pair of shorts with two girlfriends. "I was supposed to be on my way to Hawaii to surf," he

Jack Murphy arriving at the Supreme Court in New York in December 1964.

grumbled. "This has fouled the whole thing up." Ten minutes later Alan Kuhn walked in, to have handcuffs slipped over his wrists. Less cool than Murph the Surf, he spat out a line reminiscent of old James Cagney movies when he realized that Janet Florkiewicz had given them away. "That's what happens when you fool around with square broads!" snarled Alan Kuhn.

THE GLAMOROUS PUBLIC FACE

The three thieves had a strong bargaining counter, however. They knew where the jewels were. The authorities did not. Sharp lawyers worked out a preliminary deal for them. They were offered bail in return for their co-operation. And so, on November 18, Jack Murphy and Alan Kuhn flew from Florida to New York under their own steam. They were not handcuffed or compelled to come, and arrived with the laid-back air of the leisured playboys they pretended to be.

The press took their act at face value, and they became instant celebrities. The two played up to this unexpected turn of events enthusiastically. Murph the Surf's nickname ensured that he became recognized as their leader and a spokesman for the relaxed life of the beaches.

When the two were greeted by an instant press conference on arrival in New York, they casually assured reporters that they had enjoyed an early morning swim before leaving the warm south. And they had not bothered to bring any luggage with them, as they were bound to have their bail continued. New Yorkers, freezing in an iron November, could only envy the young Floridians their comfortable lifestyle.

Eva Gabor, one of the famous Hungarian actress-sisters, claimed she was a victim of Murphy and Kuhn.

Their image as classy crooks was given a useful polish by the Miami papers, which reported the unsolved theft of a quarter of a million dollars' worth of jewels in Nassau that spring – it was known that Murph and his pals had been sailing in the Bahamas at that time. "They are crack jewel thieves," the Miami Chief of Detectives was supposed to have said. "We've been trying to pin something on them for a long time."

The truth, as the more astute journalists suspected, was more mundane. Weren't the three young men mere beach bums, they asked? Murphy and Kuhn denied the suggestion indignantly. A beach bum was a hobo living by beach-combing, or a petty thief with no visible means of support living by pilfering from tourists. However it might be defined, a beach bum was undesirable in the eyes of decent society. Murph the Surf insisted he was a beach boy: a quite different animal. He and his friends were leisured, well-heeled young men who preferred to spend most of their time enjoying watersports. Actually, he and Kuhn were indeed beach bums. They had been arrested several times for vagrancy during the previous six months.

THE SEAMY UNDERSIDE

The pair were granted bail as they had predicted. It was set at $32,000, and they flew back to Florida, but they were unable to maintain the pose of elegant supercrooks whose private means lifted them above the level of petty hoods. On January 4, 1965, they were back in New York to renew their bail. As they left the courtroom, they were arrested. The desk clerk at the famous Algonquin Hotel, where Dorothy Parker and her circle of wits had feasted at the round table during the inter-war years, identified Murph the Surf as one of a group of men who had pistol-whipped him in a hold-up and made off with a paltry $250.

The following day Eva Gabor, perhaps the most talented of the three blonde Hungarian sisters who, with their worldly-wise mama, made headlines in the 1950s as the wonderfully named Zsa Zsa romanced her way to stardom, came to the police with a further complaint. Murphy and Kuhn, she said, had forced their way into her apartment, beaten her up, and stolen jewellery worth $50,000. Murph the Surf looked less and less like a gentleman thief. His bail was raised to $150,000, and he and Kuhn flew back to Miami straight away to start serious negotiations with the law. It looked as though their surfing activities were going to be seriously curtailed.

If the jewels were to be returned, they might hope for considerable remission of sentence and the dropping of some charges. The FBI had already agreed to drop the federal charge of transporting stolen property over state lines in return for their co-operation. Kuhn set out with two detectives and an assistant district attorney to try and locate the swag. An army of reporters and photographers followed the quartet from Kuhn's apartment to a succession of hotels and bars. Kuhn was observed to make a total of 50 telephone calls. A number of theories were put forward. It was suggested that an expert diver had stashed the jewels somewhere under the ocean, so the assistant district attorney hired flippers and goggles, and went diving at the indicated location. He found nothing. In the end it was a tip-off from an informer that led to the jewels' discovery.

ALADDIN'S CAVE

The party hastened to a Trailways bus terminal in downtown Miami, hotly pursued by the press. Locker 911 yielded up its secrets. The Star of India and eight other gems were there, in two brown suede pouches. The bags were wet, as though they had indeed been submerged for some time, but the water was not salt seawater. Murphy, Kuhn and Clark could no longer evade confessing that they were responsible for the jewel heist. They could, however, try to bargain for

> THE FOLLOWING DAY EVA GABOR ... CAME TO THE POLICE WITH A FURTHER COMPLAINT. MURPHY AND KUHN...HAD FORCED THEIR WAY INTO HER APARTMENT, BEATEN HER UP AND STOLEN JEWELLERY WORTH $50,000.

lenient treatment in return for bringing back the jewels that were still missing. The authorities offered the three the amazingly generous deal of a single year's imprisonment in return for restitution and a guilty plea. Alas, they could not come up with the goods because they had already been forced to sell the gems to pay for their legal costs. Even so they only drew three-year sentences when they came to trial.

The De Long ruby had already been recovered before they went to prison. A Miami gangster offered it to millionaire John D. MacArthur in return for a

$25,000 ransom. MacArthur negotiated through a writer, Francis Amstel, and when Amstel took the ransom money, as directed, to the ringing booth in a row of telephones, he was instructed to leave it there and go to an adjacent booth. There was the ruby, hidden above the door.

MacArthur was lauded as a public benefactor; excoriated as a ransom-payer who was hereby encouraging crime; and sincerely thanked by the Museum of Natural History, who were delighted to have their exhibit back. They brought out a special security case made for the Hope Diamond which had once been exhibited in the J.P. Morgan Hall. It was basically a steel safe with a glass top. And at night, the top, too, was covered by steel.

After all the publicity, 5,000 people came to look at the famous Star of India and De Long ruby in one day. The museum ruefully recognized that they would never see the Midnight Star sapphire again, as it and the other smaller gems taken would certainly have been cut up for sale in separate, unidentifiable pieces. After two years, the beach boy jewel thieves were released. The Eva Gabor case had never come to court, as she was too busy in Hollywood to return to New York and give evidence. Kuhn and Clarke slipped quietly out of the public eye.

THE SQUALID CONCLUSION OF MURPH'S CAREER

But Murph the Surf remained the brutal hoodlum he had always been. In 1968 he was one of a gang who attempted the

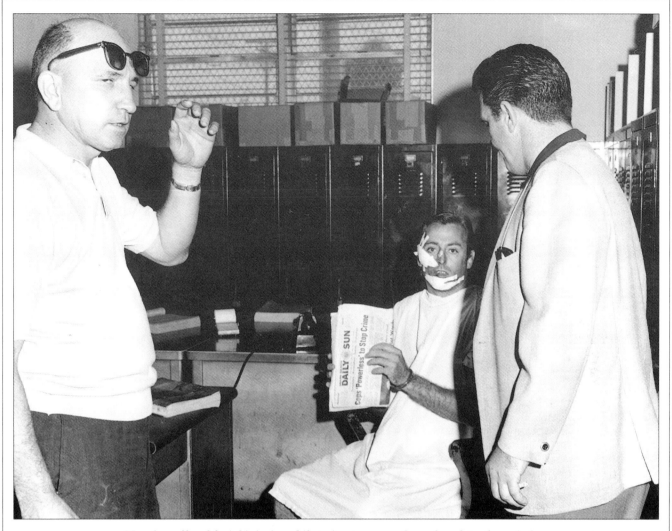

Murphy suffered facial injuries while trying to escape through a plate glass window.

violent robbery of millionairess Olivia Wofford's house. She was forced to open her safe for them, but managed to trip a secret alarm, which sent the gang rushing for safety. Murph's leap for freedom through a plate glass window only meant that he was bleeding profusely and had to be patched up when the police caught him along with his confederates.

At the trial Murphy's lawyer said that his client was psychologically incapable of telling right from wrong. Then a psychiatrist said that Murph saw himself as a sort of modern Robin Hood. Since the historical Robin Hood was a brutal mugger with a glamorized reputation given him by balladeers, this was, perhaps, not far from the mark.

In 1969 Murph added bloody murder to his criminal achievements. He and a crook called Jack Griffiths sweet-talked two secretaries into walking out of a Los Angeles finance house with half a million dollars in securities. Once this booty was safely in their hands, the two villains killed the unsuspecting girls, in the car park of Valenti's Restaurant in Miami. Then they weighted their bodies with concrete before dumping them in Whisky Creek near Fort Lauderdale. For his part in these murders Murphy was sentenced to life imprisonment.

Murph weakened that rap, too, by appealing on the grounds that he was insane. He was then committed to a top security mental hospital.

And that should have been the end of the story of Murph the Surf. But in 1985 Murphy was declared cured, and was released from prison. He came out with a new obsession, that he was put on earth to spread God's word. Thus, Murph the Surf embarked on a final career as a preacher-man. His Christian conclusions about his manifold sins and wickedness? "Well I just use this system and this experience to help me get my priorities and my life straightened out."

THE MOORS
MURDERERS

 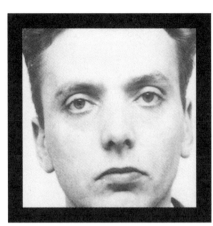

Criminals invariably hurt those least able to defend themselves, but even the most hardened criminals recognize and detest the evil that is done when the victim is a child. Ian Brady and Myra Hindley, two seemingly ordinary office workers living in the north of England, were convicted of murdering children. Their crimes horrified and continue to horrify a nation, though they were committed nearly 30 years ago.

■

THE CASE OF MYRA HINDLEY raises moral questions for society. Arguably no longer a threat to society, unlikely ever to commit such crimes again, repentant and God-fearing, she wants her release from prison. Is keeping her in prison serving a purpose or is society merely exacting its revenge? In Ian Brady's case, is this moralizing question even worth asking?

Ian Brady was christened Ian Duncan Stewart. He was the illegitimate son of a waitress named Margaret Stewart, but had been raised by a foster family, John and Mary Sloan and their four children. It was a hard, working-class environment in Glasgow, but the family was caring and loving. Brady, though, grew into a troubled adolescent. He was not known to be violent, but he got into trouble with the law a few times for house-breaking. His behaviour was taken seriously by the Sloans, the police and the courts, but was not thought to be more than "juvenile delinquency". Nevertheless, by the age of 17 it looked like he would be sent to prison unless something was done to stop his behaviour. The court, perhaps thinking that an environmental change would help Brady, ordered that he live with his mother instead of the Sloans. By this time his mother had moved from Scotland to Manchester.

The move probably did little to help Ian Brady from feeling a lack of identity within society. Not only did Brady now find he couldn't relate to the world around him, the world around him wasn't even a familiar one. It's impossible to say whether anything could have arrested the degeneration of Brady's mental condition, but without doubt the move to Manchester exacerbated it.

Crime still attracted him, however. He was sentenced to two years in Borstal for stealing and was sent first to Hatfield Prison, Yorkshire, which was designed for relatively new offenders with above-average intelligence. Here, Brady learnt how to brew alcohol which resulted in him getting drunk and, in consequence, being transferred to the tough Hull Borstal. Here he mixed with more hardened criminals and developed an interest in the Nazis and the philosophy of the Marquis de Sade. These influences fed his feeling of alienation from society.

David and Maureen Smith, two of the witnesses in the Moors Murders case.

Chief Inspector Joe Mounsey searches the moors for new graves.

Following his release, Brady managed to stay out of trouble and at the age of 21 got himself a job as a stock clerk at a chemical company called Millwards. In January 1961, a new typist began working for the company – her name was Myra Hindley. She was 18 years old, and within a short time she became infatuated with the sullen Brady. Her infatuation was inflamed by his disinterest in her and it was close on a year before they went on a date together. A few weeks later they had had sex on Hindley's grandmother's settee. Having captured her body, Brady set about capturing her mind. He introduced her to atheism, Nazism and sadism. Gradually he drew her into his insane world, which Hindley adopted as her own.

Myra Hindley and her younger sister, Maureen, were the daughters of Bob and Hettie Hindley. They lived in a small house. When Maureen was born, lack of space led to Myra going to live with her grandmother, who lived a few doors away. Her parents would divorce (after her arrest), but by all accounts they gave their children a normal childhood. Myra, a devout Roman Catholic, seems to have grown into a normal teenager, the only mark against her being an attendance problem at school and, later, at work.

PAULINE READE

It is difficult to know the precise details of Brady and Hindley's degeneration into murder because they now contradict each other's stories. Chief Inspector Peter Topping, in his autobiography, *Topping*, gives Hindley's account of the first murder: by 1963, she said, Brady had discussed with her his plans for committing the perfect murder. She claimed

Brady forced her to participate by threatening to hurt her grandmother and to show some pornographic photographs he had taken with a time-lapse camera of himself having sex with her.

Willing or otherwise, on July 12, Hindley, who had bought an old van, set out on a murder hunt. She drove around, followed by Brady on his motorcycle, until she saw young Pauline Reade who was on her way to a dance. Hindley stopped the van and offered her a lift. Pauline, who knew Myra Hindley, accepted. Hindley then enlisted Pauline's help to look for a glove she said she'd dropped during a picnic on Saddleworth Moor. On the moor they were joined by Brady. According to Hindley, Pauline and Brady went off together, then Brady rejoined her and took her to see Pauline's body. Brady and Hindley buried the body, then went home. In January 1990, in a letter to a newspaper, Brady denied this story. He asserted that Hindley actively participated in the murders and also sexually assaulted the victims.

The story of the glove lost at a picnic on Saddleworth Moor was used again, four months later, on November 23, 1963, when Brady and Hindley got into conversation with 12-year-old John Kilbride. He had spent that Saturday afternoon at the cinema with a friend, John Ryan, then gone to Ashton market to earn a few pence from the stall-holders. After a while John Ryan set off for home – he was never to see his friend again. By teatime John Kilbride's parents began to phone family and friends, then they telephoned the police. Over the coming weeks there was a massive police search for the young lad. The canal was dragged and nearly 2,000 volunteers joined in an

Two of the senior detectives who helped to bring the Moors Murderers to justice: Superintendent Talbot (left) and Chief Superintendent Benfield.

extensive search of waste ground and derelict buildings, but no sign of the boy's body was found.

John Kilbride had been approached by Brady and Hindley. His suspicions lulled by the presence of Hindley, he had agreed to help them search for the glove. The three drove to the moor, then Brady and Kilbride went off together. Hindley says she drove around for a while, then returned to where she'd left Brady. The boy's body was already buried, he said.

On June 16, 1964, the couple killed again. This time the victim was 12-year-old Keith Bennett. He was last seen heading for his grandmother's house, where he slept every alternate Tuesday. The next day his grandmother asked his mother why he hadn't come by that night. It would be more than 20 years before they knew the answer. Hindley had lured him into her car. Later, Brady

had strangled the boy and buried the body on Saddleworth Moor. The body has never been found.

On December 26, 1964, 10-year-old Lesley Ann Downey and her two younger brothers visited a fairground a short walk from where they lived. The boys returned home, but Lesley Ann never did. Her parents scoured the streets, then contacted the police. The funfair was searched, countless people were questioned, and there was massive publicity. Reports of Lesley Ann being sighted came from numerous seaside resorts in the United Kingdom and even from as far away as Europe.

Lesley Ann had been picked up and taken back to Hindley's grandmother's house, where Brady and Hindley were now living. Brady took pornographic photographs of the child, then killed her. Hindley maintained that she was aware of what was happening, but was not present, as she was in either the kitchen or the bathroom. Brady, however, has said that Hindley was present throughout and had, moreover, insisted on killing the little girl herself. She did so, he said, with a length of silk cord and would later get pleasure from playing with the cord in public.

EDWARD EVANS

In October 1965, Brady decided to kill again. This time he enlisted the help of Myra Hindley's brother-in-law, David Smith. The victim was 17-year-old Edward Evans, a homosexual, who was taken back to Brady's house and had sex with Brady while Myra Hindley was fetching Smith. The couple returned to find Brady and Evans fighting, at which point Brady took an axe to Evans. Smith helped in the clearing up. At 3.00am he felt able to go home – according to his story, he ran all the way, terrified. He described the night to Maureen Hindley and, armed with a screwdriver and a

> **IT IS THE VOICE OF LESLEY ANN DOWNEY SCREAMING, PLEADING, BEGGING, CRYING FOR HER MOTHER AND FATHER.**

carving knife, they went to a phone box to call the police. The following day Superintendent Robert Talbot called at Brady's house dressed as a baker's deliveryman and carrying a basket of loaves.

Brady was in bed and Hindley was about to leave for work. The house was clean and tidy. The body of Evans was found locked in an upstairs room. The police also found some loaded guns and an exercise book that contained the names of several film stars and also the name John Kilbride.

The investigation now took an unexpected turn. Brady consistently denied knowing anything about the murders, other than that of Evans, whose death, he

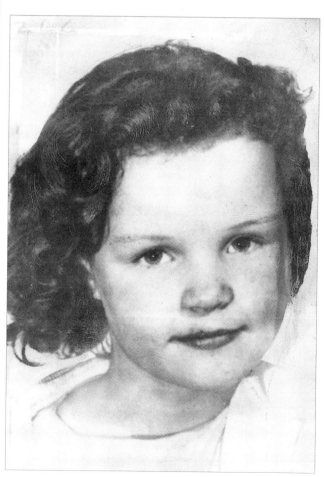

Lesley Ann Downey

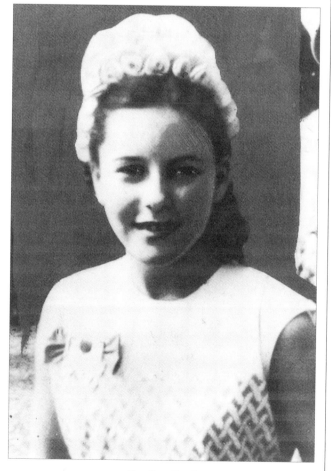

Pauline Reade

said, was an accident. Hindley, when she was arrested five days later, on October 11, and charged with being an accessory to murder, proved equally resistant to interrogation. But was it possible that Brady and Hindley might be responsible for the disappearance of the children? Smith had told an incredible story, not all of it making much sense to the police. He had spoken of bodies being buried on the moors. Could it be true? At Hindley's grandmother's house the police found a large number of photographs, some taken on what was unmistakeably Saddleworth Moor.

The Smiths were taken to the moor. So was a near neighbour of Brady's, 11-year-old Pat Hodges, who had been to the moors several times with Brady and Hindley. Together they were able to point out the places Hindley and Brady were most fond of. 150 policemen were brought in to search the area, but they found nothing except the bones of sheep. Then a young policeman saw another bone sticking out of the peat – it was a human arm bone. The police carefully excavated the scene and uncovered the naked body of Lesley Ann Downey.

The police searched Brady and Hindley's house again and in the spine of a prayer book they found a left luggage ticket. At Manchester Central Station the police recovered two suitcases, one of which contained an audio tape. It seemed innocent enough, just some radio programmes, but towards the end there were 13 minutes of stomach-churning horror that once heard was never forgotten, even by the toughest policemen. It is the voice of Lesley Ann

> ## "SHE IS DETERMINED TO GIVE THE POLICE EVERY HELP IN RESOLVING THESE MYSTERIES."
> ### MYRA HINDLEY'S SOLICITORS

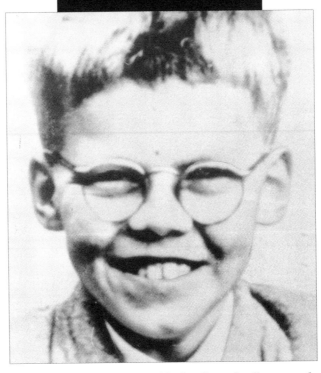

Keith Bennett, the 12-year-old schoolboy who disappeared while making his way to his grandmother's house.

Downey screaming, pleading, begging, crying for her mother and father. Fortunately we can only imagine – and it's best not to imagine too hard – what little Lesley's mother must have felt when she was asked to listen to that tape and identify her daughter's voice. Also heard were the voices of Ian Brady and Myra Hindley. In addition, there were several pornographic pictures of Lesley, giving a visual as well as audio image of that poor child's nightmare.

Brady declared that all he'd done was take some photographs of Lesley Ann Downey. He said two men had brought her to the house and that she had left with them after the photographs had been taken. Hindley was equally adamant that neither she nor Brady had killed the little girl. In Hindley's favour, she was briefly emotional when the tape of Lesley Ann was played to her, but it is of no consequence. She was also emotional when told that her dog, Puppet, had died under anaesthetic while a vet was trying to determine the animal's age. "Murderers," said Hindley to the police.

Many of the policemen investigating the case had children of their own and hearing that tape had a profound effect on all of them. Little surprise, then, that calls for Hindley's release from prison are unpersuasive and that, indeed, Brady and Hindley are often cited by the pro side when any case for the reintroduction of capital punishment is discussed.

Meanwhile, Detective Chief Inspector Joe Mounsey had continued working on the photographs found at Hindley's grandmother's house. He was able to identify the precise location of one photograph and the police began digging there. They found the body of John Kilbride.

The controversial police dig on Saddleworth Moor in 1986.

Brady was charged with having murdered John Kilbride, Lesley Ann Downey and Edward Evans. Myra Hindley was charged with the murders of Lesley Ann Downey and Edward Evans, and later with the murder of John Kilbride.

The committal – the presentation of prosecution evidence in public and before a judge so that it could be decided whether there was a case to answer – began at Chester Assizes on April 19, 1966. It lasted 14 days. Media interest in the case was extraordinary, its like probably not to be seen again until the trial of Peter Sutcliffe at the Old Bailey 15 years later. As with the Sutcliffe case, the press was hauled over the coals for what is

today called "chequebook journalism". In the Brady and Hindley case, the evidence of Smith was brought into doubt because he had received payment from a newspaper for his story. Fortunately, the original statement he'd made to the police was sufficient evidence.

Brady and Hindley were found guilty and, because the death penalty had recently been abolished, sentenced to life imprisonment.

THE LIMELIGHT

It's difficult to know why Brady and Hindley have remained in the limelight; why, with the Kray twins and Peter Sutcliffe, the Yorkshire Ripper, they remain

the most infamous "guests" of Her Majesty's prison service. Certainly, Hindley has never been long out of the newspapers. She made headlines in 1972 when Dorothy Wing, the Governor of London's Holloway Prison, took her walkabout on Hampstead Heath. More printers' ink was devoted to her when, in 1974, she attempted to escape from prison – an attempt organized with the help of a prison officer with whom Hindley was having a lesbian affair.

She made further headlines in 1989 when she announced her intention to sue ex-Detective Chief Superintendent Peter Topping over the publication of his autobiography, *Topping*. Hindley has also

The remains of Pauline Reade are removed from Saddleworth Moor, 24 years after the girl's disappearance.

attracted considerable publicity through her attempts to gain parole and through the efforts of people who have championed her case, most notably Lord Longford. The public, though, have been almost united in their outrage at any suggestion that Hindley ever be released.

Brady has repeatedly stated that he does not wish to be released from prison. Today he is apparently in a very poor physical and mental condition, though he has been removed from Gartree Prison to the maximum security hospital, Park Lane, in Liverpool, where his mental health has improved somewhat. He has gained the headlines only when responding to claims made by Myra Hindley. The couple ceased corresponding in 1971. Since then Brady has sometimes issued statements that, in the main, seem designed to warn or remind Myra Hindley that he knows the truth about her; that two bodies remain hidden.

In 1985, Fred Harrison, a journalist working for the *Sunday People*, visited Brady in Gartree Prison. According to Harrison, who wrote a book called *Brady and Hindley: Genesis of the Moors Murderers*, during several interviews Brady admitted to murders additional to those of which he had been convicted. He claimed the murders of Pauline Reade, Keith Bennett, and of Philip Deare (whose murder police had not attributed to Brady and Hindley). Later, Harrison, who had moved to the *Today* newspaper, reported the claims of a nurse at Holloway Prison who said Hindley had confessed to the murder of Reade.

Harrison's stories, though questioned by some people, succeeded in bringing the Moors case back to the public eye, in particular the fate of Pauline Reade and Keith Bennett, whose death, though widely attributed to Brady and Hindley, remained unexplained. Amid increasing publicity, Mrs. Johnson, the mother of Keith Bennett, wrote to Myra Hindley, asking that she reveal what had happened to the boy. Hindley seemed genuinely affected by the letter and, while still pondering its contents, she received a visit from Detective Chief Superintendent Peter Topping.

Myra Hindley issued through her solicitor, Michael Fisher, a statement in which she said she had viewed photographs and maps and had identified places she had visited with Ian Brady and which she knew to be special to him. She expressed gratitude for being given the opportunity to assist the police. It was a carefully worded statement which did not admit her guilt. Hindley had developed a version of events which she had come to believe; in this she was little more than a helper, an innocent.

Brady responded from his cell with a barely disguised threat. Through his solicitor, he declared his anger with Hindley's assertion that she had merely been a Trilby to his Svengali. Hindley, he said, should "be made aware that letters she wrote to him over a long period of years when they were first in prison are still in existence".

Hindley then responded through her solicitor: "She is determined to give the police every help in resolving these mysteries."

In November 1986 the police returned to Saddleworth Moor and, acting on Myra Hindley's guidance, they began a search. Newsmen shivered in their cars. Television camera crews waited impatiently. Politicians, as ever, complained about the expense. Topping approached the Home Office for permission to take Hindley to the moor. This was a matter of much debate, the security precautions being enormous – the

many threats to her life being further testimony to the public desire that Hindley never be released. The Home Secretary, Douglas Hurd, gave his permission.

On December 16, 200 policemen were taken to Saddleworth Moor – 40 of them carrying guns. Roads to the moor were blocked. At 8.30am a helicopter

> **"THE BOTTOM LINE FOR MYRA HINDLEY IS THAT SHE COMMITTED ACTS THE VAST MAJORITY OF THE POPULATION WOULD NOT BE CAPABLE OF COMMITTING. SHE CAN NEVER ATONE FOR WHAT SHE HAS DONE BUT SHE CAN BE – AND IS BEING – PUNISHED. IT IS RIGHT ... THAT HER PUNISHMENT SHOULD BE LIFELONG."**
>
> JEAN RITCHIE IN *MYRA HINDLEY: INSIDE THE MIND OF A MURDERESS*

landed – Myra Hindley had returned to the killing grounds. She later claimed to have been disoriented by the open space and concerned by the helicopters circling overhead. They had frightened her. The public, though, seemed outraged by Hindley's "finer sensibilities".

Meanwhile, winter hardened its grip on the moors and the police search had to be called off. It was a hot time for

Topping, though, who was roasted by many people for having wasted public money in a futile exercise. He was virtually accused of being a vain publicity seeker. But his actions had caused Hindley to rethink her position and several of her closest advisors were pressuring her to confess. To do so was not an easy option for Myra Hindley, as she had all but convinced herself of her innocence.

In February 1987 Myra Hindley confessed. She revisited the moor, this time amid less publicity. The police search pressed ahead, but the circus of journalists dwindled. Topping became something of a joke. There were comments that he'd next undertake a search for band leader Glenn Miller, who had disappeared during World War II. But on July 1, 1987, near where Lesley Ann Downey had been buried, police found the grave of Pauline Reade.

There was a lot of noise about a new trial and David Smith's possible involvement with the murders. A Tory Member of Parliament, Geoffrey Dickens, even claimed that another person had been involved. And then there was Brady.

He'd actually been helping the police for some time, a fact that had been kept from Hindley, it being thought that she was possessive about her relationship with Topping. Brady went to the moor, but the visit so disturbed his precarious mental state that he could not help and other bodies remain undiscovered.

T H E
MANSON
F A M I L Y

The idea of a little band of drug-crazed hippy teenagers breaking into a private house, slaughtering its occupants and daubing political slogans on the walls in their victims' blood seemed horrible beyond contemplation. The Manson "family" completely discredited the "flower power" movement, whose long hair, drug-taking and "Peace and Love" slogan offered young people an alternative to crew-cut, military-minded materialist upward social scrambling.

■

CHARLES MANSON HAS BECOME a cult figure. As he has said, he represents all things to all people – an Everyman of the '60s. A devil to some, to others he's an icon. For prison officials he's an exhibit, to psychologists a subject, to journalists copy. Being all things to all people was a technique Manson honed and used.

"Murder, death, bodies, blood!"

These words were screamed in horror and disbelief by a maid who had stumbled upon an appalling crime. It was August 9, 1969, on Cielo Drive in the Hollywood Hills. The maid had run from a house that once had been the home of movie star Cary Grant, then of Terry Melcher, son of Doris Day, and which now belonged to controversial film director Roman Polanski and his wife, actress Sharon Tate.

Those who went to investigate the maid's cries found a white Rambler in the drive. Slumped dead at the wheel was Steven Parent. Parent, who was 18, had been shot four times and his neck had been slashed. Nearby, on the lawn, lay Abigail Folger. She was heiress to the Folger Coffee millions. She had been stabbed so many times with a bayonet that her blood had soaked into her white nightdress and turned it red. Voytek Frykowski, Abigail's boyfriend, lay near the front door. A writer, producer, and drug dealer, he had been shot in the back, pistol-whipped so badly that his head bore 13 dents, then frenziedly stabbed a horrifying 51 times.

In the living room investigators discovered the body of Sharon Tate, famous for her starring role in *Valley of the Dolls*. She was eight months pregnant. She had been strangled, then stabbed with a bayonet no fewer than 16 times. A rope had been tied around her and looped over a beam. Attached to the other end of the rope, a towel over his head like a grotesque hood, hung Jay Sebring, a hair-stylist and Sharon Tate's former fiancé. On the front door, written in Sharon Tate's blood, was the word "PIG".

This ghastly sight, barely imaginable even when graphically described, shocked and appalled the police. Their first action was to arrest the only surviving member of the household, William Garretson, 19 years old, who was employed as a caretaker and lived in a house in the grounds. A dog had barked during the night, but he'd paid no attention to it, yet he hadn't heard shooting and screaming. He couldn't account for this and in front of TV cameras appeared very shaken and genuinely terrified. After two days, following pressure from lawyers acting for Garretson, the boy was released without charge. A spokesman said, "He's not involved in any way and he has been released".

Fifteen miles from the Cielo Drive murders, near Griffith Park, multi-millionaire Leno LaBianca, president of Gateway Supermarkets, lived in a Spanish-style house with his wife, Rosemary. On August 10, 1969, the LaBiancas were found dead in their home. The word "WAR" and a series of crosses had been cut into LaBianca's chest, a carving fork had been rammed into his stomach, and a cloth had been draped over his head to look like a hood. Rosemary had been strangled with an electric cord. On the

"CHARLES SAID FOR ME TO TAKE THE GUN AND THE KNIFE AND GO UP TO WHERE TERRY MELCHER USED TO LIVE. HE SAID TO KILL EVERYONE IN THE HOUSE AS GRUESOME AS I COULD."

PAUL "TEX" WATKINS ABOUT THE SHARON TATE MURDERS

Sharon Tate, found murdered on August 9, 1969.

living-room walls the killers had written in blood: "DEATH TO PIGS". On the refrigerator the words "HELTER-SKEL-TER". This horrific scene made even the most hardened policemen blanch.

NO CONNECTION

In retrospect it is amazing that the police rejected a connection between the murders. A police spokesman reassured people that the Los Angeles police department had 17 sergeants and two lieutenants working exclusively on both murders. He said: "There are some things that were of similar nature, but actually the homicides are not connected. I think the public and a lot of the media have picked up the fact that they were similar in nature, probably because of the blood and the inscriptions. But this is rather a common type of thing in homicides. We've had many cases before where the suspect has written in blood or in lipstick or various things of that nature...."

It was three months before the murders were connected. By that time there had been a third killing, that of a music teacher named Gary Hinman. This time, however, there was a clue. Fingerprints at the scene of the crime proved to be those of a hippie named Bobby Beausoleil. He was quickly traced and when picked up was found to be still wearing a shirt stained with Hinman's blood. Also identified as being at the murder scene with Hinman was a girl named Susan Atkins.

Atkins was one of a group of hippies living in a commune on a run-down ranch near Death Valley, California. They lived by stealing Volkswagens and

The home of Roman Polanski and his wife, actress Sharon Tate, under police guard after the brutal murders.

converting them into dune buggies. One of the members later detailed the bizarre lifestyle of the group: "We were constantly taking dope and stealing cars and they just sit around all day and sleep and that's about it. And we went around collecting garbage and had that for dinner and went to the store once in a while. And that was about it. They just slept and got loaded."

It was because of their involvement in stealing cars that the hippie encampment was raided at dawn one morning by the Highway Patrol. Everyone there was taken by surprise and 27 people were

arrested. The leader of the group was found by a patrolman hiding in a cabinet under the sink in the bathroom. He was an unimposing, 5ft 2-inch would-be folk singer named Charles Manson.

Most of the group were quickly released again, but among those held in the cells were Charles Manson and Susan Atkins. Atkins boasted to a cell mate that she had been involved in the Sharon Tate, LaBianca and Hinman murders. The cellmate told the police and the police told the public. On December 1 a press conference was called at which a police spokesman announced: "The

development of information from the two separate investigations of the Tate and LaBianca cases led detectives to the conclusion that the crimes in both cases were committed by the same group of people." The spokesman went on to deliver the exciting news that three people had been arrested in connection with the murders and that warrants had been issued for the arrest of three more individuals, Charles D. Watson (who was currently under arrest in McKinney, Texas), Patricia Krenwinkle, and Linda Casabien, who would later turn State's evidence. More members of what was now being called the Manson Family, or the Tribe, were arrested on the strength of her evidence. They were 20-year-old Leslie (Lulu) Van Houten, 17-year-old Steve Grogan, and Manson himself.

MANSON

It has to be said that Charles Manson hadn't had much of a life. That is no excuse, of course, because lots of people don't have much of a life either, yet are not instrumental in causing a series of horrible murders. According to Manson, his grandmother dominated the family. A strict woman, she was God-fearing, saw sin in most things pleasurable and was emotionally as dry as tinder. She drove her husband into an asylum where he died a psychotic and alcoholic, and her daughter Kathy Maddox, when aged 15 years, fled onto the streets of Ashland, Kentucky. This is where Manson was born, his father unknown, one of several customers of his prostitute mother. He was unwanted. He got his name from Bill Manson, a man with whom Kathy began living just before Charles was born.

Manson told a story to his biographer, Neal Emmons. Manson didn't know whether it was true or not, but his telling it at all is illustrative of his childhood. As a baby, he says, he was taken into a bar by his mother. A waitress said how she envied Kathy having a child. "A pitcher of beer and he's yours," said Kathy. The waitress brought the beer and Kathy handed Manson over. Days later Manson's uncle came and got him from the waitress's home.

When Manson was aged six his mother was arrested and convicted of armed robbery. She was sent to prison in West Virginia and Manson was sent to live first with his dry grandmother, then with other relatives. The world for young Manson was confusing: "turn the other cheek" Bible-bashing philosophy from his grandma on the one hand, and on the other, "eye for an eye/don't be a sissy"

> ## "THE MORE YOU DO IT THE BETTER YOU LIKE IT."
> ### SUSAN ATKINS, ABOUT THE MURDER OF SHARON TATE

urging from an uncle, who sent Manson for his first day at school dressed as a girl. Manson learned to fight, to not give up, and that one man's right was another man's wrong.

Back with his mother following her release from prison and witness to her many bisexual relationships, Manson soon got in the way and was farmed out to an uncle who brewed moonshine in Kentucky and gave Manson a liking for the stuff. From there he was handed over to the stern Order of Catholic Brothers and their Gibault Home for Boys in Terre Haute. After two days Manson realized that his mother was never coming backfor him. Charles Manson was eight years old.

Life at Gibault was harsh. The regime was strict; the few privileges existed only so that they could be taken away when a rule was broken – and Manson broke many rules. The privileges ran out, so he was whipped, for his own good, of course. By the age of 12 he had run away. He found a room in a boarding-house, hustled or stole money and lived after a fashion, scraping food out of garbage bins, until caught and sent to another institution which indulged in punishment.

The catalogue of brutality in Manson's life continued as he was sent to various juvenile institutions and, finally

William Garretson, the caretaker wrongfully arrested for the murders.

Stephen Parent, one of the murder victims found at the Tate home.

at 15, to the Indiana School for Boys at Plainfield. Here, he says, he was brutalized and describes sufferings at the hands of the guards that would have made Vlad the Impaler retch. At 16 he escaped and fled to California. He did this and that, little of it legal, and was soon back in prison.

In 1967, having spent more than half his life behind bars, he was released from California's Terminal Island prison. It is significant that he asked the authorities to let him stay there. "This is my only home," he pleaded. "I don't know if I can cope out there." Not surprisingly, he was terrified. Nobody could blame him. The world was a hostile place and he was totally unprepared for it.

Within 48 hours Manson was in San Francisco, a city that had become the capital of the "turn on, tune in and drop out" culture. Here young people took drugs and talked about things like beauty and love and peace and flower power. They didn't always express themselves very clearly, though. This was how one young woman explained the profundity of her philosophy to a television camera: "Everybody has to come to truth. The whole country. The whole world is gonna have to come to truth. And that is

not money. Truth is not in your money."

In this environment Charles Manson found himself at home for the first time in his life. He found he was able to con people and dominate people.

"I CAN DO ANYTHING I WANT TO YOU PEOPLE AT ANY TIME I WANT TO, BECAUSE THAT'S WHAT YOU'VE DONE TO ME."

CHARLES MANSON IN AN INTERVIEW WITH A TELEVISION JOURNALIST

Charles Manson is taken into custody for the Tate murders.

THE FAMILY GATHERS

Manson took a group of these followers in a converted bus from San Francisco to Los Angeles, where they settled on the old Spahn Ranch in Simi Valley, the former home of Western movie star William S. Hart. The rundown ranch was

owned by 81-year-old George Spahn. In return for treats from members of the Family – including Lynette "Squeaky" Fromme – he let the group live there for free. They thought it an idyllic life, but even the Garden of Eden had its sinister side in the shape of a serpent – and at the Spahn Ranch the serpent was Charles Manson.

"Well, when I first met him the man talked to me and he says 'why don't you come up' and the rules are, you know, there are no rules," explained one young convert. "You just look at it and just be beautiful with it and then it's beautiful to you. You know, and I love him. His so-called power, it only lies in his happiness. Yeah, that's what attracts people, he's completely happy... he dances, he sings. He looks beautiful. He looks happy...."

Not so happy were the owners of the cars Manson and his gang stole. Eventually the Highway Patrol raided the Spahn Ranch with the results already described. There they found a cache of guns and ammunition. Manson and other Family members were arrested, but the warrant was wrongly dated, a legal technicality that allowed the whole bunch to be released. Among those released was Donald Shea who was never seen again. Family members

In Los Angeles five members of the Manson "family" began a five-day trek to his trial on their knees.

Susan Atkins (left), Patricia Krenwinkle (middle) and Leslie Van Houten (right) in lighthearted mood before hearing the jury's verdict.

later said he'd argued with Manson, who'd then shot him and dismembered the body, burying the pieces around the ranch. The group was arrested again following Susan Atkins' admissions to her cellmate while in custody.

CIRCUS AND TRIAL

The trial of Charles Manson and his followers lasted over nine and a half months, which made it the longest and most expensive murder trial ever held in the United States. Charged alongside Manson were Susan Atkins, Leslie Van Houten and Patricia Krenwinkle, who often sang *en-route* to court like children on a school outing.

Susan Atkins tried to withdraw her testimony against Manson and the defence argued that Atkins' testimony was inadmissible because it was given while under the influence of LSD. The prosecution lawyer, Vincent Bugliosi, told television reporters: "Well, it's common and customary with every witness, especially a star witness, that the defence is going to attack their credibility using every device and technique available to them. I don't anticipate any problem in this particular area of LSD, speaking in the abstract; because someone takes LSD does not mean that thereafter they are forevermore precluded from telling the truth about anything. This of course is preposterous." Bugliosi added, "The defence can claim anything they want. And I'm sure they're gonna make all types of claims throughout the trial. Whether anyone wants to believe them or not is something else."

Against this background of obstructive tactics by the defence, those charged, including Manson, and Family members not under arrest tried to mock the trial and make the proceedings seem farcical. Manson frequently changed his mood and appearance. He shaved his head and cut a cross into his forehead. His followers copied him in everything he did. But through all this maniacal activity there emerged the horrible and macabre story of Manson's depravity.

Charles Manson's Great Plan was to murder rich people at random in the most revolting ways imaginable and ensure that black activists were blamed, thus fomenting racial hatred. Manson himself selected the Tate household, apparently as some sort of revenge against Doris Day's son, Terry Melcher. The LaBiancas were selected by pure chance, Family members having driven around until they found a rich person's home they could get into without too much difficulty.

Although her life had been threatened, Linda Casabien stood in the witness box for 18 days and told all she knew. She claimed that she still loved Manson. Susan Atkins said the same: "You have to have real love in your heart to do this for people." Atkins also said that killing Sharon Tate had "sent a real rush" through her. "The more you do it the better you like it," she said.

Some years later at an unsuccessful parole board hearing, Paul "Tex" Watkins explained: "Charles said for me to take the gun and the knife and go up to where Terry Melcher used to live. He said to kill everyone in the house as gruesome as I could."

How could Charles Manson have achieved this domination over his followers? Some of the defence attorneys tried to suggest that Manson used hypnosis. He didn't. What Manson had learned

A securely chained and shackled Manson leaves court after receiving a life sentence for his part in the Tate-LaBianca murders.

through the trauma of his youth and teenage years was the ability to adapt to his surroundings. He had the knack of sensing what others wanted him to be, then being it. In a strange way, Manson became a father figure to a lot of naive runaways. They did what he told them to do, just as a child does what its father tells it to do.

The Family remained loyal to Charles Manson. In his absence, Lynette "Squeaky" Fromme became its leader and spokesperson, explaining to the outside world how Charles Manson was suffering within prison, hindered by an inadequate prison law library, denied a telephone, his writings studied by the sheriff. Some years later Fromme attempted to assassinate President Ford and was sentenced to life imprisonment.

At the end of the exhausting trial, the jury took 10 days to reach their verdicts. Manson, Atkins, Van Houten and Krenwinkle were found guilty and sentenced to death. At a later trial Manson, Bruce Davis, Bobby Beausoleil and Clem Grogan were found guilty of other murders. Tex Watkins was tried separately and found guilty.

Charles Manson and other members of the Family have sought parole. Tex Watkins was turned down. Susan Atkins was told she was deemed "not suitable for parole at this time and would pose an unreasonable danger to society if released from prison." It is highly unlikely that Charles Manson will ever walk the streets again as a free man.

Maybe the clearest insight into the unholy mind of this man was a statement he once made to a television journalist when asked if he felt remorse: "Remorse for what?" he asked. "You people have done everything in the world to me. Doesn't that give me equal right? I can do anything I want to you people at any time I want to, because that's what you've done to me. If you spit in my face and smack me in the mouth and throw me in solitary confinement for nothing, what do you think's gonna happen when I get out of here? Maybe I haven't done enough, I might be ashamed of that, for not doing enough, for not giving enough. For not being more perceptive, for not being aware enough, for not understanding, for being stupid. Maybe I should have killed four or five hundred people, then I would have felt better."

Charles Manson is very angry at the world – and maybe he has every right to be. Maybe it was society that both failed and made Manson.

Manson in San Quentin Prison, 1988, showing the swastika he cut into his forehead.

THE
KRAY TWINS

People don't think of London in the same way that they think of New York, Chicago or Las Vegas – in terms of gangsters and organized crime. But there have always been gangsters in London. One of the most powerful gangs was led by Giuseppe Messina and his sons, who ran Soho in London's West End until the 1950s. As their power declined, two gangs arose that would rival them in brutality: the Richardson brothers in South London, and, in the notorious East End, the Kray twins.

■

THESE DAYS REDEVELOPMENT has destroyed most of the tangible remains of East London's rich, colourful, and often criminal history. Known to the Metropolitan Police as H Division, the district was the training ground for many of Britain's toughest policemen. It had always been a violent place: the highwayman Dick Turpin knew the area and the infamous Jack the Ripper stalked its streets. But in the 1950s and 1960s it was best known as the domain of the Krays and the "Firm".

Reginald and Ronald Kray were born in October 1933, in Stene Street, Hoxton, East London. Some six years later the family moved to Vallance Road, a broad street in Whitechapel, where they lived until young adulthood. It was a rough area and as kids the twins, with their elder brother, Charlie, joined street gangs and grew up knowing how to handle themselves in a scrap.

As East End tearaways with a liking for boxing – they become professionals for a short time – they followed in the footsteps of several generations of gangs in the teeming, hard-working but generally poor East End. They were streetwise, hard men who graduated from thuggery to running protection rackets and eventually acquired a couple of clubland venues that were soon to give them a high profile.

Their first venture was a snooker club, *The Regal*, in the district known as Mile End. The club had been having a lot of trouble from local gangs who'd do damage to the tables and generally frighten decent people away. Some people alleged that this was all organized by the Krays. For their part, they have always denied it and are probably telling the truth. Nevertheless, they put an end to the trouble and even chased away members of a Maltese gang hustling for protection money. The club became popular, the Krays made money and around them a group of men began to form – the beginnings of the Kray gang, the "Firm".

KINGS OF THE EAST END

The twins' empire began to expand. They opened a few little drinking and gambling clubs and began their own protection racket. To this day they believe – or, rather, they maintain – they were performing a service. The East End had a surfeit of gangs. Some businesses, they say, were paying out money to two or three gangs every week; when the Krays moved in, the other gangs moved out. Admittedly some of the gang members took fat lips and broken noses with them, but the local businessmen, the Krays say, were happy. The Krays were also happy. They ruled the East End.

In 1955 Ron Kray shot a man, a docker and ex-boxer, who was trying to muscle in on a garage which had taken out insurance with the twins. The shooting caused a bit of friction with Reg, and there was some trouble with the police, but nothing too unsettling resulted and Ron's reputation soared. Whether or not this led to them working for Jack Comer remains to be seen.

By 1955 criminal London was run by two men, Billy Hill and Jack Comer (known as Jack Spot). At one point Comer became concerned that Hill was going to attack him. He also had doubts about the loyalty of some of his men. He therefore turned to the Krays, hiring them as his bodyguards, though eventually he paid them off. A little while later he was "carved up" outside his West London flat. Retirement seemed a good idea. Billy Hill also retired and went to Spain to live.

Hill and Comer had retired as kings of the underworld without leaving a successor. Ron and Reg Kray saw an opportunity to move in.

Both Kray boys liked boxing and a few years on from the date of this photograph - November 1946 - they would become pros.

Mum Vi was always important to the twins, seen here in their boxing days when the ring seemed to offer a way out of the East End. They are obviously their mother's pride and joy.

Their chance came when Billy Jones and Bobby Ramsey (an old boxing chum of the Krays) opened *Stragglers*, a drinking club just off Cambridge Circus in Soho. Jones and Ramsey were having some local difficulties and called the Krays in to sort things out. They duly did, but then some Irish dockers beat up Ramsey. Ron, Jones and Ramsey retaliated and a man called Jackie Martin was severely injured. He named his attackers and the three went to prison; Ron was sent down for three years.

It was towards the end of his sentence that Ron began to show signs of paranoia. He believed people were plotting against him and his response was to

attack and try to kill them. He was sent to a mental institution.

Stragglers was soon closed down and, with Ron "inside", Reg and brother Charlie began working closely together. They opened a little club in Bow Road, which Reg called the *Two Rs*. Above it he opened a gym. Reg and Charlie ran the club with a firm hand and good business sense. It was a great success and was patronized by a few famous faces. Unfortunately, according to Reg, a small-time crook named Ronnie Marwood stabbed a policeman and turned to Reg for help. He owed Marwood nothing and knew hiding him would be dangerous, but there was a code among crooks

and Reg helped him. The police, when they learned what Reg had done, found a reason to close down the *Two Rs*. Thereafter, say the Krays, the police persecuted all their business ventures.

In 1962 they opened an up-market club in Mile End Road, called the *Kentucky*. It became popular with some rich and famous people who imagined that, by going there, they were tasting the big, bad East End with all its villainy. It was closed down by the police in 1964. Feeling persecuted, the twins decided to go legitimate with a really "posh" club called *Esmerelda's Barn*. It was in Knightsbridge and the twins began to mix with the rich and famous, becoming celebrities themselves. But they were out of their depth and lost money fast. An accountant really caused them problems, according to Ron, by not paying taxes. The tax authorities moved in. The Krays paid up and moved out.

At this time there was also a business deal that went badly wrong: Ernest Shinwell was involved in a building project in Enugu, Nigeria, and invited the Krays to invest, which they did. Later, prominent politician Lord Boothby was approached. He wanted to meet and discuss the business with an existing investor and accordingly met with Ron. The *Sunday Mirror* and the *Daily Express* newspapers picked up on the meeting and implied a homosexual relationship between Boothby and Ron Kray. Eventually the papers had to pay a libel settlement in favour of Boothby. But Ron's homosexuality became public knowledge, as did the fact that the Krays were gangsters running protection rackets. Matters weren't helped by Reg being

Reg Kray and his bride Frances Shea in 1965.

arrested for threatening a shopkeeper and being sent to Wandsworth Prison, South London, for six months.

The protection racket was booming – still run as a service, rather than a criminal endeavour, in the Krays' eyes – and

they continued to open clubs around London and even in the provinces. The only black cloud on the horizon was a persistent whisper that Scotland Yard had been told to "get the Krays" and had appointed two detectives, Leonard Read and Superintendent Fred Gerrard, to head an investigation into their activities. As this was going on, there were other pressures: Ron's mental stability showed a persistent decline, Reg's marriage went through problems and trouble with the Richardson brothers came to a head.

GEORGE CORNELL AND JACK "THE HAT" McVITIE

George Cornell, whose real name was Myers, was not a nice man. He was handy with his fists and with a knife, and apparently enjoyed the sight of people in pain. According to Ron Kray, in 1962 Cornell had murdered a London gangster named Ginger Marks. For a while he joined forces with the Richardsons.

Lord Boothby was one of the celebrities who consorted with the Krays.

At the time there was an uneasy truce between the Krays and the Richardsons, but Cornell stirred things up by trying to get the Richardsons to seize Kray territory. This was bad for the Krays, who were then engaged in very delicate meetings with the Mafia. They tried to make peace but, at a meeting with the Richardsons, George Cornell drew attention to Ron's homosexuality: "Take no notice of Kray. He's just a big, fat poof."

On March 8 there was a shooting at *Mr Smith's*, a club in Catford, South East London, and "Firm" member Richard Hart was killed. Cornell had been one of the gunmen, the only one to escape. The next night Ron Kray was drinking in an East End pub, The Lion in Tapp Street, when he received word that Cornell was in the Blind Beggar. Ron and Jack Dickson, one of the "Firm", immediately went to the Blind Beggar, arriving at the pub at 8.30pm. Cornell was on a stool at the end of the bar. The Walker Brothers' *The Sun Ain't Gonna Shine Anymore* was playing. There was a handful of customers. Cornell looked towards the door: "Well, look who's here," he said. Ron took out his gun, aimed and fired.

The murder investigation was headed by Detective Superintendent Jim Axon, later to become Chief Constable of Jersey. The word on the street was that Ron Kray had murdered Cornell and he was arrested by Chief Superintendent Tommy Butler of the Flying Squad, following which an identity parade was held at Commercial Street police station.

It is said that sometimes a shock produces amnesia. The sudden shooting of George Cornell was a shock to everyone in the *Blind Beggar*, customers and bar staff alike. Amnesia swept among them. Nobody seemed able to recall exactly what had happened or who the gunman had been. But the killing won Ron a nickname – "the Colonel".

The case of Frank Mitchell, the so-called Mad Axeman, remains a mystery. Mitchell was in the infamous but antiquated and isolated Dartmoor Prison. According to the Krays, Ron had promised Mitchell that he would arrange his escape from Dartmoor. Ron didn't expect to be held to the promise, but when the request came the twins decided to give it their best shot. On December

Ronnie Kray gently sorting out a bit of bother at the **Kentucky Club** *on the occasion of the great heavyweight boxer, Sonny Liston (next to Reg), appearing there to sign autographs for fight fans.*

12, 1966, two of the "Firm" went down to Dartmoor. That day Mitchell was on an outside working party. He managed to slip away and joined the Krays' men who sped him back to London.

Mitchell apparently wanted no more than that his case be reviewed by the Home Secretary. Nothing came of the appeals written on his behalf and nothing more was heard from Mitchell. The Krays were accused of murdering him. They denied it – and continue to deny it; they say simply that they spirited him away to some foreign shore.

Jack McVitie was used by the Krays as a "frightener", someone who encouraged people to do as they were told, but Reg believed that McVitie had become a dangerous liability. McVitie is said to have cheated the Krays, but as Reg wrote in the twins' autobiography, *Our Story*: "He had said publicly on more than one occasion that he wanted to kill me, and I had good reason to believe that it was no idle threat."

Reg invited Jack McVitie to a party at a flat. McVitie arrived looking for girls and alcohol. Reg took out a gun, aimed at McVitie's head and pulled the trigger twice. It jammed. There was a struggle. McVitie, crying, was held by one of the Krays' men. Reg plunged a knife into McVitie's face and kept on stabbing. The body was disposed of and has never been found.

THE FINAL CURTAIN

The Krays reckon they got too big, that powerful people in government told the

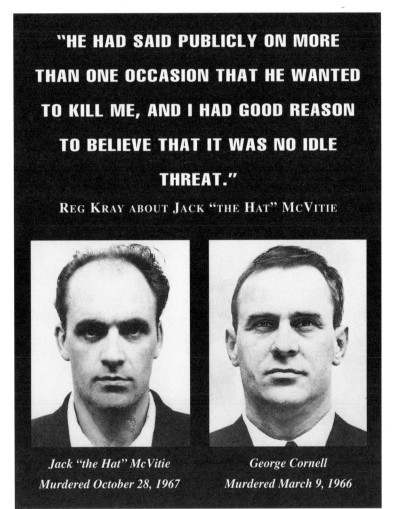

"HE HAD SAID PUBLICLY ON MORE THAN ONE OCCASION THAT HE WANTED TO KILL ME, AND I HAD GOOD REASON TO BELIEVE THAT IT WAS NO IDLE THREAT."

REG KRAY ABOUT JACK "THE HAT" MCVITIE

Jack "the Hat" McVitie
Murdered October 28, 1967

George Cornell
Murdered March 9, 1966

police to "get the Krays". Some cynics have suggested the Metropolitan Police finally moved against the Krays because the force needed some good publicity. As John Pearson observed in his book *The Profession of Violence*, the most disturbing thing about the Krays and the Richardsons is not that they became so big, but that they survived for so long.

How they survived and why the police finally went after them are perhaps irrelevant questions to ask now. What matters is that money and manpower were, at last, pitted against the Krays' organization. John DuRose, dubbed Britain's top detective, gave charge of the investigation to Detective Superintendent Ferguson Walker and Sergeant Algernon Hemmingway.

After a few months and just when some headway was being made, Walker was promoted and transferred. DuRose replaced him with Detective Superintendent Leonard Read. In the late 1940s Read had been a sprinter in the Metropolitan Police Athletic Club and won the nickname "Nipper". He had come to public attention for helping to bring the Great Train Robbers to justice. He found the Kray case was a different, bigger problem, and it was made more difficult by a widespread belief that the Krays had sources within Scotland Yard. Read personally picked his team and then set up headquarters in a nondescript office block away from Scotland Yard called Tintagel House. The Krays learned the purpose of the team, but expected the police to play by the rules. "We underestimated them – or, at least, we underestimated the low levels to which they would eventually sink in a

The message to Scotland Yard was "Get the Krays". A special squad was set up under "Nipper" Read (fourth from right).

desperate attempt to put me and Ronnie away," said Reg in *Our Story*. In fact, what the police did was to convince people that they would be protected if they would talk. Indeed, it became difficult to stop some people talking. Leslie Payne was one of those who talked. The Krays had already tried to kill him and he felt sure they would succeed. Talking, he decided, was his only chance. The barmaid at the Blind Beggar talked too.

The end came in May 1968. The twins had been to a party that finished at 5.00am. They returned to Ron's flat in Walthamstow, East London, and went to bed. Meanwhile, 68 men and women had been called to Tintagel House. They were briefed and despatched to various places around the capital.

Shortly after 6.00am they moved in. Sergeant Hemmingway applied his boot to the front door of the Krays' flat and police piled into the room. Among them were Superintendent Read and Inspector Frank Cater, one of the team who had smashed the Richardson gang and who

would rise to become Commander of the Flying Squad. Also arrested in nearly simultaneous raids were other members of the "Firm" and brother Charles Kray.

The police actually had very little evidence on the Krays and the arrests were a considerable gamble, but they believed that people would talk as soon as the twins and their closest henchmen were off the streets. They were right, but it is a measure of the fear which the Krays inspired that quite a few people needed a lot of persuading.

While they were being held on remand in a new wing at Brixton Prison, the Krays heard that members of the "Firm" were talking in a bid to lessen their own sentences. "If this was true it was serious news. We couldn't believe it – we had looked after them all so well when they had worked for us," wrote Ron Kray in *Our Story*. But the twins remained optimistic. Wrote Ron: "We knew we had a few problems, but we had such faith in ourselves and the fear we could put into people, we still believed

we were going to get out of the mess." Ron goes on to say that the feeling in the East End was the same, which was why people still paid protection money: "...no one wanted to face our wrath for non-payment of protection money once we got out again."

The police kept a firm watch on their witnesses, keeping them apart and in isolation at secret hideaways in the south of England. Some were in protective police custody for almost a year. This "shadow" operation was the responsibility of Detective Sergeant Bert Trevette. It is a tribute to him that the Krays admit their inability to get threatening messages through to those who were now turning against them.

As people talked, the case against the twins grew and the charges brought against them multiplied. They, with others, were charged jointly or individually with committing or being an accessory to the murders of George Cornell and Jack McVitie; with conspiring to murder a man called George Caruna; with causing grievous bodily harm to a man at *Esmerelda's Barn*; with demanding £5,000 with menaces from Leslie James Payne and Frederick Gore; with demanding £500 each from Payne and Gore; with conspiring to defraud; and with the murder of Frank Mitchell.

Eventually the Krays were brought to trial at the Old Bailey for the murders of Cornell and McVitie. They were found guilty. "I'm not going to waste words on you. In my view society has earned a rest from your activities. I sentence you to life imprisonment, which I recommend should not be less than 30 years." So said Mr. Justice Melford Stevenson when sentencing the Krays. People knew the Krays would go down for a long time, but nobody, least of all the Krays themselves, expected 30 years.

Six weeks later the pair were tried for the murder of Frank Mitchell. A witness told the jury that Mitchell had been shot by Frederick Foreman on the Krays' orders on December 23, 1966. The witness was not believed by the jury. The Krays and Foreman were acquitted. Reg Kray, however, received five years' imprisonment for arranging Mitchell's escape and for harbouring him.

The Director of Public Prosecutions felt after the Mitchell case that there was little to be gained from bringing the Krays to trial on the remaining charges.

In *Our Story*, Ron and Reg Kray attempt to portray themselves as people who brought a sort of law and order to a rough area where the police were wholly inadequate, who dished out a few slappings here and there, but never really hurt anyone except a hard case or two. They tell their story well, and don't seem such bad people.

But now and again they let slip a remark that gives the reader some idea of what it was like to live under their reign of terror. The police had considerable trouble getting the barmaid of the Blind Beggar to testify against Ronald Kray. When she came into court she "looked as scared as a rabbit", wrote Ron in *Our Story*. It seems not to occur to him that he was the cause of her terror. "We had sent a message to the barmaid – via the manager of the Blind Beggar – to keep her mouth shut," he wrote. "But that's all we done. We hadn't been to see her personally, we hadn't made any threats to her or attempted any physical harm on her or her family ... It was a big mistake – we'd been too soft with a potentially key witness."

Ron Kray broke down altogether in prison and he was diagnosed as a chronic paranoid schizophrenic. He was sent to Broadmoor and it is doubtful if he'll ever leave. Reg is still in prison.

Reginald Kray at the funeral of his mother, Vi, in 1982, one of the few "public" appearances he's made since being convicted.

THE McKAY
KIDNAPPING

Britain's newspapers had a good year in 1969. The world's first supersonic airliner made its maiden flight. Prince Charles was invested as Prince of Wales. And with "one giant leap for mankind", astronauts first set foot on the moon.

It was an important year for the press in other ways, too. Australian tycoon Rupert Murdoch secured his position in Fleet Street, outbidding Robert Maxwell for the News of the World, *and the Mirror Group virtually handed him the ailing* Sun, *successor to the* Daily Herald, *on a plate.*

■

Since Murdoch had inherited the respectable newspaper empire built up by his father in Australia, and secured its prominence by lowering standards of taste and discretion, there were widespread fears that his influence in England might lead to more papers relying on prurience, salacious gossip, and intrusion on privacy to sell copies. With this in mind, David Frost interviewed Mr. Murdoch on television, and drew attention to the vast financial resources that had enabled him to buy his way into the British press.

This programme, with its firm identification of Murdoch as a millionaire, was seen by two greedy and ambitious brothers, who had not found the streets of their adopted London to be paved with gold. Their plan to make their fortune would lead directly to another press sensation: Britain's first major kidnapping for ransom, their victim the wife of a newspaper magnate.

At 7.45pm on Monday December 29, 1969, Mr. Alick McKay arrived home from work. Mr. McKay, deputy chairman of the *News of the World*, had driven home in the company chairman's Rolls Royce, which was at his disposal when chairman Rupert Murdoch was out of the country.

His house was in Arthur Road, Wimbledon. This long, attractive residential street, not far from the famous tennis and croquet club, is lined with comfortable houses set in their own grounds and well back from the prying eyes of the local plebs. In appearance, it suggests the fringes of a prosperous country town, bordered by the homes of the local "quality", rather than a residential area in urban south London.

MRS. McKAY IS MISSING

As Mr. McKay came into the driveway, he noticed a sheet of newspaper blowing around. It was not a neighbourhood where litter was normal, but who could say that a passing motorist might not have carelessly dropped a page of the *People*? Mr. McKay thought little of it.

He was surprised when his wife Muriel did not answer his ring at the doorbell. Muriel was a cautious woman, who usually kept the outer and inner front doors locked and on the chain, so Mr. McKay could not, as a rule, let himself in with his own key. When repeated ringing produced no answer, Mr. McKay tried the key, and found to his surprise that the outer door was off the chain. He was even more surprised to find the inner door swinging open. On the floor in the hall was a scatter of objects that he thought would normally have been in Muriel's handbag. There was also an extraordinary tool – a slightly rusty machete or billhook – lying to one side. And a chair had been knocked awkwardly out of place. A ball of twine and a tin of adhesive tape did not normally belong in the house either.

Mr. McKay went through St. Mary House, Arthur Road, calling for his wife. Dinner for two was sitting in the kitchen waiting to be cooked. The television was on and, to Mr. McKay's mind most significant of all, the fire was blazing, but no guard screened it. Muriel was a very cautious person and since she was not in the house the unguarded fire made it apparent that she had left against her will. For, in Mr. McKay's words, "She had a great fear of fire. She was meticulous that she would always put the screen in front of the fire if she was going out for any time."

Alick McKay, who worked for the sensational and prurient *News of the*

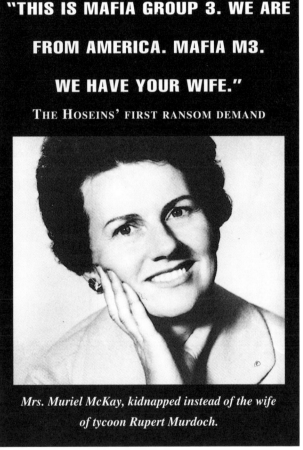

"THIS IS MAFIA GROUP 3. WE ARE FROM AMERICA. MAFIA M3. WE HAVE YOUR WIFE."

THE HOSEINS' FIRST RANSOM DEMAND

Mrs. Muriel McKay, kidnapped instead of the wife of tycoon Rupert Murdoch.

World, apparently felt he would inevitably face the possibility of scandal. Although events were to show that Mr. McKay was a devoted husband, and there is no reason to suppose that his love was anything but reciprocated, he still seemed to be answering the questions of some imaginary scandal-sheet reporter when he later said, "Now I think no man in the world could say that his wife wouldn't leave him." But he returned to the firmer ground of his own experience of Muriel with the observation, "I really believed that she wouldn't leave the dog in front of an open fire."

An attempt to telephone out revealed that things were even worse than he feared. The telephone had been disconnected and the tab giving the number had been extracted from the dial. Mr. McKay went next door and raised the alarm.

Unhappily, what Mr. McKay did next persuaded some policemen that this was quite probably just such a tale of a runaway wife as the *News of the World* might enjoy. It might even, they felt, be a stunt pulled off by the combined Murdoch press to help circulation. For immediately after reporting Muriel's disappearance, Mr. McKay telephoned Larry Lamb, the editor of the *News of the World*'s sister paper, the *Sun*. And the *Sun*, fiercely chasing the *Daily Mirror*'s ascendancy in the circulation figures, was plunging downmarket, and had no hesitation whatsoever in headlining the sensational story of the missing Wimbledon housewife.

POLICE V. PRESS

Policemen, noting that Mrs. McKay had been very nervous about intruders and there was no sign of a forced entry, speculated that she must have admitted the owner of the machete and adhesive tape of her own volition, and so she might equally well have gone away with him quite voluntarily. Middle-aged women *do* sometimes walk off without warning, as the press well knew. Papers in the Murdoch empire, intimately aware of Mr. McKay's deep and genuine distress, bridled at this suggestion.

The entire investigation of the case was bedevilled by the mutual suspicion and hostility of police and press. As a result, the authorities failed to release to the public leads that might have brought in useful information from newspaper readers, and the press gleefully ignored police requests for embargoes on information that might prove helpful to the kidnappers. At great cost to the McKay family, the fourth estate and the boys in blue learned that failure to co-operate responsibly in serious kidnapping cases can amount to murderous negligence.

The house in Arthur Road, Wimbledon, from where Muriel McKay mysteriously disappeared on December 29, 1969.

THE KIDNAPPERS EMERGE

At 1.50am a telephone call to the McKays proved their worst fears – Muriel had been forcibly abducted by criminals who wanted money.

"This is Mafia Group 3," declared the caller. "We are from America. Mafia M3. We have your wife. You will need a million pounds by Wednesday. Mafia, do you understand? We have your wife. It will cost you one million pounds."

When Mr. McKay protested that he didn't possess anything like that amount of money, the voice went on, "You'd better get it. You have friends, get it from them. We tried to get Rupert Murdoch's wife. We couldn't get her so we took yours instead. You have a million by Wednesday night or we will kill her. Understand? All you have to do is wait for the contact, that is for the money. You will get instructions. Have the

money or you won't have a wife. We will contact you again."

Now, had the entire detective force been convinced that a kidnapping had definitely taken place, there were important clues to be drawn from this call. The kidnappers were obviously raw amateurs. They had placed their call from a public call-box in Epping, and gone through the operator. Had they made it by direct dialling from a local box, it could not have been instantly traced back to source and its origins might always have remained a mystery. Moreover, the operator had listened to part of the call, and he reported, very usefully, that the caller's voice sounded American or coloured.

But the police were more startled by another aspect of the caller's rank amateurism. The demand for £1 million was so ridiculously unrealistic that it didn't seem possible the caller was serious. They opened a Crime Index File on the

case, and logged every possible useful statement and deposition. But they were, perhaps, not sufficiently alert to the warnings that came from the very experienced FBI that, unless they recovered Mrs. McKay within a very few days, she would almost certainly be killed.

On New Year's Eve a letter arrived, scribbled awkwardly all over the page, apparently because the writer was blindfolded. It was in Mrs. McKay's writing, and it merely turned the screws on her unhappy family, without producing useful information. "Please do something to get me home," it read. "I am blindfolded and cold. Please co-operate for I cannot keep going. I think of you constantly and the family and friends. What have I done to deserve this treatment? Love, Muriel."

To the annoyance of the police, Mr. McKay sent this letter to the press, who headlined it. They were equally displeased when his daughter Diane and her husband appeared on television news and made an impassioned appeal to the kidnappers to release Muriel.

When there was no response, the McKay family became desperate. They consulted a medium in England and called in a famous Dutch psychic, Gerard Croiset. Those who believe in clairvoyance hail this as one of its successes, since Croiset reported that Mrs. McKay was being held in a white farmhouse to the north-north east of London, near a disused aerodrome. Sceptics note that attempts to follow Mr. Croiset's lead turned up only one deserted farmhouse, and that proved to be a false trail. But true believers enthuse that it was very close to the farm where the kidnappers were in fact living. Sceptics also observe

that the police had already pinpointed the district by taking the machete to its manufacturer, and learning that this type of tool was popular in the Bishop's Stortford area of Hertfordshire. Unfortunately, so many machetes had been sold that it was a very imprecise clue.

It was increasingly worrying that communications now came only in the form of frantic letters scribbled by Mrs. McKay. And it looked more and more likely that these had been written some time previously. In an attempt to force the kidnappers to renew direct communication, the police set up Mrs. McKay's doctor to issue a half-true statement that she was ill and on drugs which she urgently needed. The implication was

that she might die on her kidnappers' hands if they didn't return her. The fact was that she took cortisone for her arthritis, so that she might be in considerable discomfort without a renewed prescription, but her life was not at risk.

TWO ATTEMPTED DROPS

The ruse galvanized the kidnappers into action. They renewed their demands for money, and flatly turned down Mr. McKay's offer of £20,000 as hopelessly inadequate. They sent a fragment of Muriel's clothing as "proof" that she was still alive. And, at last, they dictated a plan for Mr. McKay to get half a million pounds to them on February 1. He was to take the money in the company Rolls

Alick McKay, flanked by his family, appeals to his wife's kidnappers for evidence that she is still alive.

Royce to a telephone kiosk on the A10 road where he would receive further instructions.

The police promptly took charge. Two armed detectives were to travel in the car, posing as Mr. McKay and a chauffeur. Two suitcases were prepared with top layers of genuine £5 notes and a massive packaging of counterfeit bundles underneath. The cases were bugged so that the kidnappers could be followed if they made off with them. Their entrapment seemed certain.

But the handling of the final drop was hopelessly bungled. The instructions pointed to a country lane and a rendezvous indicated by some paper flowers, so unmarked detective cars were sent to reconnoiter the spot before the Rolls turned up. Motorcycle police outriders accompanied the spurious "Mr. McKay and his chauffeur". They wore "Hell's Angels'" leathers, but this could

not disguise from even inexperienced villains that this was an armed and guarded convoy, not a discreet ransom delivery. Not surprisingly, the kidnappers made no attempt to pick up the money, and the mission had to be written off as a complete failure.

> ## "I AM BLINDFOLDED AND COLD. PLEASE CO-OPERATE FOR I CANNOT KEEP GOING."
>
> MRS. MURIEL MCKAY

Scotland Yard sadly assumed that that was the end of it. They'd blown the operation, and there could be no further chance to get Mrs. McKay back and arrest her kidnappers. But they had underrated the villains' extraordinary greed. Mr. McKay's son Ian received yet another call the following day. He was told that the kidnappers knew the deliv-

ery car had been followed, and there would be no further chances if the next drop went wrong. The caller claimed that he was pleading with his bosses to spare Muriel's life. "I am fond of her – your mum – you know. She reminds me of my mum," he said.

Three days later, renewed instructions reached the McKay family. Mr. McKay was to make the drop personally, accompanied by his daughter Diane. There must be no outriders and no snooping unmarked patrol cars checking out the territory. The police made their plans accordingly.

They were still unwilling to let Mr. McKay – let alone Diane – approach men who were probably armed and dangerous. Once again, armed detectives would impersonate Mr. McKay and his chauffeur, and a woman policeman, made up to look as much like Diane as possible, would also be in the car. The

The bugged suitcases containing ransom money which the kidnappers failed to collect, fearing a trap.

The blue Volvo car traced to the Hosein brothers. It was seen in Arthur Road and in the vicinity of the pick up.

Police mounted a massive search for Muriel McKay around the home of the Hosein brothers.

only back-up would be an armed plain-clothes man hidden in the vehicle.

This much more hopeful expedition followed the kidnappers' trail of messages from telephone box to telephone box until, at Epping station, they were given spoken instructions. They were to leave the Rolls and then take a taxi to Bishop's Stortford, where they would

No stone was left unturned in the hunt for Mrs. McKay. Her body was never recovered, and the Hosein brothers refused to disclose her fate.

find a minivan parked on the forecourt of Gates' Garage. They should leave the cases containing the money there and go straight back to Epping.

Taxi driver Rob Kelly was hired for this extraordinary journey. He was left under the impression that his passengers really were Mr. McKay and a woman friend – he didn't know about Diane – in

a fur hat and camel-hair coat. He was rather frightened when another man – the armed plainclothes bodyguard – was furtively added to the party at the top of the road. The approach to the destination was weird, too. As Rob Kelly reported, "He said, 'I want you to drive past the garage slowly, turn back onto the main road, come in back on the road again and when I tell you to stop pull up as near to the hedge as possible and stop.'"

In fact, the drop went without a hitch. The cases were left in the garage forecourt and the taxi drove straight back to Epping, relying on disguised watchers to see who picked up the cases and on the bug to lead to their destination.

Alas, for human ingenuity! This meet was aborted by completely innocent civilians. A garage hand saw one of the kidnappers loitering around Gates', and told him to clear off. A couple who stopped at the garage for petrol saw the abandoned cases, and one of them stood guard over them, while the other telephoned the local police. Verdict: a complete fiasco! Almost....

ARRESTS

However, the disguised watchers had seen a blue Volvo cruise past the garage repeatedly, and slow to observe the cases. Its number was XGO 994G.

The chase was over. A blue Volvo holding two "Arab"-looking men had been seen cruising along Arthur Road, Wimbledon, on the day Mrs. McKay disappeared. A blue Volvo had also been seen hanging around the vicinity of the first dropping point in the Essex country lane. Both cars had been included in lists of sighted vehicles, but their recurrence had not taken on any significance.

The license number of this Volvo led straight to the Trinidadian Asian brothers Arthur and Nizamodeen Hosein, living at Rooks Farm, Stocking Pelham. Arthur's fingerprints matched those on the ransom demands, the envelopes, and a cigarette packet dropped in the Epping call-box. His palmprint was on the page from the *People* picked up in the McKays' drive. Nizam was identified as the driver who had brought the Volvo to Bishop's Stortford and been ordered off the forecourt. The farm yielded a sawn-off shotgun, a tin of adhesive tape like the one left in Mr. McKay's house, the exercise book from which pages had been torn for Mrs. McKay's despairing notes, and some paper flowers like those used to mark the first ransom drop point.

The kidnappers were caught, but of Mrs. Muriel McKay, there was no trace. Nor has there been from that day to this, and the Hoseins have never confessed.

THE MURDERERS

Arthur Hosein came to England in 1955 and worked as a tailor's cutter in Hackney, east London. He was imprisoned for six months for desertion during his national service, but back in Civvy Street he married a German girl and settled in Essex, opening his own trouser-making business in Mare Street, Hackney.

Nizamodeen, the youngest of Arthur's six brothers, came to join him when he was 21. Arthur was small and shrewd, dominating Nizam who was taller and stronger. Arthur supplied the brains of their enterprises and Nizamodeen the brawn.

Arthur had boasted hugely of his great success in prosperous England and Nizam expected to join him in the good life. It was a shock to find that the owner of Rooks Farm was failing utterly in his dream of becoming the Squire of Stocking Pelham. The trouser-making business wasn't earning enough to support the lifestyle of a country gentleman, and Arthur's pretensions only called down ridicule on his head. He tried to join the local hunt, but since he couldn't ride and couldn't afford the subscription, this rather simple exercise in social climbing was doomed to failure. The villagers mocked him as "King Hosein".

Both brothers were totally materialistic, greedy and pretty stupid. Both thought that the television programme pinpointing Rupert Murdoch's wealth showed them the way to a life of comfort. They went to the *News of the World* offices and identified the company chairman's car. They tailed it home after work – back to Wimbledon. More sophisticated villains would have paused at that point. St. Mary House is a very comfortable residence of good size, but hardly a millionaire's residence.

Arthur and Nizam didn't even have the wit to consult a Post Office directory and find out who they were kidnapping.

Rooks Farm, Stocking Pelham, where the Hosein brothers, especially Arthur, tried to live like country gentlemen from the meagre proceeds of their business.

They thought they were getting Mrs. Murdoch when they got Mrs. McKay. And their threats and ransom notes showed that they assumed Mr. Murdoch would hand over a million pounds to Mr. McKay on their terms without putting a police tail on them.

When they were arrested, each tried to blame the other. Nizam was probably telling no more than the truth when he said he acted entirely on Arthur's prompting. But his own crass stupidity and greed made him a more-than-willing accomplice. Arthur's attempt to set up Nizam as the crook who had acted behind his back could not hold up against the fingerprint evidence. The brothers were convicted of kidnapping and extortion, for which they drew long sentences, in addition to the life sentences they received for the murder of Mrs. McKay.

For murder her they did – there can be little doubt of that although there is no evidence. It is most unlikely that she lived far beyond the New Year. But what became of her body has never been revealed. The police wondered whether the ferocious guard dogs which wandered around the farm at Stocking Pelham might have been allowed to dispose of her remains. The local villagers were more inclined to believe that she had been fed to the farm pigs: omnivorous beasts that would make short work of a cadaver added to their swill. This theory could have been tested, were the pigs available. The cortisone Mrs. McKay took should have shown up clearly in samples of their blood. Unfortunately, all of Arthur Hosein's porkers were sent off to slaughter not long after Muriel McKay's disappearance. We shall never know for sure how the evil pair disposed of their helpless victim.

The children of Muriel McKay at the trial: from left, son Ian, and daughters Diane and Jennifer.

THE GREEN BERET KILLER

1970 was the year of Charles Manson's arrest for the horrific murders of Sharon Tate and her house guests, followed by those of Mr. and Mrs. Leno LaBianca. So it was appalling to learn that, in February 1970, the hippies had struck again. Another household had been violated. Another family had been savagely done to death. Their blood, too, had been used for crude graffiti.

■

DR. JEFFREY MACDONALD was an army captain in the prestigious "Green Berets": the crack special operations unit of the American army, trained, like Britain's SAS, for particularly hazardous roles. MacDonald was an excellent example of the good soldier. Born into a poor family on Long Island, he worked hard and graduated from Princeton University. While still a student there in 1963, he married a girl from his hometown of Patchoque. Colette was carrying a baby for the handsome young pre-med, whose suave and easy manners made him a popular date for many women, before and after the marriage.

But his happy and healthy sexual opportunism did not mean he was idle or profligate. He accepted the responsibility of marriage and was accepted by Colette's family. When their daughter Kimberley was born, it spurred Jeffrey to complete his medical studies at North Western University, and in 1969 the newly-qualified practitioner found his niche in the army. By this time, the young couple had a second daughter, Kristen, and they lived in successive military married quarters. By 1970, the doctor was a captain; the family were living at Fort Bragg, a large military base in North Carolina.

The MacDonald house at 544 Castle Drive was not a billet in civilian territory – Military Police provided security. On February 7, the MPs were preparing for the extra duties inevitable on a Visitors' Day, when hordes of civilians would pour onto the base. But the visitors that day were to find themselves on a base in a state of shock from the carnage wrought by four non-military kids.

Early in the morning, Jeffrey Mac-Donald telephoned the Military Police. His voice was weak and croaky: his message alarming and imprecise. "Help! Stabbing! Hurry!" he urged. Perceiving something to be very wrong, duty police raced over to Castle Drive.

In the living room, they found signs of a struggle. In the main bedroom, the Captain lay in a state of collapse with wounds to the head and chest. Next to him, Colette lay dead. She was savagely battered and covered with blood. Tiny stab-wounds dotted her torso and abdomen. Jeffrey's pyjama jacket had been folded over her. On the wall, the word "PIG" had been scrawled in her blood. Five-year-old Kimberley lay dead in the next bedroom, her skull shattered by two savage blows. Two-year-old Kristen lay dead in another bedroom. Fifteen of the pinpoint stab wounds had penetrated her body, together with 20 stabs from a broader-bladed knife.

The murder weapons were found outside the back door. They were a wooden club, a knife, and an icepick which had created the small but deep wounds. The Captain said he had never seen them before. They had all been wiped clean of fingerprints. MacDonald was taken to the military hospital. He had a severe stab to the chest which had punctured a lung, and more superficial bruising and abrasions to the head.

His story indicated that Manson now had imitators on the east coast. The family had gone to bed, he reported, except for him. He had stayed up, reading and dozing in his pyjamas on the couch in the sitting-room. He awoke with a start to find four hippies in the house. Three of them were men: the fourth was a blonde woman in a floppy hat who carried a lighted candle and led the others in chants of "Kill the pigs!" and "Acid is groovy". Jeffrey struggled with them, but they overpowered him and tied his hands before clubbing him over the head. Before oblivion overtook him, he heard Colette screaming, "Jeff! Jeff! Help! Why are they doing this to me?"

When he finally came round, the house was cold and silent. The marauding hippies had gone. The Captain went upstairs to find bloodstains on the floors and walls: his whole family had been brutally massacred.

The Military Police were working under severe handicaps. Their normal employment does not involve solving casual serious crimes, let alone the notoriously difficult "stranger murders" that can give experienced detectives serious problems. The boys in the gaiters and white helmets are normally used to breaking up drunken brawls, pursuing enlisted men who have gone AWOL, and perhaps handling the odd case of pilfering. They are usually in closed barracks too, where guards on the gates mean all entries and exits have been checked, and the whole community can be sealed off for immediate investigation in a crisis. But Fort Bragg was an open base. The public had the right to enter and pass through parts of it. It was not possible to close everything down at once and hope the hippies would be caught in the trap.

SUSPICIONS

Despite these limiations, however, the Fort Bragg MPs were astute enough to note very quickly that the sitting room was surprisingly undisturbed for the supposed site of a furious struggle. True, some things were disarranged. But a fragile coffee table in front of the couch should surely have been overturned, if not smashed, as MacDonald wrestled with his brutal and spaced-out assailants.

In Castle Drive the marauders had encountered a man trained in unarmed combat. Even barefoot in his pyjamas, he should have given them something to

Jeffrey MacDonald claimed his family was murdered by drug-crazed hippies.

remember him by. There was no sign in the living room that this had happened.

The military CID team took all the necessary photographs of the crime scene, and drew up their plans of what had been found and where. They collected pieces of physical evidence, like the pyjama jacket, and took samples of the blood that liberally bespattered the house, carefully labelling the points from which they had come. Then they waited for forensic laboratory reports.

They enjoyed one advantage over civilian cops. The house was Uncle Sam's. They were Uncle Sam's men. They did not have to complete their investigations and hand the house back to the owners to be cleaned and refurnished. They could seal it, holding the site-of-crime as evidence for as long as they liked. And in fact, 544 Castle Drive was to be preserved intact as a grisly undisturbed memento of the murders for no less than nine years. This is probably the longest any murder site has ever been held in such a way.

Before the investigations had got very far, the funerals were held. The tragedy was deeply felt by family, friends and the wider public. Colette had been pregnant again, so that, as with Sharon Tate, the hippies had ruthlessly taken two lives in one go. Jeffrey MacDonald's mother found this aspect of the murders particularly distressing.

Colette's stepfather, Alfred Kassab, was most supportive of his stepson-in-law. Freddy Kassab had married Colette's mother when the girl was 13, and they had formed a close and devoted family unit. Freddy had been delighted that his stepdaughter won such a handsome and presentable partner, with a promising career ahead of him. Like any middle-American, he was outraged that members of the Alternative Society could wreak meaningless havoc among decent respectable conservative families. The MacDonalds, after all, unlike the members of Sharon Tate's house party, had no questionable association with illicit drugs; no unsavoury personal

addiction to flagellant sessions or sexual orgies; and no home movies of their own fornication that would certainly *not* pass a censor anywhere.

The public shared Kassab's outrage. As the case of Colonel Oliver North has shown, by and large, America loves its serving army officers if they are good-looking, polite and obey orders. West Point and the other military academies of America give the USA its only real taste of the sort of regimented and disciplined good manners and respect for elders that the English are used to meeting in public schoolboys. "Manners Makyth Man", says the motto of Winchester College, and if the sentiment is a little extreme, it is none the less certain that well bred deportment is one of the easiest ways of winning instant admiration and sympathy. Jeffrey MacDonald profited by this.

And well it served him as the forensic scientific reports started coming in. Blood grouping had become more sophisticated than the simple A, B, AB, O and Rh positive or negative that is used (for example) to determine paternity. It was possible to differentiate between the blood samples found in the house, and allocate each, precisely, to one of the family members.

Significantly, no other blood was found there. Combat-trained Jeffrey MacDonald, struggling with three young men in a state of drugged intoxication, had failed to give any of them a bloody nose. It was extremely unlikely that any hippy would have the strength and agility of a mature man kept fit by army PE instructors. Yet, as far as forensic evidence could demonstrate, the intruders seem to have emerged entirely unscathed from their fracas with a startled and

Jeffrey MacDonald talking with his defence lawyers during the 1970 hearing.

enraged army officer. Furthermore, in flagrant breach of one of the first laws of forensics, they seem to have left no microscopic physical clues at the scene of the crime: no fragments of skin or cloth under the fingernails of their resisting victims. All they'd left were their murder weapons, carefully wiped clean of clues. Coupled with the barely disturbed sitting room, it looked odd.

Things looked far worse when the individually matched blood samples were checked against the plan of the house, and compared with Jeffrey MacDonald's story. By his account, he had been downstairs the whole time; Colette and the girls upstairs in bed. He had heard Colette cry out for help. Then, after his period of unconsciousness, he went upstairs and found his wife and daughters, murdered in their beds.

But the bloodstains told a very different story – Colette and Kimberley had both bled in the master bedroom; Colette had bled profusely in Kristen's room. Yet all three females had been found in their separate rooms as though each had been attacked separately. If the hippies had aroused Kimberley and attacked her when she came into the master bedroom, why had they carried her back to her own room? If Colette had rushed in to protect Kristen, and been clubbed down there, why and how had she made her way back to her own bed? Why didn't she leave an obvious trail of blood?

There was Jeffrey's blood in the master bedroom, too. Was this compatible with a little continuing bleeding as he went upstairs after coming round from his concussion?

More damning still were the fragments of thread found on, around and

MacDonald and his chief attorney, the flamboyant Bernie Segal, in 1975.

under the bodies. By all the laws of forensic science there should be minuscule traces of the killers' garments left behind. But the minute scraps of fabric found apparently came from Jeffrey's pyjamas. How had they got there? He said nothing about picking up or moving his dead wife and daughters when he found them.

THE INQUIRY

On April 6, six weeks after the tragedy, MacDonald was asked to take a lie detector test. He instantly agreed. By the time the appointment could be set up, however, he had changed his mind and refused. The army charged him with the murders of Colette, Kimberley and Kristen, and sent the case to an official inquiry rather than a formal trial.

Jeffrey refused the army lawyer he was offered, and hired the flamboyant civilian attorney Bernie Segal. And Segal did a wonderful job for his client.

He went directly on the offensive, and charged the Military Police with total incompetence. Twenty officers had trampled all over the house in their investigation, he asserted, treading blood everywhere and obliterating any traces the intruders might have left. Their own clumsiness had destroyed any fingerprint or forensic evidence that could have been of use. The military had lost vital evidence – a thread found under Kimberley's nail, for example. No hair samples had been taken from any of the victims to compare with stray hairs hoovered up in the house. Most astonishing of all, they had thrown away MacDonald's pyjama pants, and now were making all this fuss about fibres that supposedly came from the jacket.

Bernie Segal also succeeded where the MPs had failed, by producing the hippy girl in the floppy hat. Her name was Helena Stoeckley and, though her hair was not blonde, she often wore a blonde wig. She was 18 years old, and confessed to being so far out on mescaline on the night of the murders that she couldn't say for sure whether she had been there or not.

In October, the inquiry concluded that there was insufficient evidence to find against Captain MacDonald, and the case was thrown out of court.

Jeffrey was discharged honourably from the army and then moved to California. Here he pioneered emergency room medicine at St. Mary's Medical Center in Long Beach. He also adopted a West Coast lifestyle distressingly similar, in some ways, to that of the hippies who had destroyed his family. He grew his hair long, dated a succession of pretty girls, moved into a seafront condominium, and bought a 30-ft boat. He also revelled in the publicity from his personal tragedy, and took the opportunity of repeated appearances on TV to attack the army.

Provost-Marshal Colonel Kriwanek at Fort Bragg did not enjoy hearing his officers' competence and integrity attacked. He agreed that the file on the MacDonald murders should stay open, and the MacDonald house sealed for further investigation.

He won support from an unexpected source. Freddy Kassab, determined originally on helping his stepson-in-law bring the murdering hippies to justice, had studied the inquiry report very carefully, and he was not satisfied: "I read this transcript through, oh, innumerable times. Maybe 20, 30 times. And the more I read it through, the more I realized that the story as he told it had to be a fabrication."

Kassab went to Fort Bragg and was allowed by the investigators to look over the house where the murders were comittted. He joined forces with CID

> **"NONE OF HIS STORY HOLDS TOGETHER. I MEAN NONE OF WHAT HE SAYS HE DID. HE CLAIMS TO HAVE BEEN ATTACKED IN THE LIVING ROOM. HE CLAIMS TO HAVE SUSTAINED TEN ICEPICK WOUNDS ACROSS HIS ABDOMEN. NOW, THOSE TEN ICEPICK WOUNDS, NOBODY HAS EVER SEEN. NO DOCTOR IN A HOSPITAL EVER SAW THEM."**
> ALFRED KASSAB

Colonel Pruett, who had eight agents still working on the case.

After Pruett re-opened the house and scrutinized the situation, the army recommended that charges in the civilian courts be brought against ex-Captain MacDonald. It took Freddy Kassab two years to persuade the Justice Department to act on this advice. It was five years after the murders before a Grand Jury in North Carolina handed down indictments against MacDonald. Nor did this result in a speedy trial. The US Court of Appeals endorsed MacDonald's legal plea that the long delay violated his civil rights. Freddy Kassab insisted that the case be taken forward to the Supreme Court.

BACK TO COURT

Bernie Segal argued passionately that this was unfair and that so delayed a trial could not possibly serve the cause of justice. The Supreme Court disagreed and, in June 1979, Jeffrey MacDonald at last stood trial in Raleigh, North Carolina, for the murder of his wife and daughters nine years earlier.

The prosecution had assembled a formidable array of forensic evidence. Jeffrey's pyjama jacket, which he admitted folding and placing over Colette's body, was shown to contain 48 small holes. Folded together, these matched the 21 icepick wounds inflicted on Colette.

The scientists had pieced together the blood trail through the house into a plausible scenario. A quarrel between Jeffrey and Colette had taken place in the master bedroom – possibly over his womanizing or the children's bedwetting. As it escalated, Jeffrey knocked his wife down. Colette seized the nearby club and hit him with it. Kimberley woke up and rushed into the room to help her mother. As Jeffrey seized the club from Colette and lashed out with it, he accidentally

Identikit picture of Helena Stoeckley.

struck Kimberley and cracked her skull. He picked the child up and took her back to her room. Fearing she was fatally injured, he made it look like a deliberate attack by an outsider and hit her again.

Colette rushed into Kristen's room to defend her baby. Jeffrey followed her and clubbed her down, breaking both her arms. He carried her back to the master bedroom where he killed her with 16 knife thrusts. He then stabbed Kristen 17 times. Finally he attacked all three bodies with the icepick. After wiping down the weapons, he stabbed himself in the chest and called the police.

Jeffrey's lame account of everything being a blur after he was hit over the head by a male intruder was far less detailed and persuasive. His defence made no serious attempt to counter the telling scientific evidence point by point. Instead, Bernie Segal again attacked Military Police methods, and argued that all the evidence was so old and out of date that it proved nothing. When the jury was taken to see the house, Segal jeered that it had been completely altered since the murders, so that the jury was only getting five percent of an impression of the real scene of the crime.

He could not, however, counter their impression that the building fitted the prosecution's story of the fight that moved precisely, with the identifiable bloodstains, from room to room.

Helena Stoeckley was trundled out again as the blonde hippy woman with the floppy hat, but her testimony was rambling and contradictory. She didn't know where she'd been on the night of the murders. She certainly had not worn her blonde wig that night. She couldn't remember ever chanting "Acid is groovy!" After the trial she was to tell totally contradictory stories about the murders, sometimes she confessed to being there, sometimes she withdrew the confession. She identified certain young men as having been her companions, but they all easily established absolute alibis.

Bernie Segal had hoped to rely on Jeffrey MacDonald's sterling character and admirable personality as the keystone of his defence. Unfortunately, the

defence lost one of its cornerstones when the judge disallowed psychiatric evidence on his state of mind in 1970. Segal was reduced to praising his client and abusing the circumstantial evidence.

The jury found Jeffrey MacDonald guilty on all three counts of murder, but made it murder in the second degree in Colette's and Kimberley's cases, first degree only in Kristen's. Their reasoning was impeccable. Kimberley had been injured fatally by accident. Colette had been killed in the process of a quarrel; but Kristen had been murdered in cold blood, simply to substantiate MacDonald's tale of the fictitious hippy intruders.

The judge handed down three terms of life imprisonment. To Alfred Kassab's undisguised satisfaction, the judge also refused MacDonald bail during the long drawn-out series of appeals following the trial; these lasted until 1982. MacDonald went to prison, where he has remained ever since.

MacDonald stood trial nine years after the murders were committed.

THE YORKSHIRE
RIPPER

In October 1975, a woman named Wilma McCann was murdered in Leeds, in England's northern county of Yorkshire. She was hit on the head, then stabbed. Three months later Emily Jackson was also murdered in Leeds. A little over a year later, in February 1977, Irene Richardson was found dead in Roundhay Park, Leeds. She had been stabbed. It was clear that Leeds had a serial killer, a phenomenon comparatively rare in Britain and unknown to most of the population.

■

I N CRIMINOLOGICAL CIRCLES a British murderer is popularly credited with marking the start of modern serial killing. That killer was Jack the Ripper. In 1888 he killed a number of prostitutes in the East End of London. In 1977 a newspaper likened the Leeds killer to Jack the Ripper and dubbed him "the Yorkshire Ripper".

When Peter Sutcliffe was tried for the Yorkshire Ripper murders, the question of his guilt was never in question. Instead, the jury were required to assess whether Sutcliffe was sane or insane. It was Peter Sutcliffe who stood in the dock at the Old Bailey, but for many people it was the credibility of psychiatric evidence that stood trial.

On October 30, 1975, 28-year-old prostitute Wilma McCann left her home in Scott Hall Avenue, Leeds. She went out for a drink – quite a few drinks, in fact – and the following morning her body was found on a bleak, frosty recreation ground. She was lying on her back. Her bolero jacket and pink blouse were open, her bra pulled up. Her white flared trousers had been pulled down below her knees. Her panties had not been pulled down. She had been struck on the head twice, viciously, with an implement like a hammer, and her skull had shattered. Her hair was matted with blood. Her body bore the marks of 14 post-mortem stab wounds.

It was on January 20, 1976 that the killer struck again. Emily Jackson was 42 years old. She was married with three children and lived in a respectable suburb of Leeds called Churwell. She was a part-time "good-time girl", an occasional prostitute whose husband indulged her peccadillo. He went with his wife to the

Gaiety pub, then known for its "fun-loving" patrons and their would-be clients. About an hour later Emily was seen climbing into a car.

She was found the next morning on her back, breasts exposed. She'd been struck twice on the back of the head with a hammer-like object, then frenziedly stabbed some 50 times and her corpse further marked with what appeared to be a screwdriver. Her killer had also stamped on her right thigh, leaving the impression of a size seven rubber wellington boot.

On May 9, 1976, a woman named Marcella Claxton was attacked in Leeds. It was not realized at the time that her assailant was the Leeds killer. Nor was it realized by the police, press or public that this was the third attempted murder. In fact, failed attacks went back to July 1975, when Anna Rogulskyj was attacked in Keighley, not far from Leeds, and the following month, when Olive Smelt was attacked in the town of Halifax.

The area known as Chapeltown was and is Leeds' red-light district. It was once a "posh" suburb with leafy, tree-lined streets and large, rather magnificent houses. But its poshness faded long ago.

It is now drab, soulless, home to a high proportion of prostitutes and drug dealers. In nearby Bradford the red-light district was and is an area around Lumb

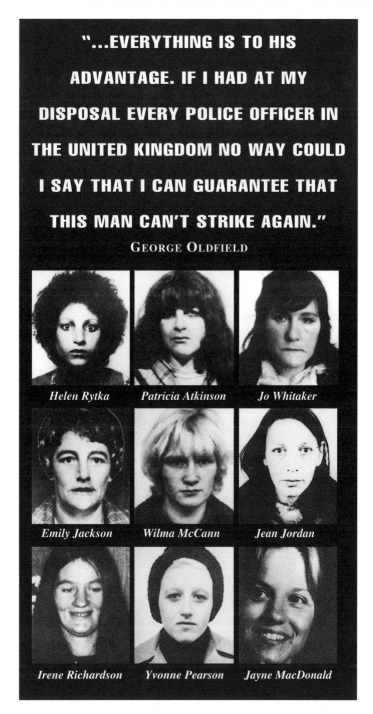

"...EVERYTHING IS TO HIS ADVANTAGE. IF I HAD AT MY DISPOSAL EVERY POLICE OFFICER IN THE UNITED KINGDOM NO WAY COULD I SAY THAT I CAN GUARANTEE THAT THIS MAN CAN'T STRIKE AGAIN."

GEORGE OLDFIELD

Helen Rytka   Patricia Atkinson   Jo Whitaker

Emily Jackson   Wilma McCann   Jean Jordan

Irene Richardson   Yvonne Pearson   Jayne MacDonald

Lane – a derelict landscape of crumbling buildings and sleaze. Both areas were to know a paralyzing fear over the months and years to come.

Irene Richardson lived in Cowper Street, Chapeltown, in a rundown rooming house. 28 years old and a mother, her two children being in foster care, she worked the street corners part-time in an effort to make some needed cash. Her sad, squalid life was cut horribly short on February 5, 1977. The next morning her body was found in Roundhay Park. Her skull had been shattered by three hammer blows, her body brutalized by a frenzied attack with the blade of a knife.

The Yorkshire press was not slow in making a connection between the three murders – nor in recalling Jack the Ripper, the infamous murderer of prostitutes in London's East End almost a century earlier. The Leeds serial killer soon had a name: the Yorkshire Ripper.

Patricia Atkinson was 32, a slim, attractive divorcee with three children. On April 23, 1977 she set out for her local pub, The Carlisle, dressed in blue jeans and shirt, with a black leather jacket. She drank a great deal that night and was fairly drunk when she left the pub at closing time and headed for home, alone.

The next night some friends went round to Patricia's flat. They found her body on the bed, covered in blankets.

She was naked, her clothes having been torn from her. Her skull had been crushed by four heavy hammer blows and she'd been stabbed several times. One of the bedsheets bore the imprint of a size seven rubber wellington boot.

THE RIPPER MAKES A MISTAKE

June 25, 1977, and Jayne MacDonald was walking home in Leeds. A white Ford Corsair parked and the driver got out. He followed the girl. Her body was found the following morning by a group of children. She'd been bludgeoned on the back of the head three times, and stabbed once in the back and numerous times in the front.

There was no doubt that Jayne MacDonald was a victim of the Yorkshire Ripper. But her murder was very different and it changed the public perception of the crimes. Up till now the murders had seemed unreal, the victims the inhabitants of a red-lit netherworld of sex-for-sale. It was a world with which most people never came into contact. But Jayne MacDonald was only 16 years old and she was not a prostitute. Now every woman felt like a potential victim and the fear in Leeds was almost tangible.

The most experienced policeman in West Yorkshire was put in charge of the case. His name was George Oldfield and he publicly staked

> UP TILL NOW THE MURDERS HAD SEEMED UNREAL, THE VICTIMS THE INHABITANTS OF A RED-LIT NETHERWORLD OF SEX-FOR-SALE. BUT NOW EVERY WOMAN FELT LIKE A POTENTIAL VICTIM ...THE FEAR ... WAS ALMOST TANGIBLE.

The man in charge of the Ripper case, George Oldfield (left), with Yorkshire police supremos Ronald Gregory and Jim Hodson.

his reputation on catching the killer. The police appealed for help and opened telephone hotlines. Very soon they were swamped with information. The investigation became unwieldy, almost impossible to control and conduct meaningfully. It involved over 300 officers, 12,500 statements were taken and some 10,000 vehicles checked.

Meanwhile, in July 1977, a woman named Maureen Long was attacked on some waste ground in Bradford. The assault was extremely savage and Maureen Long was badly injured, but she was not killed. She was able to describe her assailant: he was over six foot in height, aged about 36, and had collar-length fair hair. Was the Ripper beginning to make mistakes that would lead to his capture?

The police certainly thought so when it came to the next murder. The victim this time was Jean Jordan. 21 years old and born in Scotland, she was the mother of two children and lived with her lover in a council-owned house in Manchester. On October 1, 1977, she met the driver of a red Ford Corsair. He offered her a brand-new £5 note, which she accepted. She got into the car and then directed the driver to an area where prostitutes took their clients. There the driver smashed Jean Jordan's head into a bloody pulp. He struck no fewer than 11 times with a hammer, but was prevented from further abusing the body by the arrival of another car. The Ripper crossed the Pennines back to Leeds in the knowledge that he had left his first clue, the £5 note.

Amazingly Jean Jordan's body was not discovered and after eight days had passed the murderer thought it was safe to return to the body. He drove back to

The Ripper's father speaks of his shock: "It's a terrible, terrible thing."

Manchester and to the murder scene. The body lay where he had left it, pulled under the cover of some bushes. But Jean's handbag was nowhere to be found and the murderer had to leave without the note. Angry, he further abused the body with some broken glass, even attempting to remove the head. Delivering several fierce kicks to the body, the murderer got back into his car and left the scene.

The next day the body was discovered. Identification was difficult, Jean Jordan's head being unrecognizable, but she had been reported missing and a fingerprint was found at her home. The police also found what the murderer had not – the new £5 note. They did not immediately recognize its significance, but soon learned that the new note was traceable by its number.

Bank officials were able to identify the note as one of a batch sent to the

Shipley and Bingley branches of the Midland Bank. It had been among the notes issued to no more than 30 firms to pay wages. Unfortunately, those 30 firms collectively employed 8,000 people, any one of whom could have been the murderer. Or maybe none of them was the killer. The note could have been taken from a wage packet and handed across a shop counter, then given to someone else in change. It could have passed through several hands before reaching Jean Jordan and there was no guarantee that it had been given to her by the murderer. A poor clue then, but a team of detectives nevertheless pursued the lead – and eventually it brought them face to face with the Ripper.

Two months later, in December 1977, the Ripper tried to kill again. Returning to his old stamping-ground of Chapeltown, in Leeds, he attacked Marilyn Moore. He swung a hammer at her, but lost his balance. She screamed and the Ripper, scared, ran away. Miss Moore needed 56 stitches, but she'd lived – and she helped to create a photofit picture of the killer.

1978 saw the Ripper claim three victims: in January, Yvonne Pearson, a 22-year-old professional prostitute with two young daughters, had gone to the Flying Dutchman pub and been picked up by a bearded man and driven off with him in his car. On March 26 a passer-by spotted what he thought was the arm of a mannequin sticking out from beneath an upturned sofa discarded on some wasteground. Also noted was a putrid smell; the police were called.

This victim had been struck with a hammer and jumped on, breaking her ribs. Beneath one of her arms was found a copy of the *Daily Mirror* newspaper. Curiously, it was dated four weeks *after* she had been killed, indicating that the murderer had returned to the scene of the crime.

Ten days after Yvonne Pearson had gone missing, 19-year-old prostitute Helen Rytka was killed in Huddersfield. A strikingly attractive girl, one of twins born to a Jamaican father and an Italian mother, Helen worked the car trade with her sister Rita. They were very careful. They touted for trade outside a public lavatory, only one going off with a

client; the other girl remained behind and took the car number. The first stayed with the client for 20 minutes, then returned to the public lavatory. On this

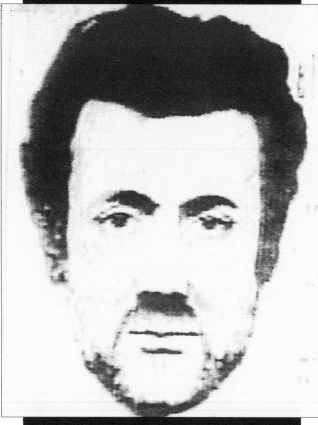

IN THE END, AS IS SO OFTEN THE CASE, THE RIPPER WAS NOT CAUGHT THROUGH DETECTIVE WORK, BUT BY SIMPLE 'GOOD COPPERING'.

A photofit of the Ripper came from a description given by victim Maureen Long.

night, though, Helen was tempted by a promised quickie for £5 and broke the system. She was never seen alive again. Three days later a police dog found her

body. It bore the tell-tale Ripper hallmarks of a blow to the head and repeated stabbings.

Spanish-born Vera Millward worked the notorious Moss Side area of Manchester. The mother of seven children, she had turned to prostitution to support her family. She was very ill, crippled with violent stomach pains. On May 16 she went to get some pain-killing drugs from the local hospital. Her body was found next day, dumped on a pile of rubbish in a car park. Her skull had been shattered.

By this time the police investigation had brought them into contact with the murderer no fewer than four times. Maybe he felt threatened; he didn't kill again until April 1979, almost a year after the murder of Vera Millward. This time he found his victim in Halifax: Josephine Ann Whitaker, a 19-year-old clerk with a building society. Once again the Ripper had chosen a victim who wasn't a prostitute.

"I'M JACK!"

It was now that the police received an audio cassette. It began "I'm Jack". The speaker had a distinctive regional Geordie accent. The police believed the tape came from the killer. A million-pound publicity campaign was launched, substantial rewards were offered, and a confidential memorandum was distributed among other police forces instructing them to eliminate from their inquiries anyone who did not have a Geordie accent. This was an understandable but serious mistake. The Ripper was not a Geordie. The Ripper did not have a Geordie accent.

The Ripper was a lorry driver named Peter Sutcliffe, the eldest son of John and Kathleen Sutcliffe. He was ill-suited to the rough, tough area of Bingley where he was born and brought up, and his father's "man's man" approach to life was alien to him. He wasn't a big drinker, unlike his brothers, or a womanizer, though he took considerable and perhaps excessive pride in his appearance. Intelligent, though not academic, he left school at 15, getting a job as a grave digger.

Peter Sutcliffe was regarded as rather strange, but it is difficult to determine whether he betrayed a genuine oddness that would eventually manifest itself in psychotic killing, or whether he was untrained for his environment, there being some evidence that serial killing might be a defence mechanism of those who feel like aliens in normal society.

For Sutcliffe that feeling might have been based on the ideals he invested in his mother and, perhaps, through her in women in general. Certainly the discovery in 1969 that his mother had been having an affair with a neighbour seemed to affect Sutcliffe deeply. By this time, though, he had met his future wife.

Her name was Sonia Szurma. Born in August 1950, she was 16 years old and sampling the heady delights of under-age drinking with her friends in The Royal Standard pub when she met Peter Sutcliffe in 1966. Eight years later they were married. Less than a year after that

A weeping Sonia Sutcliffe leaves court during the trial of her husband.

The home of Peter Sutcliffe in Garden Lane, Heaton, Bradford.

Sutcliffe made his first murder attempt.

By some accounts the marriage was a strange one, Sonia being the dominant partner. But Sutcliffe worked hard and soon the couple moved out of Bingley to a large – and palatial by Bingley standards – house in middle-class Heaton, Bradford. Sonia never suspected that her husband was the Yorkshire Ripper.

Between May 1978 and September 2, 1979, the Yorkshire Ripper didn't kill. Some speculated that the Ripper had killed himself – it is a widely held belief that serial killers do not suddenly stop killing – while others thought he may have been arrested for another crime and imprisoned, nobody suspecting he was the murderer. But Peter Sutcliffe – who had by now been interviewed five times by police – was merely taking a break.

He put the speculation to an end on September 1, 1979, when he spotted a 20-year-old Bradford University student, Barbara Leach. He jumped on her, dragged her body into some bushes and stabbed her eight times. Then he dumped the body in a recess designed for a dustbin and covered it with a piece of old carpet. Barbara's corpse was discovered the following afternoon.

Another year went by. Then, on August 18, 1980, the Ripper killed an attractive 47-year-old civil servant named Marguerite Walls. She had worked late at her office because she was about to go on holiday. Her body was found two days later. She had been struck with a hammer, but had been strangled and not stabbed. The police dismissed her as a Ripper victim. A murderous attack on a doctor from Singapore named Upadhya Bandara was similarly not attributed by the police to the Ripper.

Finally, in November 1980, in Headingley, a Leeds suburb known internationally for its cricket ground, the Yorkshire Ripper killed 20-year-old Jaqueline Hill, a student returning to the Leeds University halls of residence.

During this time George Oldfield had had a heart attack and been temporarily replaced by Superintendent James Hodson. Oldfield returned to head what was now as much a personal vendetta as an investigation, but the police were obviously floundering, helpless under the sheer weight of the massive inquiry and subjected to considerable and sometimes unfair criticism. George Oldfield was removed from the case and Superintendent Hodson brought back in his place. In the end, though, the Ripper was not caught through detection, but by simple "good coppering".

In Sheffield two policemen, Sergeant Robert Ring and Constable John Hyde, were on vice duty. A man had picked up prostitute Olivia Rievers. A routine check of the number plates on the man's Rover car revealed them to be false. The man was arrested. At first the police could find nothing incriminating, then one of the arresting policemen remembered that the man had asked to relieve himself and he returned to the spot. He found a hammer and a sharp knife. Another knife was later found hidden in the police station lavatory.

Three days later the man, whose name was Peter Sutcliffe, confessed to the Ripper killings.

PSYCHIATRY ON TRIAL

The trial was a media circus. One newspaper, the *Daily Mail,* had no fewer than 32 reporters and cameramen on the scene. Sutcliffe was treated by press, public and police as guilty. The Solicitor-General issued a warning that by British law Sutcliffe was to be regarded as innocent until proven guilty.

The trial, though, had less to do with Sutcliffe's guilt than with his mental condition. Both the prosecution and the defence counsels had agreed to a plea of

James Hodson in the Ripper incident room. Hodson took over the case after illness and mounting criticism forced out his predecessor, George Oldfield.

Peter William Sutcliffe, 35, long-distance lorry driver, is bundled into court, within sight of a hostile crowd.

guilty on the grounds of paranoid schizophrenia. But when the trial began on May 5, 1981 the judge, Mr. Justice Boreham, insisted that Sutcliffe's sanity be decided by a jury.

The reason was that Sutcliffe had told two versions of why he'd begun his killing spree. In the first version he said he'd once been humiliated by a prostitute and had begun killing for revenge. In another story he said that he'd heard the voice of God instructing him to kill prostitutes and all women of easy virtue. The jury had to decide which of these stories was true. For Sutcliffe their decision would determine whether he would be sent to prison for life, with no chance of release, or to an asylum from where he might one day walk free, adjudged a sane man.

The trial progressed amid much discussion about whether or not a jury was capable of understanding, let alone judging, psychiatric and other, often crucial, specialist evidence. Eventually, by a verdict of ten votes to two, the jury concluded that Sutcliffe was guilty – and sane. He was sent to prison for life.

Peter Sutcliffe was taken to Parkhurst Prison on the Isle of Wight, where he was kept in the top security wing. In March 1984, he was transferred to Broadmoor, a hospital for the criminally insane. His mental condition had deteriorated dramatically.

The Ripper case is rarely far from the public eye. It has been the subject of several books and there are the inevitable comparisons made in the seemingly endless stream of books about his Victorian counterpart. Peter Sutcliffe made headlines again when, in January 1983, he was attacked and his face cut by a fellow prisoner. And Sonia caused a sensation when she won a libel award of £600,000 against *Private Eye* magazine in May 1989 (it was reduced at an appeal hearing in October of that year).

THE BLACK
PANTHER

In 1973 British newspapers reported that 15-year-old Lesley Whittle was an heiress. Her father, George, was a coach driver who built up his own successful coach business, and when he died he left £100,000 in trust for his estranged wife Dorothy and their daughter Lesley. Since £82,500 would pass, untouched, to Lesley when she came of age, she was momentarily newsworthy as a schoolgirl inheriting a lot of money.

■

BUT FOR THE PRESENT, Lesley and her mother were leading a perfectly normal middle-class life in the village of Highley, Shropshire. The interest on £100,000, paid out by trustees, was not in itself a source of enormous wealth such as headlines about the "schoolgirl heiress" might suggest. But the alluring phrase had caught the attention of a predator.

On January 14, 1975, Lesley Whittle did not come down to breakfast. When her mother went to see what was keeping her, she found Lesley's bed abandoned. A further search revealed three Dymo-tape messages in the sitting-room – £50,000 ransom for the return of Lesley was demanded. The family was instructed to collect the money in used notes, and take them early in the evening to a public telephone box in a Kidderminster shopping mall, where they would receive further instructions. A sinister warning read: "You are on a time limit – if police or tricks, DEATH."

Lesley's family told the authorities. They accepted the police advice that her brother Ronald should go to the call-box to collect the instructions. The police, meanwhile, proposed to log all calls coming in and out of the box.

Unfortunately, they learned that a freelance journalist had picked up the story of the kidnap. Lesley's safety was the first consideration, as the police feared the kidnapper might harm her if he discovered calls to the box were being checked, so they pulled Ronald Whittle out of the box at 9.30pm, before any instructions had come.

They did not realize the cunning kidnapper had ordered an early rendezvous to allow himself an opportunity to watch

The Whittle home at Salop, from where Lesley was abducted by the Panther.

the call-box and see whether police turned up at the time he had specified. It seemed all clear, so he went away again to make his call at a later hour. But by the time he telephoned at 11.00pm, the call-box was empty.

The following night Ronald tried again, but both he and the kidnapper spent a frustrating evening. The kidnapper proposed to have the ransom drop made at a Dudley freightliner base. Before calling Ronald, he went there to reconnoitre the territory, and was disturbed by security man Gerald Smith, who asked him why he was prowling around the place. The intruder promptly shot Mr. Smith, pumping bullets into his back. (Mr. Smith lived for 14 months before succumbing to his injuries, so that in law this killing was technically "attempted murder" rather than murder. The victim must die within 12 months of the assault for the crime to be categorized as murder.)

Even so, the killer-kidnapper might have made contact with Ronald Whittle that night and Lesley's life might have been saved. But a wicked hoaxer had rung the police with a false message for Ronald Whittle, who spent the rest of the night on a wild goose chase.

BATHPOOL PARK

The following night, Ronald Whittle finally made telephone contact with the man who had kidnapped his sister. Lesley's taped voice told him to carry the ransom straight to a telephone box near Kidsgrove, where he would find further instructions awaiting him.

Unfortunately, Scotland Yard, who had just been brought into the case, were shocked to find that no record had been made of the used notes' serial numbers. They insisted on Ronald Whittle delaying his journey while the numbers were copied. It was 3.00am before he reached the phone box, where a Dymo-tape message on the ledge told him to take the ransom money to nearby Bathpool Park.

The place was utterly deserted when he arrived. Earlier in the evening, a courting couple had driven out to the park, and been disturbed and then puzzled by an electric torch which appeared to be signalling to them. They watched for a while, but, as it seemed to be coming no nearer, they paid it no further notice and resumed their love-making.

The kidnapper's nerves were badly upset, though. He was a precise and careful strategist, and he had timed Ronald Whittle's probable journeys. He was already late. The courting couple's car which pulled in and proved unresponsive to his signal was worrying. The arrival of a police panda car – carrying out a routine check that nothing was amiss in the empty parkland – completely panicked him and he fled.

Today the police know that kidnap investigations must be very carefully co-ordinated if they spread across the boundaries of several different forces – four separate forces were engaged in the hunt for Lesley Whittle. Her death, unfortunately, was one of those which went to prove that ordinary policemen on

Lesley Whittle. Press reports brought her to the attention of the Panther.

Dorothy and Ronald Whittle, the mother and brother of kidnap victim Lesley, showing the strain of the lengthy and troubled negotiations for her release.

the beat from one force must not be allowed to stray accidentally into the hot-spots of a major crimewatch mounted by another. The whole incident of the panda car proved so embarrassing that, to this day, it has not been established which force was responsible and who were the officers on duty.

Bathpool Park was searched the following day, but very discreetly, so that the kidnapper should not be further alarmed by thinking his rendezvous had been checked by the authorities. This time, the need for discretion overcame the need for thorough searching, and a vital clue was actually missed. Two schoolboys found an electric torch near an entry to the underground drainage systems of the park, after the police had left the area. They thought nothing of it and, following the good old schoolboy principle, "Finders keepers", kept it without telling anyone.

And with that, the kidnapper of Lesley Whittle went to ground and made no further attempt to collect the ransom.

A week went by before anything material rewarded the police investigation. And then it was plain routine "cop-

> **"YOU ARE ON A TIME LIMIT — IF POLICE OR TRICKS, DEATH"**
> THE BLACK PANTHER'S
> DYMO-TAPE MESSAGE

pering" that gave the CID men their break. A beat constable checking out a car park, 150 yards from the freightliner base where security guard Gerald Smith had been shot, noticed that the registration plates on a Morris 1300 car didn't match the number on its tax disk. The car had stood there, uncollected, for some days. It turned out to be stolen.

It contained a treasure trove of clues: the gun which had been used to shoot Gerald Smith; Lesley Whittle's slippers; a tape recording of her voice; a box of Dymo-tape messages; a mattress; and, most important of all, a box of bullets which could be matched with those used in three earlier shootings which were already under investigation.

Now the police could put a name to the kidnapper. They had photofit likenesses of his appearance. Only they still didn't know his identity. He was a short, athletic white man. The police nicknamed him "The Brace and Bit Man" from his habitual method of breaking and entering.

THE POST OFFICE KILLER

Around 1965, police in Yorkshire discovered that they had a very adept burglar on their patch. He was highly professional. He always wore gloves and left no fingerprints. He never dropped careless clues or indulged giveaway habits like fouling the premises he entered, or eating like a greedy schoolboy from his victims' fridges. He could only be picked out by his efficient and quiet means of gaining access to people's houses. He would drill a hole in the window frame, and insert a piece of wire or a narrow knife blade to free the catch. No noise. No visible mess. No awkward circle of glass on a rubber sucker to dispose of. Just a silent entry through a window which could be closed again from the inside if it was visible from the street, so that no beat policeman ever suspected his presence.

In fact, the "Brace and Bit Man" was so successful that, right up to the point when as "the Black Panther" he was the most wanted man in England, he was never arrested for burglary. He was one of those really successful criminals of whom one normally never hears: the men who avoid the courts or conviction for the whole of their careers.

There was just one weakness to the Brace and Bit Man's professionalism. He didn't seem to have very good inside information on the likelihood of a good haul. His takings were tiny.

In 1967 he changed his strategy. Instead of making his expert entries to suburban houses, he started burgling sub-Post Offices. There would always be *some* useful money there – not as much as could be found at a main Post Office, of course, but enough to be getting on with, and far less securely locked up than that within main Post Offices. A series of raids on sub-Post Offices in Yorkshire, Lancashire and the North Midlands showed how the Brace and Bit Man was now targeting his jobs to ensure a worthwhile take.

In 1972 he was seen for the first time, and proved to be armed and violent. Mr. Leslie Richardson, the sub-postmaster at Haywood, Lancashire, woke up to find a hooded intruder bearing a shotgun in his house. The man threatened Mr. Richardson in a thick West Indian accent. Mr. Richardson ignored his threats, and attacked him without hesitation. The gun discharged, injuring Mr. Richardson, but fortunately spending most of its force blowing a hole in the ceiling. Yet, Mr. Richardson was un-deterred. He pulled the man's mask off, and found to his amazement that he was looking at a white man.

The cunning burglar, who had hoped any description would set the police looking for a West Indian, fled forthwith. And the police had their first general description of the Brace and Bit Man.

Not that it helped a great deal. Nearly all serious burglars are male. The majority of males in England are white.

In February 1974 the Brace and Bit Man killed for the first time. He had broken into Donald Skepper's sub-Post Office in Harrogate, menaced Mr. Skepper's 18-year-old son with his shotgun, and forced him into his parents' bedroom to find the safe keys. When Mr. Skepper woke up to see his son in the hands of a hooded gunman, he bravely leaped out of bed, shouting, "Let's get him!"

The Brace and Bit Man made no mistakes this time. He shot Donald Skepper dead at point-blank range and ran away.

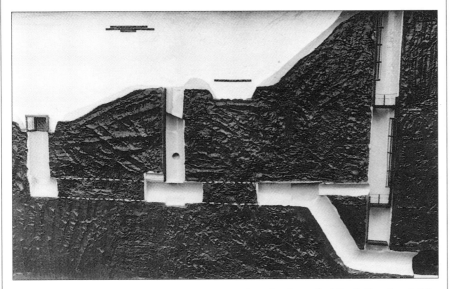

A plan of the drainage complex in Bathpool Park where the Black Panther held kidnap victim Lesley Whittle until her murder.

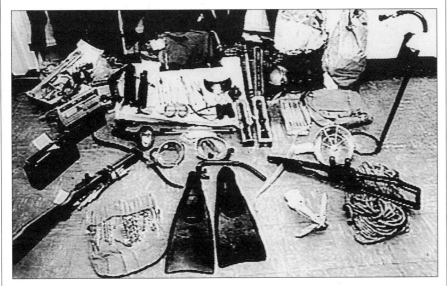

The array of combat gear found at Neilson's home. Neilson insisted that his wife, Irene, train with him in combat and survival techniques.

In September the Black Panther killed sub-postmaster Derek Astin near Accrington. Mr. Astin was recuperating from an operation when he awoke to find the hooded marauder in the house and grappled with him. Mrs. Astin woke up, and tried to use a vacuum cleaner as a weapon with which to help her husband. In the melée the gun went off, Mr. Astin's arm was almost severed, and the gunman fell backward downstairs. Even in the turmoil, Mrs. Astin was impressed by the acrobatic speed and strength the villain showed as he sprang to his feet and made off. Tragically, Mr. Astin bled to death from his wound.

Now the police dubbed this man "the Black Panther". It was, perhaps, an unduly romantic nickname for an essen-tially squalid villain, but it summed up his effective self-concealment in dark clothes and a black hood, coupled with the impressive stealth of his entries, and the steel-muscled agility with which he could recover his balance and escape from a tight spot.

In November 1974, the Black Panther murdered Sidney Grayland at his sub-Post Office in Langley, near Birmingham. The Panther had an ammonia bottle taped to his torch on this occasion, and when Mr. Grayland grappled with him, it backfired and squirted over his mask. Blinded and enraged, the Panther tore the hood off and kicked Mr. Grayland before shooting him in the stomach. When Mrs. Grayland came in, her dying husband said, "Watch it, Peg. I have been hit." Fearing that Mrs. Grayland could identify him, having seen him without his mask, the Panther battered her savagely, and left her for dead.

But Mrs. Grayland survived, and helped the police assemble the photofit picture of the killer. It was severely criticized later as being misleading. The killer's hair looked quite different from normal when Mrs. Grayland saw him, as it had been flattened by the mask, then ruffled when the mask was torn off.

The Post Office offered a £25,000 reward for information that would lead to the arrest of the killer. The public responded, but the misleading photofit hampered the investigation and all the information gathered as a result of it had to be discounted.

Police about to enter the underground network of tunnels used as a kidnap base by the Black Panther.

VITAL CLUE

This, then, was the ruthless and violent villain who had Lesley Whittle in his clutches. But no one knew where, in his wide-ranging territory, he might have hidden her.

At last, seven weeks after Lesley's disappearance, the vital clue to her whereabouts turned up. The two school-boys who had found the torch finally took it to the police. A Dymo-tape message was taped to it: "Drop suitcase into hole." It was clear they had picked it up close to the point where the courting couple had seen a torch flashing. Bathpool Park was thoroughly searched again by police with tracker dogs. The reference to a hole directed attention to the subterranean passages below the park.

In addition to the park's normal drainage system, British Rail had built a network of tunnels and conduits in the 1960s to carry off water from a new railway tunnel replacing the old Victorian excavation. The Black Panther, it transpired, knew all about the old Victorian railway line, and proposed to use it as an emergency escape route. He had found on entering the network a vast underground hideaway at his disposal, much of it equipped with the platforms and ladders used by the engineers who had constructed the courseways.

After fully exploring the complex, the killer made his base on a platform toward the bottom of the main shaft. Here he had hidden Lesley Whittle. Her body was found by the police on the second day of their search. She was hanging, naked, by a wire noose around her neck. She had been dead ever since the police panda car inadvertently aborted the ransom pick-up.

The body of Lesley Whittle is removed from the Black Panther's hideaway in Bathpool Park, seven weeks after her disappearance.

Chief Superintendent Bob Booth, who led the hunt for Lesley, described the Panther as "evil" and "terribly wicked".

ARREST AT LAST

The hated Black Panther was now the most wanted man in England. Scotland Yard took over co-ordinating the kidnapping investigation team with the sub-Post Office murders' team. An angry Ronald Whittle revealed that, apart from external delays, the Panther's taped instructions had been so inexact that he had been unable to follow them expeditiously. He blamed the press for giving the case such high-profile coverage, which he believed had contributed to the panic that had led the Panther to kill his victim.

But for all the determined search, the Black Panther evaded discovery. Eight months went by, and still the police were no nearer to catching him. In the end he was taken by good old-fashioned "coppering". P.C.s Stuart Mackenzie and Antony White, on patrol in a panda car, saw a man with a large hold-all moving furtively through Mansfield Woodhouse in Nottinghamshire. As a matter of routine, they stopped him. The man responded by pulling a shotgun and ordering them to drive him to the safety of a nearby village.

As they approached the village, and P.C. Mackenzie slowed down, the gunman's attention wavered. P.C. White immediately made a grab for the gun which went off, injuring his hand. Fortunately, the main force of the blast expended itself through the roof of the car. P.C. Mackenzie ground the vehicle to a halt opposite a fish and chip shop, and two men from the queue ran to assist the policemen.

The phenomenally fit and athletic Panther put up a remarkable struggle and in the course of it was severely bruised and suffered a bloody nose and massively swollen black eye.

He was taken to Kidsgrove police station. His hold-all contained masks and burglary equipment which pretty clearly identified him as the Black Panther, but he resisted questioning for 12 hours, and refused to give his name or confess to anything. Finally he cracked and revealed that he was Donald Neilson, a self-employed decorator from Bradford.

A quick search of his home turned up a dreadful collection of weaponry and equipment. Neilson, it transpired, was a survival and combat freak, who collected guns, camouflage clothing and quantities of assault and combat equipment. His armoury included knives, a sawn-off shotgun, a .22 rifle with telescopic sights, a crossbow and hundreds of rounds of ammunition. There were also two rolls of wire, identical to that used to hang Lesley Whittle.

Gruesome evidence: the wire noose that killed Lesley Whittle.

At last Neilson confessed. He was the Panther; indeed, he seemed to take a perverse pride in the evil skills that had won him the nickname, but he denied murdering anybody. All the deaths had been accidental. The sub-postmasters had startled him and the guns went off by mischance. Lesley Whittle had been left safe and sound on the platform with the wire noose clamped round her neck to prevent her from trying to escape. Unfortunately, Neilson's hasty return from the aborted ransom mission had startled her, and she slipped and fell off the platform to her instant death. That was to be his defence.

THE CAREER OF DONALD NAPPEY

Donald Neilson was born Donald Nappey in 1947. A small, aggressive boy at school, he resented the teasing his surname brought. He grew up into a rather rigid, non-smoking, non-drinking lad, whose favourite recreation was going to dances in Bradford. He was apprenticed to a carpenter, but found his metier in National Service in 1955. His rigid personality made him a slow learner, but what he finally mastered he mastered fully. He enjoyed training for jungle warfare against the Mau Mau in Kenya and active service against the EOKA terrorist organization in Cyprus.

He married Irene Tate, two years older than himself, while he was still in the army and immediately drew her into the secretive, private world where he felt safest. Their wedding was so private that

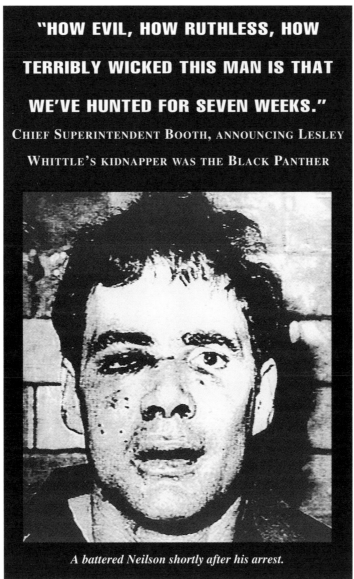

"HOW EVIL, HOW RUTHLESS, HOW TERRIBLY WICKED THIS MAN IS THAT WE'VE HUNTED FOR SEVEN WEEKS."
CHIEF SUPERINTENDENT BOOTH, ANNOUNCING LESLEY WHITTLE'S KIDNAPPER WAS THE BLACK PANTHER

A battered Neilson shortly after his arrest.

Irene's twin sister was not invited. When Donald left the army, Irene became a surrogate military unit, ruled with a rod of iron, cut off from friends and reduced to wearing shabby clothes.

Her spare time was given over to "training" with Donald; training in breaking into empty houses – starting with her parents' home; training in survival and combat exercises in woods and parklands. Donald started to build up his collection of weapons, and wore combat fatigues so obsessively that neighbours nicknamed him "Castro". When the couple's daughter, Kathryn, was born, Donald abandoned his hated surname and called himself Neilson. Deeply resentful of his low earnings, in 1965 he began to put his training and military gear to use in highly proficient burglaries.

His trial took place in Oxford, outside the area where he had aroused so much fear and loathing. The proceedings lasted three weeks, and Neilson put forward his limp defence that he was simply accident-prone. The prosecution made a lot of his claim that it was necessary to leave Lesley Whittle naked and noosed around the neck if he had no intention of harming her. Donald could give no rational explanation for not having fastened her feet or hands as well.

The jury agreed with the prosecution that he had lost his nerve or his temper, and deliberately pushed Lesley to her death when his ransom meet had gone awry. In sentencing him to life imprisonment, the judge commented, "In your case, life must mean life."

GARY
GILMORE

As a criminal, Gary Gilmore was a no-account recidivist failure. In and out of prison from the time he was 15, spending 18 of his 37 years behind bars, he never committed any really lucrative robbery; never associated with any great gangland figures or truly skilled thieves. He was a nickels-and-dimes thief, holding up gas stations and late-night stores. The murders for which he was executed were senseless shootings of harmless night-shift workers.

■

No, GILMORE'S MAJOR importance is constitutional, not criminal. He was the man whose obstinate machismo led the US Supreme Court to overrule one of its earlier decisions. He caused the USA to step back towards barbarism. After 10 years during which execution had been deemed "cruel and unusual punishment", and therefore unconstitutional, Gary Gilmore insisted on being shot for his crimes. He, more than any other individual, brought about the restoration of capital punishment in America – in 1976.

Gilmore had little hope of growing up an honest and worthy citizen. His father was a professional thief. Gary started stealing when he was 10, and by the time he was 14 he had, on his own admission, broken into 50 or more houses. He was sent to a reformatory, the McClaren School for Boys.

However, as experience has shown, custodial sentences for determined adolescent offenders are very unlikely to prove rehabilitating. Incarceration serves the useful purpose of preventing them from mugging old ladies, but, with the best will in the world, reformatory staff have little hope of overcoming the peer group pressure on the bad boys to link arms and unite against punitive authority. The finest classrooms and tool shops will never make approved lessons interest the young crook as much as the skills of housebreaking, auto theft and disposal of stolen property which can be learned in a University of Crime.

A CRIMINAL CAREER

Gilmore graduated from the reformatory as a violent and dangerous criminal. At the age of 22 he succeeded in earning a

15-year sentence for armed robbery. He spent much of his prison time in maximum security jails; quite often in solitary confinement. His internal rage and hatred was not exclusively focused on respectable society: he and a fellow convict beat and knifed another prisoner so severely that the man nearly died. While Gilmore had some talent and some intelligence, it was completely warped and he was without question unfit to mingle in decent society. Like many convicts, he had some skill as a draughtsman, but this was not the same as having the creative vision of an artist. He had also read and reflected a lot, like many prisoners who have spent time in solitary, but the impression that he was a more interesting man than the average stick-'em-up hoodlum was misleading.

Gilmore's mental horizons were bounded by the petty criminal's usual mind-boggling egocentricity and short-sightedness. He valued nothing more highly than his own gratification, and was quite incapable of perceiving the consequences of his actions, let alone accepting responsibility for them. He could produce momentary ingratiating charm to wheedle his own way with other people, or flashes of self-deprecation if that was the best way to get others to serve his immediate ends. But he was simply not gifted with any real capacity to feel consideration for others, and was incapable of true self-assessing shame, from which he might have moved forward to self-control.

His reaction to frustration was rage. He did not try to hold it back and reacted with violence against those who impeded his wishes. When he could not impose his will on the world, he turned against himself. In Oregon Prison he made 16 suicide attempts, once swallowing a razor blade. He also tried to drag others into his self-destructive cycles, twice making suicide pacts with other inmates.

"HE IS A PRODUCT OF THIS INSTITUTIONAL SYSTEM THAT WE HAVE. IT DIDN'T WORK."
RONALD STANGER, GILMORE'S ATTORNEY

FINAL FREEDOM

On April 9, 1976, he was released on parole from a 15-year sentence for armed robbery. He was obviously a hopeless case. There could be no reasonable prognosis for his becoming a useful citizen, but relatives in Provo, near Orem, Utah, agreed to sponsor his parole and give him a roof over his head. His uncle Vern

Vern Damico, who did his best for his errant nephew, Gary.

Damico and his married cousin Brenda did their best for Gary.

They found him a job in a factory. They helped him buy a car. They nursed the delusion that there was no reason why he shouldn't go. After all, like many institutionalized recidivists, Gary made a big point of intending never to go back to jail. To the unwary, this familiar tune may sound like a firm purpose of amendment.

The first tiny sign that it wasn't all going to be easy soon showed. Vern accepted that a man who'd been locked up in teetotal conditions for a long time welcomed the opportunity to enjoy a few cans of beer again. It didn't really cross anyone's mind that Gary was a little too enthusiastic about relaxing with the booze after all his enforced relaxation without any.

Furthermore, Gary's whining objections that the car obtained for him wasn't as good as he wanted should have set off alarm bells. The inability to accept frustrating reality without angry complaint is one of the first triggers of criminality. Gary's very dubious skirting around the bounds of legality as he set about exchanging the car for a truck and welching on his agreements to pay instalments showed (yet again) that he hadn't really changed.

Probably no one was desperately surprised that Gary proved a bad workman. A long-term ex-prisoner is hardly likely to be good at time-keeping, once it depends on his own efforts. His gratitude to the man who has overlooked his past and employed him need not be expected to last much more than a few days and weeks. The temptation to slope off and pilfer soon triumphs over the wish to obey benevolent authority. Dealing in stolen guns on the side was not a desirable activity. But gun-happy American society saw a lot of it, and Gary's relatives meekly tolerated his coming in with firearms which he wanted them to hide.

NICOLE

Real trouble, however, came when Gary fell in love. Like many long-term convicts, he had lost the art of relating easily and sociably to women. He had remained resolutely heterosexual throughout his incarceration, firmly resisting all opportunities to participate in the homosexual scene which exists in every jail that permits any association between prisoners. So unlike, say, John Dillinger, who kept his charismatic skills with women well honed by daily seductions of young men whenever he was incarcerated, Gary emerged into the free world utterly unable to practice normal social intercourse with attractive women. He was either rude and self-absorbed, or proffered crude and tasteless sexual propositions. Naturally, these invited and received rebuffs or, if Gary's coarse sexual invitations were accepted, the object of his intentions was herself usually pretty disturbed.

Nicole Baker was just 19 when the 37-year-old Gilmore met her. She had already been married three times, and she had two children. Although she was young and attractive, any mature man

would have realized that her emotional life was likely to be as messily confused as the slummy surroundings in which she lived. Gary was blind to any drawbacks.

The Damicos had mixed feelings about his insistence that he was moving out and going to live with Nicole. They

"HE KILLED THEM INSTEAD OF KILLING ME."
NICOLE BAKER

Nicole Baker, who had a destabilizing effect on Gilmore.

doubted whether his association with her would prove a stabilizing influence. It was not really part of the terms of his parole that he should leave his relatives' emotionally secure home and shack up with a teenager who was only a few removes from being a wayward girl. But, on the other hand, Gary's own instability was not proving an entirely welcome addition to the Damicos' happy home life. They felt they could do without his

persistent unthinking selfishness, and the worried approaches from people like his employer and the man whose car Gary was supposed to be buying: approaches which indicated that Gary's ideas of "going straight" were not those of the honest workaday world.

The cohabitation of Gary Gilmore and Nicole Baker proved a disaster. They lived together for six weeks. Gary sketched her: accomplished drawings, which brought out the little girl quality he found appealing (and unthreatening) in her. But Nicole was not willing to be a doormat. She was not impressed when he went back to stealing, nor was she prepared to stop seeing other men. They fought, and, more than once, possessive Gary threatened to kill the girl whose name he had tattooed on his forearm.

On July 13 they had a final explosive quarrel. Gary kicked Nicole out of the house. Fearing his rage, she went into hiding. Now Gary became obsessed with finding her. On July 19 he went to his mother's house, and took back a stolen gun he had left with her.

MURDER

That night he committed the first of his two murders. He took Nicole's sister for a ride in his truck, and left her in the parked vehicle while he walked into the Sinclair gas station in Orem. Max Jensen, a 24-year-old married student, was on duty, working out his summer vacation there as a forecourt attendant.

Gilmore pointed his gun at Jensen and made him empty his pockets, then he told him to lie face down on the floor. Jensen obeyed, and Gary shot him twice through the head, saying as he did so, "This one's for me and this one's for Nicole." He ransacked the place, making off with all the loose cash he could find – a beggarly $125.

The following night he drove the few miles to Provo on his own. He took his truck to a service station, claiming it was overheating. The mechanic told him it would take just 20 minutes to fit a new thermostat. Gary declared that he would walk around, rather than wait.

He walked into the City Center Motel, almost next door to his uncle's house, where he forced the young manager, Ben Bushnell, to lie down. Like Max Jensen, Bushnell was a married student at Brigham Young University. Gary shot him twice through the head, and made off with a cashbox which, once again, contained about $125.

Now his hopeless incompetence came fully into play. He decided to get rid of his incriminating gun by dumping it in nearby bushes – an almost sure-fire way of ensuring it would be found and traced back to him – but he bungled even that silly plan. He caught his wrist on the bush as he was depositing the gun; it went off, shooting him in the hand. He went back to the garage trailing blood. As soon as the mechanic heard about the murder, he telephoned the police.

Gary asked a friend to drive him to the airport. The friend suggested he ought to go to hospital instead. Gary promptly telephoned his cousin and parole sponsor, Brenda, asking for her help. Brenda pretended she was coming

Gilmore (with beard) at the time of his arrest in Salt Lake City.

over to fetch him but, sensibly, she telephoned the police and told them where he was. She felt unhappy about having to do this, as most of us would. But Gary's shallowness meant that he ultimately accepted the inevitability of her action.

Once in prison again, Gary's first priority was to see Nicole. He was far more interested in that than in any questions of his defence. Nicole believed that his murders were intimately connected with their separation. "He killed them instead of killing me," she observed.

TRIAL AND AFTERMATH

The trial was unremarkable. The defence called no witnesses. Gary had never denied to his lawyers that he intended to kill the attendant when he went into the Sinclair gas station: he'd been building up a "head of steam" for some weeks,

and knew he was going to release it by killing. And having done so once, he knew it was inevitable that he would go on killing. To the suggestion that sex might provide a better release than murder, Gilmore offered the astonishing response, "I don't want to mess with questions of sex. I think they're cheap."

As that half-educated pseudo-morality suggests, it was the state's reformatory system that seemed to be on trial as much as Gary Gilmore. Here was a man who had been in the hands of law enforcement and rehabilitating officials for more than half his natural life. All they had produced was a monster who could cold-bloodedly kill twice for no sensible reason; feel no remorse and not a shred of concern for his victims and their families; and who had the almighty gall to think himself gifted with superior

The legal arguments over, Gilmore makes his final journey, January 17, 1977.

taste to sympathizers who wondered whether sexual frustration had contributed to his growing tension. Well might defending lawyer Ronald Stanger remark, "He is a product of this institutional system that we have. Since the age of 14 years he was under the care and control of the rehabilitation system. It didn't work. Why didn't it work? With Gilmore, that's the question."

It wasn't a question that the authorities wanted to answer. District Attorney Noall Wootton recognized that Gilmore had not been rehabilitated and did not believe he ever could be. He rightly saw him as a perpetual menace to society and treated the question as one of economics,

with Gilmore as some form of subhuman life form that it would cost taxpayers' money to keep alive in captivity:

"It just wasn't realistic to think that he'd ever be rehabilitated. One of the things I thought at the time, but I didn't argue it, was that you could give him life in prison. The only thing we could do, probably, is lock him up in a cage like he was a gorilla at the zoo. But even with gorillas, somebody's got to go in and clean out the cage once in a while. And the only logical conclusion is that the man just has to be destroyed."

It was no surprise that the jury found Gilmore guilty and no surprise that the court followed the existing Utah state

law and pronounced the death penalty. The murders, revolting as they were, would normally have caused no ripples outside Provo and Orem.

Nor would there have been any concern that the execution was suspended while its constitutional validity was questioned. The Supreme Court had agreed in 1972 that one state's capital penalty represented cruel and unusual punishment, and so it was tacitly banned. In practice, no one had been executed in America for 10 years, and Death Rows up and down the country were filled with convicted murderers who would never go to their destined deaths at the hands of the law. Gilmore, having expressed his preference for execution by shooting rather than hanging (as the state law of Utah permitted) would simply have stayed in prison while his lawyers appealed for a stay of execution.

However, Gilmore changed all that. He fired his lawyers when they made the successful appeal on his behalf. He told a fellow prisoner, "They're figuring to give me the death penalty, but I have an answer for that. I'm going to make them do it. Then we'll see if they have as much guts as I do."

His vaunted "guts" didn't represent quite as much fortitude as he claimed. In November he was granted a visit from Nicole. By prearrangement, she smuggled in an overdose of Seconal to him, concealed in a balloon stuffed inside her body. Gilmore entered into another of his suicide pacts with her and, at the appointed time, he took the Seconal, and she took Seconal and Dalmane. Her three-year-old son led neighbours in to her comatose body when he couldn't wake her up. She was taken to hospital to have her stomach pumped. Her favourite picture of Gary was clasped to her bosom, and when she recovered she had to be sent to a mental hospital. In her own interests, she was not allowed to communicate with Gilmore again.

Gilmore's suicide attempt may have been more show than reality. He was quickly discovered and transferred to the prison hospital. The sheriff's department swore that Gilmore would be closely guarded from then on.

THE CONSTITUTIONAL BATTLE

Gary's legal actions thereafter formed a sort of suicide attempt, though. His new lawyers demanded, on his behalf, that the execution proceed. Gary had spent too long in prison already, they were instructed to say. He wanted the law to take its course.

All manner of pressure groups recognized the danger of letting one ignorant villain force a vital constitutional point on continental USA. From the left, the American Civil Liberties Union led the legal struggle to keep Gilmore alive, supported by the Socialist Workers Party of America. From the right of the political spectrum, Citizens Against Pornography also showed an awareness that capital punishment appeals to baser instincts than many of its supporters realize. The Right to Life group turned their attention from abortion for a moment to join the agitation to keep Gary from execution.

Gary callously dismissed all these people, whose lives of dedication and commitment to the welfare of others contrasted so strongly with his own useless self-gratification: "They always want to get in on the act, basically. I don't think they've ever done anything effective in their lives. I would like them all, including that group of reverends and rabbis from Salt Lake City, to just butt out.... If this is my life and it's my death, it's been sanctioned by the courts that I die, and I accept that."

But how genuine was he? He made yet another attempt to poison himself, taking an overdose of Phenobarbitol after a courtroom telephone failed to connect him with Nicole. An embarrassed prison warden had to admit that the guard over Gary Gilmore had been slackened, since the cost of watching him constantly in case of suicide was proving prohibitive.

Gilmore was by now a celebrity. Agent Lawrence Schiller represented his interests as first a photo-journalist, then the writer Norman Mailer wrote books and articles on him. By the time the Supreme Court had decided that Utah was constitutionally entitled to enact the death penalty, Gary Gilmore was, for the first time in his life, a rich man.

And what did he want to do with this money? He offered it to his lawyer in return for a smuggled suit of clothes that he might use to try and effect his escape! So much for his genuine determination to race to the grave. His lawyer, naturally, turned the idea down flat.

In the end, there was nothing anyone could do to stop the execution. With the laconic last words, "Let's do it", Gary Gilmore was strapped to a chair in front of an absorbent mass of plywood, sandbags, and a dirty mattress. Five volunteer police marksmen aimed from behind a curtain at the target pinned over his heart. The four live bullets in their randomly distributed guns all found their mark. (The fifth, a blank, was to allow any executioner who later regretted his participation in the execution to believe that he had had no part in it.) After living on for two minutes, Gary Gilmore expired, his role in changing American legal history for the worse completed.

The chair in which Gilmore was executed. Over the back is the black hood he wore.

SON OF SAM
SERIAL KILLER

It takes a lot to frighten a New Yorker. Some say that's because violent death in New York is so common it barely makes the newspapers anymore. But New Yorkers were scared when a killer who called himself the Son of Sam stalked the streets of the Big Apple. David Berkowitz was illegitimate and adopted. He felt robbed of a personality and tried to be many people. Increasingly alienated, he eventually found a personality, somebody he was happy being. He was famous – as the Son of Sam.

■

IN 1641 JONAS BRONCK established a farm on a piece of land opposite Manhattan Island. The area took his name – it's now known as the Bronx – and eventually became one of the most densely populated residential areas in the USA. Today the South Bronx is noted as a hotbed of crime, but moving further north one finds some quieter areas.

In one of these, Buhre Avenue, at one o'clock in the morning on July 29, 1976, Donna Lauria and Jody Valenti were sitting in a car. Donna, an 18-year-old medical technician, and Jody, 19 years old and a student nurse, were saying goodnight. Donna half opened the car door to get out. Suddenly a man appeared out of the darkness. He pulled a gun out of his pocket, aimed at Donna and pulled the trigger. A bullet hit her in the neck. A second bullet struck Jody in the thigh. Donna was raced to hospital for treatment, but she never made it. Jody described her killer as aged about 30 with curly black hair.

Bordering the Bronx is another of New York's five boroughs, Queens. It was named for King Charles II's queen consort, Catherine of Braganza. Predominantly residential, like the Bronx, it has several neighbourhoods: Astoria, College Point, Corona, Douglaston, Flushing, Forest Hills, Jackson Heights, Jamaica, Kew Gardens, Long Island City, Maspeth, Rego Park, Saint Albans, and Sunnyside. It was in the oddly named neighbourhood of Flushing, on October 23, 1976, that Carl Denaro and his girlfriend Rosemary Keenan were sitting talking in Rosemary's Volkswagen, in front of a tavern. A shot was fired and Denaro was hit. He survived – and a .44 bullet was found on the floor of his car.

A month later, again in Queens, two teenage girls were shot at and injured. Sixteen-year-old Donna DeMasi and 18-year-old Joanne Lomino were returning home from a visit to the cinema. They saw a man standing in the shadows and became scared. They walked faster and got to Joanne Lomino's home. The man followed them. It was just 12.30am. The man came up to them and began to ask a question. Suddenly he produced a gun and began shooting. A bullet lodged in Joanne's spine, paralyzing her for life. A .44 bullet was found lodged in the woodwork of the house.

The Queens attacker was described by several people, but they said with certainty that he had blond hair. The police didn't connect the shootings with the murder in the Bronx of Donna Lauria.

In Forest Hills, Queens, on January 30, 1977, 26-year-old Christine Freund went with her boyfriend John Diel to see the popular boxing movie *Rocky*, which made a star of Sylvester Stallone. About midnight they were sitting in Diel's car. Suddenly gunshots shattered the passenger window. Christine, shot point-blank in the face, died immediately. Later her boyfriend voiced the opinion of many, including the police department, that there was a serial killer on the loose. "This man has got to be caught," he said.

"Because he will injure or kill a lot more people if he's not caught..."

By now the police had connected all the shootings. They had been carried out with the same gun, a .44 caliber Bulldog

"THIS MAN HAS GOT TO BE CAUGHT – BECAUSE HE WILL INJURE OR KILL A LOT MORE PEOPLE IF HE'S NOT CAUGHT..."

JOHN DIEL, WHOSE GIRLFRIEND WAS ONE OF BERKOWITZ'S FIRST VICTIMS

Christine Freund, blasted by shotgun at close range.

Virginia Voskerishian, disproved police theory.

Stacy Moscowitz, fatally wounded in the head.

Bobby Violante, blinded by the .44 caliber killer.

pistol. Fired at short range this cumbersome weapon was lethal. The mystery gunmen thus acquired the nickname that would stick throughout the investigation: the Forty-Four Caliber Killer.

NEW YORK BATTLEFIELD

Police Commissioner Mike Codd held a press conference on March 10, 1977: "We all think the commonsense approach would be, in reading the newspapers and seeing the coverage that it is getting on television, that any young girl or fella would not park for any great length of time in an automobile in any desolate location, especially dark ones and especially late in the evening." It was a frightening warning.

Mike Codd added that he had over 60 detectives working full-time on the case, that the police were receiving lots of phone calls, and letters were pouring in from all over the United States. Every clue was being followed up. "We hope, er, that the right lead will come one of these days and, er, we'll eventually make an arrest."

The Police Commissioner was wrong about one thing. It wasn't just people sitting in cars who were at risk from the maniac.

On March 8, 1977, Virginia Voskerishian was heading home to Exeter Street in Queens. A student at Barnard College, she stepped aside to let a young man pass. He pulled out a gun and shot her dead, with .44 caliber bullets.

Five weeks later, on April 17, 1977, close to where Donna Lauria had been killed in the North Bronx, Valentina

The bulletin board at the 109th Precinct in July 1977, a year after the first Son of Sam killings. By this point the psychopathic killer had struck seven times.

Suriani and Alexander Esau sat in their parked car. Valentina, aged 18, was a student of acting at Lehman College. Alexander worked with a tow truck. In the car they embraced, then kissed. A gun was fired. Both were killed. Again the bullets were .44 caliber.

This time a letter was left, addressed to Captain Joe Borelli. One part read: "I feel like an outsider. I am on a different wavelength than everybody else, programmed to kill. I love to hunt, prowling the streets looking for fair game, tasty meat. I am the Son of Sam."

The name "Son of Sam" caught the public imagination. New York became obsessed by the killings, and with the obsession came terror. A little while later there came a second letter. This one was received by James Breslin, a columnist on the *New York Daily News*. It began: "Hello from the gutters of New York City which are filled with dog manure, vomit, stale wine, urine and blood... Sam's a thirsty lad. He won't let me stop killing until he gets his fill of blood."

Sam almost got his blood soon enough. On June 26, 1977, Judy Placido

and Salvatore Lupo were sitting in Salvatore's car. They'd been to a discotheque. Suddenly their world exploded. Shot at point-blank range, both suffered severe injuries but, incredibly, neither was killed. Witnesses spotted a man running away and were able to describe him. The problem presented to the police by these descriptions was that, while the weapon used in the killings was the same, the killer was variously described as having either blond hair or curly dark hair. There were either two killers or a single killer who wore a wig. A photofit picture that was issued gave both images.

FIRST DATE, LAST KILLING

On July 31, 1977, Bobby Violante, 20 years old and a clothing salesman, and 20-year-old telex operator Stacy Moscowitz were on their first date. They'd been to see a movie, *New York, New York*, then gone for a meal. At 1.45am they were cuddling in Bobby's car under the yellow light of a street lamp on Shore Parkway, near the Coney Island fairground. They kissed – and a bullet ripped into Stacy's head. She died the next day. The irony was that she'd only recently been talking with her sister and estimated the chances of coming face to face with the Forty-Four Caliber Killer as several millions to one against. Bobby took the full impact of the shot in the face and was blinded.

Nobody knew it, but Stacy would be the last victim of the Forty-Four Caliber Killer, or the Son of Sam as he was becoming better known. There was a witness to the murder: Mrs. Cecilia Davies, who initially remained silent for fear that the Son of Sam would kill her, came forward to say that at 2.00am she had seen a yellow Ford Galaxie illegally parked near a fire hydrant. A young man had taken a parking ticket off the windscreen and driven away.

The police checked the parking ticket records and identified the car as belonging to David Richard Berkowitz, who lived in Yonkers. They paid a visit to his apartment. Outside they found the yellow Galaxie. They opened it. Inside they found a rifle in a duffel bag and a letter to the commissioner of police. Written in Sam's unmistakable hand, it threatened a shooting in Long Island. "I think we've got him", said Detective Ed Zigo.

For six hours the police staked out the apartment. They rushed forward when a plump, dark-haired man went to the car. He smiled at them warmly. When asked his name, he replied, "I'm Sam." David Berkowitz couldn't have been more helpful. He cheerfully confessed to the killings and to having written the "Son of Sam" letters. A search of his apartment revealed a cache of weapons.

Berkowitz had been arrested in the nick of time. He'd planned on that day, August 10, to go on a killing spree, shooting aimlessly at the crowds in the upper-class area called the Hamptons. He'd slept late that morning, though, and failed to carry out his plan. Instead, he decided to go to a nightclub in Riverdale and open fire there. The duffel bag in the back of his car contained two .22 rifles and an Ithaca 12-gauge shotgun.

ADOPTED

David Richard Berkowitz was born on June 1, 1953, an illegitimate child who was the result of a liaison between a lady

One of the letters that would eventually help the New York Police Department track down the Son of Sam.

named Betty Falco and her lover of long standing, married businessman Joseph Kleinman. Although Berkowitz knew about his adoption from an early age, the discovery that he wasn't born in wedlock seemed to affect him profoundly.

David was adopted by Nathan and Pearl Berkowitz, a respectable Jewish couple. He was spoiled as a child and behaved badly, throwing tantrums and being destructive. Pearl died when Berkowitz was 13 years old. Her death was a considerable shock to him. Even worse, he couldn't adjust when Nathan re-married in 1971, and his resentment towards his stepmother and step-sister was such that he left home. He joined the army, served in Korea (where he experimented with drugs) and, on returning to his home city, New York, took a variety of dead-end jobs, before ending up working in a lowly capacity in the postal service.

The news that the crazed killer had at last been caught spread through New York like wildfire. On the one hand neighbours expressed total surprise, even shock, at David Berkowitz being revealed as the Son of Sam. "He was really nice to us," said one. "I'm shocked to hear it was him because I would never have thought it was," said another. A third said, "Right in my own back yard, you know you never believe it...."

On the other hand, relieved New Yorkers were happy Berkowitz had been caught. One made a particularly chilling comment, unintentionally likening New Yorkers to soldiers in a war zone: "I'm just so glad they caught him because I have a child of my own. And you worry every night when he goes out, if he's ever coming back."

Another New Yorker told a TV camera: "The panic's over. Everyone was afraid, everyone was pointing the fingers at this one, pointing the fingers at that one. Afraid to sit on a stoop. No one wanted to go out, come home at night. It's over, they got him."

For the police questioners, meanwhile, a bizarre story was unfolding. Berkowitz said that orders to kill had been transmitted to him via a black Labrador belonging to a neighbour named Sam Carr. He also said that demon voices originated from Carr, that Carr was his "Infernal Father". On investigation the police discovered that, although Carr had never met Berkowitz, he had received a number of letters from him complaining about his dog barking and howling.

Berkowitz further claimed that he'd tried to firebomb Carr's house and shoot the dog, but that the dog had survived – proof, said Berkowitz, that it was the devil in disguise. He was admitted to Kings County Hospital for psychiatric examination.

Two weeks later, David Berkowitz was taken to court and the formal proceedings began. The prosecution, in the shape of the Kings County District Attorney, produced a report from a forensic psychiatrist, Dr. David Abrahamsen, which maintained that "...while the defendant shows paranoid traits, they do not interfere with his fitness to stand trial." Mark Heller, Berkowitz's attorney, declared that Berkowitz was innocent on the grounds of insanity and produced two

David Berkowitz (centre) was taken into custody after a tense six-hour stake-out at his apartment. Nearest to the camera is Detective Edward Zigo.

psychiatrists who stated that, in their professional opinion, he was suffering from advanced paranoid schizophrenia.

There was some debate about whether or not Berkowitz was fit to stand trial, but eventually he pleaded guilty. His defence of insanity was accepted and the full trial never went ahead. He was jailed for 365 years.

Once in prison Berkowitz wrote a diary. In it he explained that as a child

he'd had severe nightmares that sent him running hysterically into his parents' bedroom. As he grew up, he said, the demonic "voices" caused him to behave badly. He began lighting fires. From late 1975 and throughout 1976 he started no fewer than 1,488 fires, several of them causing serious damage. He then shot a few neighbourhood dogs and wrote threatening letters to neighbours. He also wrote about how demons had possessed him and ordered him to kill.

As he writes, his handwriting changes. First he is calm, almost naive in his review of his current position in Kings County Hospital. Then the handwriting quickly changes as Berkowitz is supposedly possessed by demons. He writes of killing whores and

> **THE POLICE RUSHED FORWARD WHEN A PLUMP, DARK-HAIRED MAN WENT TO THE CAR. HE SMILED AT THEM WARMLY. WHEN ASKED HIS NAME, THE MAN SIMPLY SAID, "I'M SAM."**

their offspring. Then it changes again, the content of his writing becoming more intellectual. He made a request for a direct telephone link to the office of Detective Keenan and writes of the need for the police to set up a Demon Task Force – "a monumental step in the annals of justice and historical law" – and of a Demon Hospital for the specialized treatment of the possessed.

In his diary he writes about hearing the demons – about how they were in the walls of his apartment and how he kicked at the walls. "Nothing happened. It just didn't have any effect. I could hear deep in the wall a lot of sounds. Voices, thousands of them. Screams. Funny sounds. Music... I tried to do what they said, but they were never satisfied.... I wasn't a bad person, but they were making me do bad things. I didn't want to. I did everything they said to do, and still they weren't satisfied."

Interestingly, perhaps significantly, in November 1975 he took time off work, locked himself in his apartment room and apparently prepared himself for the mission he was planning to undertake. The following month he went out to kill. He stabbed 15-year-old Michelle Foreman. He didn't kill her, but inflicted terrible injuries on her. Her screams frightened Berkowitz, but he felt satisfied with the attack and celebrated by dining at a cheap restaurant.

In February 1979 Berkowitz admitted that his story about Sam Carr and demons was a lie. He contacted the prosecution witness David Abrahamsen, the only psychiatrist to have refuted his claim of demonic possession and insanity. Abrahamsen was permitted to visit Berkowitz in Attica Prison.

The story Berkowitz told revealed a man who was clever, whose murders were premeditated and planned in minute detail. "I went to so much trouble to succeed and I took such huge risks. I familiarized myself with the streets and possible escape routes from those central areas. Also I managed to learn all the streets by repeated trips into the area. I mean, there were nights in which I travelled all through a certain area...."

He explained that knifing someone was harder than he'd imagined, so he'd bought the .44 pistol. Then he had spent time making elaborate plans. Queens, he said, was special to him. "Shooting someone in Queens was an obsession."

Unfortunately, while Dr. Abrahamsen got Berkowitz to reveal a lot about the inside of a serial killer's mind, as a Freudian he interpreted almost everything as sexually motivated. As a result, his reading of Berkowitz is limited. He put forward the notion that Berkowitz began killing because of the discovery that he was the unwanted result of Betty Falco's affair with Joseph Kleinman. He then tried hard to establish that Berkowitz had been conceived in a parked car. Berkowitz was symbolically attacking Betty Falco and Joseph Kleinman when he shot people in parked cars, Abrahamsen suggested. Abrahamsen also put forward the idea that Berkowitz received sexual gratification from the killings, but Berkowitz denied this: "I had no sexual feelings," he said. Abrahamsen seems to have disregarded parts of Berkowitz's story or reinterpreted them to suit his own conclusions.

Berkowitz killed because he felt the world hated him and laughed at him. The demons were of his own creation. People were his tormentors; women tormented him the most. He was a soldier at war with them. He was able to kill without remorse. He wrote: "Some pretty girls at 18 lived three times over, with all the attention they got. If a pretty girl dies, what the hell, she had a good time."

Zigo displays some of the weapons found at the time of Berkowitz's arrest.

THE HILLSIDE
STRANGLERS

Serial killers crop up again and again in the annals of crime history – but their numbers have increased dramatically in recent years. It is estimated that every year in the United States alone 7,000 people fall victim to this particular type of killer. Few things are more terrifying than living in a town which is prey to a serial killer, even when that town is the weirdo capital of the western hemisphere, Los Angeles.

■

IT OFTEN HAPPENS – as in the cases of the Yorkshire Ripper and Son of Sam for example – that the trial of a serial killer develops into a trial of psychiatry, with defence and prosecution psychiatric experts battling to persuade a judge and jury that the accused is or is not insane. The case surrounding Kenneth Bianchi was no exception, but it was singular in the extreme – maybe even unique. Did the mind of Bianchi harbour multiple personalities or was he a consummate actor?

Yolanda Washington was a prostitute. Tall and black, she worked a beat around Hollywood Boulevard in Los Angeles. On October 17, 1977, her body was found on a hillside near Forest Lawn cemetery. She had been stripped naked and strangled with a piece of cloth. An autopsy revealed that she'd had sex with two men, one, interestingly, a non-secretor (someone who doesn't secrete blood with their saliva or sperm). But both men could have been customers, with neither being responsible for her death.

Los Angeles does not have a reputation for peace and tranquillity and the nature of a prostitute's job makes her a target for perverts, weirdos, and psychopaths. Prostitute murders are so common they sometimes don't even rate a comment in the newspapers. The murder of Yolanda Washington was one such non-event in the daily life of LA.

So, too, was the discovery the following month of a second woman's body. This time the victim was young, barely 15 years old. Judy Miller was found naked and strangled, and the autopsy revealed she'd had sex with two men, one a non-secretor. She had worked Hollywood Boulevard, just like Yolanda.

Her body had been dumped from a car in Alta Terrace Drive, in the small town of La Crescenta. Judy's parents had three children and lived in a motel room. Judy had run away, they said.

Five days after Judy Miller's body was found, but before she'd been identified, a third victim was discovered. This was 20-year-old Lissa Kastin. She was found dumped near the golf course of the Chevy Chase Country Club in Glendale. She was naked, strangled, and had had sex with two men. But Lissa Kastin was a dancer who for some time had been working as a waitress. She wasn't a prostitute.

It was clear that a serial killer was on the loose. What made this one so frightening was the speed with which he killed. Within the last three weeks of November 1977, the corpses of seven women were discovered: that of Jill Barcomb, an 18-year-old prostitute, was found on November 10, at Franklin Cyn Drive and Mulholland. Kathleen Robinson, a 17-year-old prostitute, was discovered on November 17, at Pico and Ocean Boulevards. She turned out to be the only victim left clothed by the killer. Kristina Weckler, a 20-year-old art student who studied

in Pasadena but lived in Glendale, was found on a street corner near Glendale. Dollie Cepeda, 12 years old, and Sonja Johnson, 14 years old, were discovered on a rubbish dump. They were found by

PROSTITUTE MURDERS ARE SO COMMON THEY SOMETIMES DON'T EVEN RATE A COMMENT IN THE NEWSPAPERS. THE MURDER OF YOLANDA WASHINGTON WAS ONE SUCH NON-EVENT.

a nine-year-old boy who thought they were discarded store mannequins. They had been raped and sodomized. Another boy was found who'd seen the girls on the night they vanished. He had seen them go up to a large, two-colour sedan and speak to someone on the passenger side. This meant there were two men in the car. The girls were generally nervous about speaking to strangers, but one was known to admire policemen. Could the men have posed as policemen? The body of Jane King, a 28-year-old scientology student, missing since November 9, was found in some bushes off the Golden State freeway.

Lauren Wagner, an 18-year-old student, was also found in some bushes, this time in Cliff Drive, Glendale. In this case there was a witness who had seen Lauren abducted. Beulah Stofer said she had seen Lauren's car pull up. A big dark sedan with a white top had pulled alongside it and two men jumped out. There was an argument, then Lauren had got in the other car and been driven away. Mrs. Stofer had heard her say: "You won't get away with this." She was able to describe the men. One had bushy hair, was Latin-looking and

Prostitute Yolanda Washington, the Stranglers' first known victim.

Lauren Wagner was last seen alive getting into a dark sedan.

Sonia Johnson's body was found on a rubbish dump.

Jill Barcomb was another prostitute victim of the Stranglers.

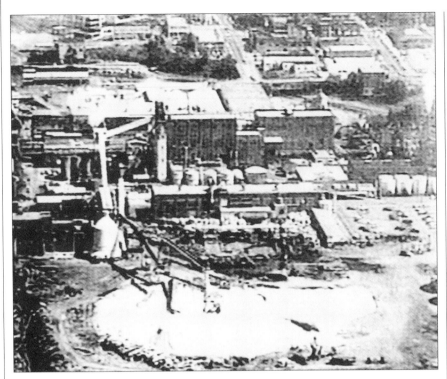

The vacant lot on Alvorado Street where the body of 17-year-old prostitute Kimberley Martin was found.

older. The other was, taller, younger, and had acne scars on his neck. Later that day Mrs. Stofer received a phone call. The speaker had an East Coast accent and he told Mrs. Stofer to say nothing to anyone or she was as good as dead.

The press gave maximum coverage to the murders, adding to the rising panic in Los Angeles. Women refused to go out at night. Even prostitutes defied their pimps and stayed indoors. The police responded by creating a task force that included members of the various police departments involved: the Los Angeles Police, the Los Angeles Sheriff's Department and the Glendale Police. However, they did not publicize the fact that the bruising on and semen in the victims' bodies showed that there were two killers working in partnership.

As the police investigation ground on, Chief Daryl Gates announced several times at press conferences that his men were closing in on the killer. But when the suspects were arrested, they were able to clear themselves and the investigation continued. In truth, the authorities were no nearer to catching the killer.

Within two weeks Kimberley Martin was found dead in a vacant lot on Alvorado Street within sight of City Hall. A prostitute, 17-year-old Kimberley worked for a phone-in agency. Customers would ring up, state their requirements, and give their address and phone number. A customer had phoned and offered $150 in cash for a blonde wearing black underwear. He gave his address as the Tamarind Apartments in Hollywood. The telephone number he gave was later checked – it was the number of the Hollywood Public Library. A check of the residents in the Tamarind Apartments, however, produced a wit-

ness named Kenneth Bianchi who said he had heard screams. Was the murderer a resident there?

1977 passed without further murders that could be attributed to the Hillside Strangler, as the murderer had become known, but on February 17, 1978, 20-year-old Cindy Hudspeth was found in the boot of her orange Datsun halfway down a cliff. The car had been pushed off the Angeles Crest Highway, north of the town of Glendale. Cindy, a part-time waitress, was naked. The autopsy revealed that shortly before her death she had been raped by two men. A palm print was found on the car, but it was too smudged to be of value. However, the police investigation produced one interesting but disturbing piece of information: Cindy Hudspeth had lived opposite victim Kristina Weckler.

With the death of Cindy Hudspeth the murders stopped as suddenly as they had begun. It is so commonly believed as to have become accepted as fact that serial killers don't stop killing unless they are prevented from continuing. If the killings stop then it is because the killer has been caught (for the murders or for some other crime), commited suicide, or moved away. The police assumed that the Hillside Strangler(s) had left the area.

BELLINGHAM

Bellingham, in Washington State, is the most northerly Pacific coastal town in the United States. The bodies of two students, Diane Wilder and Karen Mandic, were found in their abandoned car. Police inquiries produced Karen's boyfriend. He told the police that Karen and Diane had taken a job house-sitting a property in the exclusive Bayside area of town. A new burglar alarm was being fitted, he said, and the building's security supervisor had offered the girls $100 to do the job. For security reasons they had been told not to tell anyone, but Karen had divulged the secret to her boyfriend.

The police questioned the security man. He denied ever having heard of the girls and maintained that someone must have been using his name. The police believed him, until they found at his home some items taken from premises he'd been guarding. This prompted a search of his truck where they found keys to the house in Bayside. They also found a scarf which was identified as having belonged to Diane Wilder. Even faced with this body of evidence, the security supervisor, whose name was Kenneth Alessio Bianchi, continued to deny murder.

Kenneth Bianchi was born on May 22, 1951, to a New York prostitute, but he was given out for adoption at birth. Throughout his life Bianchi maintained the appearance of a clean-cut all-American man, and nurtured an ambition to be a policeman. But for all his professed aspirations, Bianchi was also lazy, prone to stealing, and a liar. Married, but quickly divorced, he had eventually moved to Los Angeles, where he lived for a short time with a cousin named Angelo Buono.

> **"I ASKED HIM IF HE'D EVER KILLED ANYBODY. HE THOUGHT HE WAS TALKING TO KENNY. HE DIDN'T THINK ANYTHING OF IT. HE SAID, 'I DON'T KNOW. WHY DO YOU WANT TO KNOW?' I SAID, 'WELL, WHAT DOES IT FEEL LIKE?' HE SAID, 'I DON'T KNOW.' I SAID, 'WELL, WE SHOULD FIND OUT SOME TIME.' HE SAID, 'SURE. OK.' "**

The body of waitress Cindy Hudspeth being hoisted from the cliff over which her car was pushed by the killers.

The police looked into Bianchi's background. They found he'd moved from Los Angeles to Bellingham the previous May. They also discovered that, when in Los Angeles, he had been living at the Tamarind Apartments. The police in Bellingham contacted their colleagues in the Los Angeles Police Department. The link between the Tamarind Apartments and the Hillside stranglings was eventually made and it turned out that Bianchi was in the Los Angeles task force's suspects file (admittedly a long document with between eight and nine thousand other names). A further search of Bianchi's home was carried out and jewellery from victims of the Los Angeles murders discovered. Still Bianchi continued to deny involvement in the killings.

Then he was put under hypnosis. During these sessions a second personality emerged who called himself "Steve". He was foul-mouthed and vicious. He hated Kenneth Bianchi, thought himself a better person and was striving to be dominant, to come out and stay out. "Steve" freely admitted to committing the murders in Bellingham, and eventually admitted to the crimes in Los Angeles as well. He also implicated a second person, his cousin, Angelo Buono. "Steve" claimed that he had killed four girls in Los Angeles and that Buono had killed five.

"How did you two decide to kill girls in the first place?" the police asked of his other persona, "Steve".

"Just sitting around shooting the shit," he replied nonchalantly. "I asked him if he'd ever killed anybody. He thought he was talking to Kenny. He didn't think anything of it. He said, 'I don't know. Why do you want to know?' I said, 'Well, what does it feel like?' He said, 'I don't know.' I said, 'Well, we should find out some time.' He said, 'Sure. OK.' And we did."

A week or so later they had gone out. "Steve" had killed first. Referring to Yolanda Washington, though unable to recall her name, "Steve" explained that Buono had picked her up in his car, then driven round the corner to where "Steve" was waiting for them. He got in the back of the car with the girl, had sex, then killed her. "We dumped her body off and that was it".

Several psychiatrists were convinced that Kenneth Bianchi was a genuine multiple personality, which meant that his evidence would be inadmissible in a court of law. The police were appalled, convinced that Bianchi was faking.

A prosecution expert, Dr. Martin T. Orne, watched the videotaped interviews held by defence psychiatrists with the hypnotized Bianchi. He couldn't decide whether or not Bianchi was genuinely hynotized. One thing that worried him was that the character of "Steve" seemed to develop during the course of the hypnotic sessions. This didn't seem right. In his opinion, "Steve" was a character invented by Bianchi and being developed by him in the same way as an actor fleshes out a character in a script. If "Steve"

> **"WHY SHOULD WE CALL SOMEONE INSANE SIMPLY BECAUSE HE OR SHE CHOOSES NOT TO CONFORM TO OUR STANDARDS OF CIVILIZED BEHAVIOUR?"**
>
> JUDGE RONALD GEORGE WHEN ASKED WHETHER BUONO AND BIANCHI'S CRIMES IN THEMSELVES PROVED THEM INSANE

was genuine then he would be a fully developed alternative personality and wouldn't undergo this fleshing out.

Increasingly convinced that Bianchi was faking hypnosis, Dr. Orne tried an experiment. Under hypnosis Bianchi was made to hallucinate that his lawyer, Dean Brett, was sitting next to him. Bianchi went through the motions of shaking hands with Brett. This was a big mistake. Dr. Orne had never known a genuinely hypnotized subject try to touch their hallucination. Finally, Dr. Orne casually mentioned that genuine multiple personalities generally have more than one alternative personality. At the next interview with Bianchi, the personality of someone called "Billy" appeared.

It was the police who eventually destroyed Bianchi's insanity plea. Watching Bianchi's taped sessions with Dr. Ralph Allison, detectives Frank Salerno and Pete Finnigan picked up "Steve" saying that his surname was

A special police task force was set up to track down the serial killer.

"Walker". For the two policemen the name "Steve Walker" set some distant bells ringing.

As it turned out the bells were very distant indeed and it is testimony to the two men's grasp of the case that any bells rang at all. In Bianchi's papers they found a letter written by Bianchi to California State University. The letter was signed "Thomas Steven Walker". Bianchi had placed an advertisement in a newspaper offering a job in psychology. One applicant had sent his academic papers and Bianchi had used these to obtain a diploma in psychology from California State University. The applicant whose papers Bianchi had used was named Thomas Steven Walker.

In court the defence stuck to the story that Bianchi was a genuine multiple personality, but at the hearing in Bellingham on October 19, 1979, the "evidence" of the police and prosecution psychiatrists, Dr. Martin Orne and Dr. Saul Faerstein, made the more convincing argument. Bianchi was found sane and immediately pleaded guilty to the murders in Bellingham and to five murders in Los Angeles. Under Washington State law his admission of guilt meant that he could be sentenced without trial before jury. He was offered and accepted a plea bargain, his sentence being commuted from the death penalty to life in prison if he testified against Angelo Buono.

BUONO

Born on October 5, 1934, Angelo Buono and his sister, Cecilia, were taken to Los Angeles by their mother following her divorce from their father. He got into trouble with the law and as a consequence spent time in reformatories. By

Kenneth Bianchi under hypnosis. Was he a genuine multiple personality or simply faking the condition to escape punishment?

the age of 14, Buono had graduated to stealing cars. He married four times, slept with lots of women, and set up his own business as a car upholsterer. Sometime after Bianchi moved to Los Angeles in 1976, Buono and his cousin had become small-time pimps. He was reputed to hate women and to gain enjoyment from humiliating the women who worked for him. Some of Buono's girls said Buono and Bianchi had beaten them, threatened them with death, and forced them into prostitution.

In August 1976, for example, Buono's call-girl agency had received a telephone call from a wealthy New York lawyer. He wanted a girl sent to his home in Bel Air. The girl who turned up was Becky Spears. Only 15 years old, she seemed thoroughly miserable and clearly hated prostitution. The lawyer

asked a few questions. Becky explained that she was from Phoenix, Arizona, and had been encouraged to come to Los Angeles by another girl, Sabra Hannan, who promised her well-paid work with Angelo Buono. Soon afterwards, she said, Buono and his cousin, Bianchi, had threatened to kill her if she didn't prostitute herself for them.

The lawyer was deeply upset by Becky's tale and immediately bought her an air ticket back home to Phoenix. Becky's departure infuriated Buono, who threatened the lawyer and only ceased to do so after the lawyer sent a "heavy" round to Buono to suggest that backing off would be a very sensible decision.

The police were able to trace both Becky Spears and Sabra Hannan. Both confirmed the basics of the lawyer's story, that they'd been offered jobs as

Angelo Buono in court. His cousin, Bianchi, agreed to testify against him, identifying him as one of the two Stranglers.

models by Buono and Bianchi, then had been forced by the two men to accept a less savoury form of exposure.

Buono and Bianchi were clearly not fine, upstanding citizens, but no part of this sorry tale linked Buono to the killings, and there was no evidence against him beyond Bianchi's testimony. To add to the prosecution's difficulties, Bianchi now began to back-track on the plea-bargaining deal he'd made with them, and refused to give evidence against Buono. The Los Angeles District

Attorney, downhearted, announced the decision not to charge Buono with murder. Instead he was to stand trial for the

> "I WOULD NOT HAVE THE SLIGHTEST RELUCTANCE TO IMPOSE THE DEATH PENALTY IN THIS CASE WERE IT WITHIN MY POWER TO DO SO."
>
> JUDGE RONALD GEORGE AT THE END OF BUONO'S TRIAL

lesser crimes of pimping, rape and sodomy. Whether or not the District Attorney's proposal was carried out

would be up to Judge Ronald George. Hardly anyone doubted that he would accept it. Buono and his counsel looked confident on the day of the hearing when the judge was due to give his pronouncement. Even the police were convinced the murder case against Buono would be dropped.

In the event Judge George refused to consider such a possibility and said that if the District Attorney would not prosecute then he would refer the case against Buono to the Attorney General, which is exactly what he did. This decision was remarkable. It was certainly within the judge's remit, but was interpreted by many to be an arrogant interference with accepted legal practice. Others believed it to have been a brave move, there being ample evidence against Buono. Apart from Bianchi's testimony, Buono had been identified by several people as being in the company of some of the victims, and a piece of fibre discovered on Judy Miller's eyelid proved to be similar to material found in Buono's house.

The trial of Angelo Buono began on November 16, 1981, and lasted until 1983. It was the longest murder trial in American history. Over 250 witnesses were called. Bianchi, who was number 200 in this long line, had been persuaded to co-operate with the prosecution, the judge having reminded him that a breach of his plea-bargaining agreement would result in him being sent immediately to the notoriously tough environment of Walla Walla Prison in Washington. Bianchi got the message: for five months

he occupied the witness stand and played the double-role of his life.

Buono's defence lawyers made a valiant and determined effort to get their client off the hook that Bianchi had succeeded in hanging him on. They used every weapon in the advocate's armoury to cast doubt on Bianchi's evidence. They challenged Bianchi's testimony on the grounds that it was inadmissible, Bianchi being a multiple personality and having given evidence while under hypnosis. Then they asserted that Bianchi had committed all the murders and was trying to shift the blame onto Buono. The judge refused to accept either argument and the case preceded on the evidence presented by the state.

THE VERDICT

On November 14, 1983, the jury reached their decision, finding Buono guilty of murdering Lauren Wagner, Judy Miller, Lissa Kastin, Kristina Weckler, Dolores Cepeda, Sonja Johnson, Jane King, Kimberley Martin and Cindy Hudspeth. The jury, perhaps mindful that Bianchi had escaped the death penalty through plea-bargaining, stated that Buono should escape it too. He was sentenced to life imprisonment. Judge Ronald George said: "I would not have the slightest reluctance to impose the death penalty in this case were it within my power to do so." But the decision of the jury had to prevail.

Buono was sent to Folsom Prison, where he will probably remain for the rest of his life. Bianchi was sent to Walla Walla. The earliest he can expect parole is 2005, by which time he will be 54, a mere 5 years older than Bianco was at the time of his conviction.

Crocodile tears? Bianchi weeps in court.

JIM JONES
GUYANA MESSIAH

In November 1978, a United States congressman named Leo Ryan, accompanied by an NBC camera crew and other journalists, flew to Guyana in South America to investigate reports that a thousand American citizens were being exploited at a town there called Jonestown. Four days later Ryan and four companions were about to fly home. Suddenly there was gunfire and the men dropped to the tarmac, dead.

■

A SHORT TIME LATER Reverend Jim Jones, the leader of the community at Jonestown, told his followers to drink a soft drink containing cyanide. They did so. 913 people died. It was the most amazing mass suicide in history.

James Warren Jones was born in the small Bible Belt town of Lynn, Indiana. It was a town that lived close to death, the principal trade there being coffin-making. Jim Jones's father was the local bar-fly and a lifelong member of the Ku Klux Klan. Jim Jones later described him as "a mean old redneck racist".

His mother seems to have been particularly odd. She wore trousers and smoked in the street, which in those days in small-town Indiana was more shocking than buying your groceries without any clothes on. She believed in reincarnation and told young Jim Jones of her adventures up the Amazon river – her tales were in part derived from the *National Geographic* magazine, to which she subscribed. She also spoke about black magic, omens and suchlike.

By the age of 12 Jones was delivering hell-fire sermons to fellow children and officiating at the funerals of family pets. When he was aged 16 he married and became a Methodist preacher, eventually being given his own parish church in Indianapolis. Jones felt he had a mission to help the poor and the weak. He attracted a great many black and underprivileged members to his church, but the largely white congregation eventually objected and the church was taken away from him.

At the age of 22 he opened the Community National Church in a rundown part of Indianapolis. He wasn't an ordained preacher and he had no money, but he managed to finance his church by importing and selling monkeys. He also joined the Communist Party and, at the time when Julius and Ethel Rosenberg were executed for spying, he conceived the strange philosophy of "revolutionary death" that would reach a terrifying conclusion in the jungles of Guyana.

Jim Jones created one of the first genuinely multi-racial churches in the United States and his greatest efforts were directed towards the poorest and most helpless people in the country. He and his wife adopted black and Korean children and gained a reputation for looking after the interests of minorities.

However, madness was already creeping into his behaviour, alongside his liberal crusading ideas. He was obsessed by the idea of the apocalypse. He had read that Brazil would be the safest spot in the world in the event of a nuclear holocaust and in 1962 he moved there, leaving his disciples in charge of the church in Indianapolis. Two years later he left Brazil and returned to Indianapolis, stopping *en route* in was shortly to become the independent state of Guyana.

Back in the United States he discovered that events had rolled on dramatically. Voices raised against racial inequality now included the powerful peace oratory of Martin Luther King and the violent preaching of Malcolm X. Jones persuaded 100 of his followers to hand over all their possessions to his

church and join him in a migration to another supposedly nuclear-safe spot, Redwood Valley in California. Here they set up a New Temple and self-contained society, from which they spread out to

"I ONLY KNOW JIM JONES AS A MAN WHO CARES FOR HUMANITY,"
MARCELINE JONES, WIFE OF JIM JONES

Happier days: Jones preaching, with his wife, Marceline, at his side.

San Francisco and Los Angeles. The membership of his temple swelled to nearly 20,000 as his reputation grew. He opened day-care centres and food kitchens and targeted minority groups.

One convert recalled how he'd gone along to the Temple, but not gone back again. Jones "called me later and says, 'why didn't you come back to the Tem-

ple?', so I thought no one, no pastor, ever asked me to come to the Temple before, or why wasn't you in Church, so I went back and he offered me to sit down in the seat where he was sitting at the table to eat...."

PERVERTED

It is difficult to know when Jones's motives became perverted. He certainly arranged fake displays of healing and urged his followers to believe he was the embodiment and even the reincarnation of Jesus Christ. His services were exhilarating, alive, joyous, with soul and gospel singers, dance groups, and appearances by celebrity preachers such as black activist Angela Davis.

Jones's congregations grew. He had the ability to make each individual feel wanted and in return his followers willingly gave him their money, their property and their support. The money and property were to make Jones's Temple very wealthy, and the support meant that Jones was able to deliver the Temple's members' votes as a block vote, which gave him considerable political influence. He allegedly lent this support to the Democrats in the 1976 Presidential Elections and was openly courted by local politicians, even becoming a member of the City's Housing Commission.

But there were rumours. Investigative journalists accused Jones of running his Temple as though it were a private empire and there were claims of bizarre

The village of Jonestown, Guyana, where Jim Jones imposed a harsh regime on his cult members.

sexual practices and savage punishments. Certainly the evidence mounted that Jones encouraged members of both sexes to sleep with him. Indeed, sex almost became an obsession. He advocated sexual openness and public urination, and he seemed to derive considerable pleasure from exposing himself. Furthermore, the sheer quantity of money involved in Jones's Temple began to be appreciated by outsiders. It was claimed that millions of dollars were regularly being sent from San Francisco to banks in Switzerland and Panama, even that an officer in the city administration had been involved in establishing the overseas accounts.

Many people remained in ignorance of the press allegations about Jim Jones while others refused to believe them. Welfare agencies continued to place children – more than 100 of them – in the

custody of his church and Jones continued to wield political influence. But he also became increasingly paranoid and there were several spectacular defections from the Temple. One couple, Elmer and Deanna Mertle, were long-time and senior members of the Temple who suddenly discovered just how much their lives were controlled by Jim Jones. Their home and everything in it was owned by him; the only people they knew were fellow Temple members; even some of their children lived with Temple members and were committed followers. Jones made threats, one of which smeared Elmer Mertle as a child molester; the Mertles made it through this hell.

On Memorial Day, 1977, there was an anti-suicide rally in San Francisco at which Jim Jones gave a speech. Instead of the expected anti-suicide exhortations,

Jones actually supported suicide. There were some to whom this did not come as a surprise, though, for as early as 1976 he had demanded his followers drink what he told them was poison. They had done so to show their solidarity with Jones by laying down their lives. It was, they thought, a symbolic act.

Pressure in the press was now mounting, and the Mertles were dedicated to fighting Jones and his Temple. Another voice raised against the Temple was that of Grace Stoen. The wife of the Temple's lawyer, Tim Stoen, she had, at the insistence of her husband, allowed Jim Jones to father her child, John-John. Breaking from her husband and from the Temple, Grace began petitioning in the courts for the return of her son. Tim Stoen told Jones that Grace would almost certainly win her case, though it could be prolonged if the child was taken out of the United States. As press speculation mounted, Jones upped and left San Francisco. Stoen would eventually defect and rejoin his wife but John-John stayed and was among the death toll at the end.

Jones had spent three years building a village in Guyana for his followers. In 1977 he airlifted nearly 1,000 of them from San Francisco to this new base. They were crowded into huts and were expected to work in the fields from dawn until dusk. Food was short and every day Jones, who liked to be called Dad, would urge his followers to make still greater efforts. Local politicians supported Jones, unaware of the daily diet of humiliating punishments. One described the place as idyllic: "Jonestown to me is a community where seniors, young people, middle-aged people of all different races can live together in a harmonious way, where there's no so-called generation gap, there's no sexism. Women perform as many duties as the men do. They operate heavy machinery, they operate the metal shops, the carpentry shops...

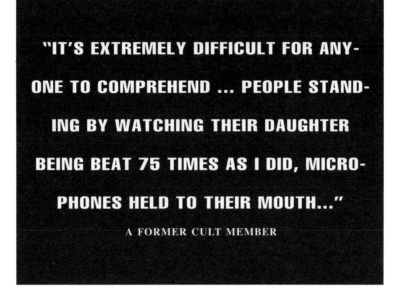

"IT'S EXTREMELY DIFFICULT FOR ANYONE TO COMPREHEND ... PEOPLE STANDING BY WATCHING THEIR DAUGHTER BEING BEAT 75 TIMES AS I DID, MICROPHONES HELD TO THEIR MOUTH..."

A FORMER CULT MEMBER

there's no elitism. So I would say it's a community that belongs to the people."

HORRIFIC TESTIMONY

Soon angry ex-members were telling a different story. Many spoke quietly, struck with the horror of what they had seen, of what they had done, and perhaps even more horrified that they could have allowed themselves to became so totally dominated by Jim Jones. One woman related the following tale to television reporters:"Well, the children were scared of this thing called Bigfoot. What they do is this. If a child has done anything that most children do – you know, all children try different things out to see how far they can go – it's considered very bad there and they are sent out to see Bigfoot. They're taken into the forest and... a well for drinking water. Two people will already be in the well, swimming, and it's dark and you can't see, and the child's thrown in there and the people who are in there will be grabbing at the child's feet, or pulling him down, making sure he comes back up for breath. You can hear the child screaming all the way there and all the way back."

According to the testimony of these people, Jones demanded that the children scream how sorry they were. If the children didn't scream loud enough, Jones would have them taken back to the well.

One man, his eyes and voice almost numb with disbelief at what he had witnessed, and participated in, explained how he was engaged in getting protection and aid for Jones's followers. "It's extremely difficult for anyone to comprehend people being in a cult group, standing by watching their daughter

The bloody end met by the Congressional party sent to investigate the cult.

being beat 75 times as I did, watching children being beat, microphones held to their mouth while they're screaming so that everyone throughout the building can hear them scream also... it's incredibly difficult for anyone to believe a story like this."

Against this background of former cult members telling horrifying stories, the allegations against Jones grew. He was accused of fraud, in particular the appropriation of welfare cheques from elderly members. Some said the cheques were handed over voluntarily. A former member said, "voluntarily only because they knew if they didn't that they could be beaten."

In the light of what was waiting only a short time in the future, one story told by an ex-member is particularly significant. "She says there are mass suicide rehearsals going on in Jonestown. For example she says that Jim Jones has mass meetings and he orders everyone to drink a brown liquid. After they drink the liquid he says that it is a fatal poison that is going to act on you in an hour, two hours, whatever." Jones would then preach at his followers, getting each to stand up and say how happy they were to be dying for the glorious socialism. "And Debbie told me she wanted to die so bad that she was hoping this was for real. But then Jim Jones at the end of an hour or two says that was a test."

The same source also explained how Jones had armed guards patrolling the perimeters of Jonestown and that Jones had publicly told his followers that anyone trying to escape would be shot. The Temple's attorney dismissed such allega-

tions. "There's no bodyguards in Jonestown... I have not seen any guns."

But the rumours were growing and eventually Congressman Leo Ryan agreed to accept an invitation to visit

> ## "NOW WE'D LIKE YOU TO STAND UP EACH OF YOU AND TELL ME HOW HAPPY YOU ARE TO DIE FOR THE GLORIOUS SOCIALISM."
>
> STATEMENT CREDITED TO JIM JONES

Jonestown. Accompanied by a party of cameramen, reporters, and the relatives of four of Jones's followers, he flew to Guyana. He also had the backing of the House Foreign Affairs Committee in Washington. This made Ryan's trip an official government investigation, which effectively forced Jones to allow Ryan's team into the camp or risk having their funds from the United States, stopped.

Nevertheless, on arrival in Jonestown, Ryan and his party were greeted by a group of Jones's followers, who had a petition asking him to go away. Ryan persisted. Jones then declared that only Ryan would be allowed into the town. Ryan replied that if the newsmen weren't allowed in with him, the result would probably be a Congressional investigation. Jones had to give in. On November 17 Ryan and his party landed at the Port Kaituma airstrip. A commitee of the Temple's legal representatives escorted the visitors into Jonestown.

Described by Jim Jones as "Heaven on Earth", Jonestown at first glance seemed very pleasant. Congressman Ryan saw a well-run nursery, dancers and cult members who claimed they were happy in Jonestown and who ridiculed the notion that they were being held prisoner there. Ryan seemed satisfied with what he saw. At a meeting he

The scene of self-inflicted carnage at Jonestown.

told the followers that he'd had a few conversations with people "who believe this is the best thing that ever happened in their whole lives".

But there was a nagging feeling that Jonestown as it appeared to Ryan and his followers was an elaborate charade. Within a few hours Jones was confronted by journalists with some of the Congressman's accusations. He was visibly breaking down under their questioning when a family sought Ryan's help, asking to be allowed to leave with him. Other people seized the opportunity. Jones began to wail about betrayal and had to be calmed down by his aides.

A man named Don Sly then attempted to knife Ryan, but was pulled off by Jones's security guards. Sly was cut in the struggle and blood spurted over Ryan. Later, a man named Larry Layton asked to join Ryan's party. The defectors viewed his request with concern. Layton was known as very pro-Jones – indeed he was called "Jones's robot".

As Ryan and others were waiting with the pilot of the aircraft, a tractor and trailer appeared. Inside the plane, Layton opened fire with a gun. Men appeared on the trailer outside and began shooting. Congressman Ryan was killed; a photographer for the *San Francisco Examiner*, Greg Robinson, was wounded; so, too, was Robert Brown, an NBC cameraman; and NBC reporter Don Harris. The three wounded men were then shot repeatedly in the head. Several journalists and defectors were injured. Larry Layton was later tried for his part in the shooting of Ryan and his party, but the jury could not reach a verdict and he went free.

Meanwhile, back in Jonestown something incredible took place. Jim Jones

After the massacre San Francisco police kept a close watch on the People's Temple.

had his lieutenants prepare two 50-gallon drums of a soft drink called Kool-Aid and lace it with Valium and cyanide. Then he called his followers together, told them that Congressman Ryan had been murdered and said they must now all kill themselves. 913 people took the drink and died, including children, given the lethal drink by their parents in a grand betrayal of the most supreme trust.

"The children were crying," recalled one survivor, as he explained how Jones told the parents "not to tell the children that they were dying, not to tell them it was painful, he was telling them it wasn't painful." A tape recorder was left

running throughout the last minutes. It is horrible, with Jones telling his followers that death was sleep, that suicide was "a revolutionary suicide protesting the conditions of an inhumane world". Finally, only Jones and a nurse, Annie Moore, were left. They shot themselves.

As television news programmes and newspapers carried pictures of US military detachments collecting the bodies, and as the death toll mounted, a handful of survivors told their stories. Public reaction was one of disbelief that parents would kill their children, then themselves, because one self-styled messiah told them to do it.

JOHN GACY
MASS MURDERER

Norwood Park is neither part of the city of Chicago nor part of the city of Des Plaines. The city police departments of the two conurbations have no jurisdiction over crimes committed there, and have to leave them to the county sheriff's department. In December 1978 the citizens of Norwood were not a little surprised to find the Des Plaines police staking out 8213 West Summerdale Avenue, home of nice Mr. Gacy, the fat and friendly building contractor who had lived there for seven years.

■

THE WATCH BEGAN on December 13 after a muddy and dishevelled Gacy had been less than willing to comply with a request that he go and be interviewed by detectives at Des Plaines Police Headquarters. The interview was unsatisfactory from the police point of view, and the decision was taken to put a tail on Gacy and to keep a close watch on his house.

On December 19 Gacy invited the two officers keeping watch to have breakfast with him. What they smelt on entering the house gave them grounds to ask for a search warrant.

Police flocked to the house, and astonished neighbours watched as a stream of bodies was carried out. First one; then another; finally seven from a crawl space to the front of the house. Another eight were found covered with quicklime in a subterranean trench.

By the time the house and garden had been fully excavated, 28 corpses had been brought to light. The puzzling comment Gacy had made to neighbours, about the house, in which he lived alone, becoming too crowded for him, now made perfect sense!

UPS AND DOWNS

John Wayne Gacy was born in 1942. He had suffered a severe accident when he was 11: a swing struck him on the head, following which he suffered blackouts and headaches. When he was 16, a blood clot on the brain was diagnosed, but this was dissolved by medication and the blackouts ceased. Then he was discovered to have a heart condition.

Gacy overcame these problems, though, and went to business college. On graduating he became a shoe salesman, and married a colleague in the business. His father-in-law set him up managing a fried chicken fast-food business in Waterloo, Iowa. Gacy was a popular and successful local businessman. He worked hard. He liked to be liked. He and his wife had a son and a daughter. It seemed a tragedy to all who knew him when his world fell apart in 1968. He had to give up the fried chicken business; his wife divorced him; and in 1971, Gacy returned to his birthplace, Chicago, to start over again.

He set up as a building contractor. It was at this time that Gacy bought the house at 8213 West Summerdale Avenue. Soon he met up with an old flame, Carole Hoff, and they married on June 1, 1972.

This marriage, too, only lasted four years, but this time, Gacy's position in the community seemed assured. He became a member of the Junior Chamber of Commerce. He was also active in the Democratic Party, and had cards printed to mark his rise to the organizing position of precinct captain. He made donations to charity and to the party, and was photographed shaking hands with Michael Bilandic, Chicago's mayor.

Among his most attractive activities were the charity entertainments he put on for children. As Pogo the Clown, in

white face and ruffled costume, he would do conjuring tricks and hand out balloons at parties or in children's wards in hospitals. The mother of one of the boys

"I'D JUST AS SOON SHOOT YOU AS LOOK AT YOU."
Gacy, to Jeffrey Rignall, a victim he spared

Jeffrey Rignall survived an horrendous ordeal at the hands of John Gacy.

whose body came out from Gacy's house in later years recalled, "He was a very nice man to work for, and he liked the kids. And my son told me he was a politician, and he says, 'Boy! if you stick

with that guy you could go far. He's got a lot of connections.' See, and this is what the boys liked about him."

The high point of Gacy's public life came after he had organized three fund-raising events for President Jimmy Carter's re-election campaign. As a loyal Democrat, he was introduced to First Lady Rosalynn Carter when she came to Chicago and, to her subsequent embarrassment, was even photographed with her.

BRUSHES WITH THE LAW

The dark side of Gacy's life went back a long way. His father was of Polish extraction, his mother of Danish. His childhood was not happy: his father drank and beat him, and at least one of the family's friends abused him sexually.

Those who knew him best, when he achieved success in business, were aware of him as a braggart who tried to buy popularity with gifts. The collapse of his marriage in 1968 came after attempts to seduce young men who worked for him in the fried chicken business, handcuffing them in the backroom and offering them money for sex. One potential victim objected strongly, and refused Gacy's request that he practise fellatio on him. When Gacy attempted to sodomize him, the lad escaped and went straight to the police. It became apparent

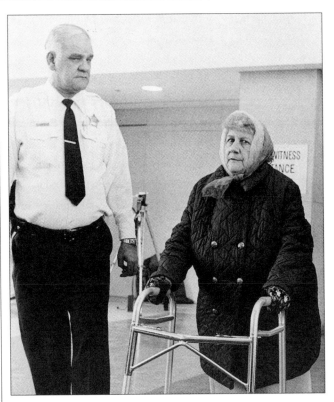

Mrs. Marion Gacy resolutely refused to believe the charges brought against her son, John.

The younger sister of John Gacy, Karen (right), described their family life as "sometimes very stormy".

that the boy was going to press charges, so Gacy hired thugs to beat him up. It made a nasty little story in court, and Judge Peter Van Meter had no hesitation in handing down a 10-year sentence.

However, 26-year-old Gacy's ingratiating skills came into play at once. He was a first offender. He became a model prisoner and resolutely eschewed all homosexual advances made to him in prison. In this way he won parole after serving a mere 18 months.

Gacy's attempt to go straight in Chicago was not very long-lived. In the year he arrived there, he was arrested for picking up a teenage boy and trying to force him to have sex. The case was discharged when the adolescent plaintiff failed to appear in court.

A young man who went to West Summerdale Avenue looking for work as a building labourer later revealed that Gacy pulled a gun on him, trying to force him to engage in sexual activity. The fat contractor snarled, "I killed a guy before." The young worker did not believe him. Gacy was probably telling the truth, although on this occasion the threat of violence did not become reality.

When he married Carole, friends who came to his home for the reception noticed an odd smell. Gacy explained that water was leaking into the crawl space. Well before the marriage broke down, Gacy was cruising gay areas of Chicago and showing sexual interest in good-looking young employees. Two of them, John Butkovich and Greg Grodzik, disappeared. A detective hired by Greg's mother was unable to trace him.

At home Gacy became increasingly violent. He beat up Carole until she left

him in 1976, and within a year he had come to police attention again.

A boy complained that Gacy had taken him to Norwood Park, held him at gunpoint, and subjected him to brutal sexual abuse. Gacy admitted the use of a gun and the ferocious sex, but claimed that the boy was a willing masochistic partner who was now trying to blackmail him. The gun had been nothing more than an exciting sexual prop. Chicago police kept a half-hearted eye on him for 30 days, but nothing more untoward turned up, and the matter was dropped.

JEFFREY RIGNALL

The following year, Gacy made a pickup who refused to co-operate with him. On March 21, Gacy met 27-year-old Jeffrey Rignall on North Broadway in New Town, Chicago and invited him to join him in his sleek black Oldsmobile for a drive and a joint. Rignall agreed, but within minutes of his entering the car, Gacy pulled over to the curb and slapped a chloroform-soaked rag over his passenger's face. Rignall eventually came round sufficiently to be aware that the car, which was travelling very fast, had pulled off at a motorway exit.

The next thing he knew, he was naked and tied into a sort of pillory or rack in Gacy's basement. Gacy was naked, too, his gross hairy belly protruding obscenely. The fat man gloated over his victim, showing him various whips and promising to use them on him. He kept his promise. For hours, he tortured and sodomized Jeffrey Rignall. From time to time he slapped the chloroform over his face to quieten him, and then waited for him to regain consciousness before whipping and raping him again.

There was no hope of escape, he told Rignall, claiming to be a policeman. "I'd just as soon shoot you as look at you," he sneered. The sexual assaults were so painful that Rignall wanted to die. But when he begged Gacy to release him, promising to leave town and say nothing about the incident, he was surprisingly granted his freedom. Gacy then chloroformed him once again. When Rignall came round, he was fully clothed, under a statue in Lincoln Park, Chicago. His wallet and money were untouched, but his driving licence was missing.

He was bleeding from the rectum; his face was burned by the repeated applications of chloroform; and hospital tests showed that the heavy doses of the drug Gacy administered had permanently damaged his liver. But, at least, he was alive and free.

Jeffrey Rignall went to the police. The Chicago Police Department's lackadaisical attitude to his complaint astounded and enraged him. Since he did

Gacy as "Pogo", the lovable persona he presented to children at charity events. He would use conjuring tricks in his sexploits, too.

not know his assailant's name or car number and could not give them an address, they told him there was little they could do. They held out no hope of the fat sadist ever being caught and evidently had no intention of trying to track him down.

So Jeffrey Rignall did it himself. He hired a car and took it along the route he vaguely recollected travelling in the Oldsmobile. Gacy's car was a very distinctive vehicle, and when Rignall came to the expressway exit he thought he remembered his torturer taking, he parked beside it and watched the traffic

for hours. During one of his vigils, he spotted Gacy's car leaving the highway.

Rignall tailed the Oldsmobile to West Summerdale Avenue and noted the house number, 8213. He had some knowledge of real estate documentation, as he had once worked for a law firm. Through land records he found Gacy's name, and triumphantly went to Chicago Police Department with the information, at the same time offering himself as a positive identification witness against Gacy.

To his astonishment, Chicago's finest were still loath to take serious action against this monster. They told Rignall that the man he named had been convicted of sodomy in Iowa and sent to prison – but they did not act. It is not clear whether they thought Rignall was a cannabis-smoking pervert who had willingly got into a strange man's car, and deserved all he got, or, more sinister still, whether a glad-handing contributor to the Mayor's various political funds and chosen charities was being given a free hand to beat and sexually abuse strangers if that was his pleasure.

Rignall had to press the Chicago police to issue an arrest warrant. When the cops finally met with Rignall at Norwood Park, they suddenly announced that there would be no arrest. Norwood Park was out of their jurisdiction, and he would have to start all over again with the county sheriff's department. Rignall did no such thing. He and his lawyer,

Gacy's house at 8213 West Summerdale Avenue, Norwood Park.

Fred Richman, had Gacy arrested on a misdemeanour charge of battery and proceeded to open a civil suit against him. Chicago police still would not issue the felony indictment that was obviously called for, and, as he had done the year before, Gacy tried to turn the tables on his accuser. He counter-sued Rignall. Things were getting too hot for comfort by the middle of 1978, however, and in the end he settled Rignall's $3,000 medical bills out of court.

DES PLAINES POLICE STEP IN

The real pressure started soon after 9.00pm on December 11, 1978, when Mrs. Elizabeth Piest of Des Plaines went down to the Nisson Pharmacy to fetch her 15-year-old son Robert back for her birthday party. Robert asked her to let him go and talk to a contractor living nearby about a vacation job first. "I'll be right back," he promised. But he wasn't.

After half an hour, Mr. and Mrs. Piest and their son and daughter Ken and Kerry went looking for Robert. When they couldn't find him and went to Des Plaines police, their reception contrasted wonderfully with Chicago's suspicious bearishness in the Rignall case. Police Captain Joseph Kozenczak was sure that this was not the sort of family nor Robert the sort of boy to give rise to a runaway escapade. Convinced there had been foul play, he put Des Plaines youth officer Ron Adams on the case.

> ## "IT'S FRIGHTENING. THAT'S THE ONLY WORD I CAN USE. FRIGHTENING. FRIGHTENING."
> MEDICAL EXAMINER DR. ROBERT STEIN, ON THE CADAVERS AROUND GACY'S HOME

Adams found out from the drugstore that Gacy was most likely the contractor Piest had gone to visit. He telephoned Gacy at 9.30am on December 12, and was rudely brushed off. "I don't talk to any kids. I can't help you. I don't know anything about it," was all "Pogo the Clown" would say. Captain Kozenczak was far from satisfied.

He learned about Gacy's Iowa sodomy conviction, and became more than ever convinced that the man knew something about Robert Piest's disappearance. He took some colleagues to Norwood Park to interview the suspect, but got nothing helpful out of Gacy: just vague mutterings about talking to "one of the boys about some shelves" discarded from the revamped Nisson Pharmacy. When Kozenczak asked him to come down to the station to make a formal statement, Gacy dragged out an opportune phone call about an uncle who had just died for as long as he could manage.

The police waited politely, and insisted that they wanted him to come with them, but he burst out, "Hey, I got a lot of important work to do. I can't be going down to the police station. I know this kid is missing but that's not important to me." Kozenczak was absolutely furious. "Well, it's important to the parents," he snapped. But he was helpless. Without evidence to bring charges, he had no option but to let Gacy go.

From then on, he determined that Gacy should feel the real heat of constant observation. Unfortunately, on the first day, Gacy managed to give his tail the slip. He had been out to his car during the night and put something he wanted to dispose of in the boot. When he saw watchers outside the house, he leaped in the car and roared away to a racing start that left them standing.

His journey took him to Interstate Highway 55 and the Des Plaines River. Clearly it was in some way upsetting, for his car went mysteriously out of control on the way back, and had to be towed out of a ditch. It was a muddy, confused and glassy-eyed Gacy who presented himself at Des Plaines Police Headquarters to make a voluntary statement. The statement was not very helpful, though.

Still, Captain Kozenczak and Assistant State Attorney Terry Sullivan succeeded in persuading a judge to issue a search warrant, even though there was little more than suspicion against Gacy. The search of 8213 West Summerdale Avenue turned up only a sales slip from the Nisson Pharmacy. This would, in the end, be invaluable evidence, for it had been made out to Robert Piest, and proved that he had been in Gacy's house.

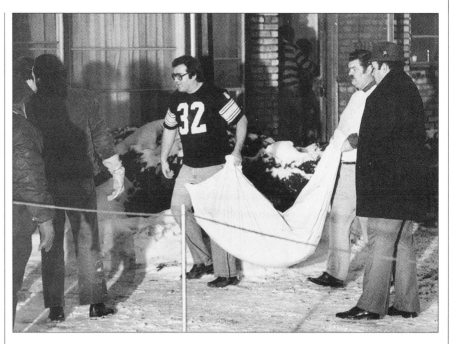

A total of 31 bodies were recovered from Gacy's house and garden.

The significance of the slip was not evident at first, and Gacy's attitude to the persistent police tail became patronizing as the conviction grew that he had well and truly beaten the cops. Hence his swaggering gesture of offering breakfast to the two officers on duty on December 19. When they remarked on the smell in the house, Gacy casually said that he had disconnected his drain sump pump, and water had got into the crawl space.

That was the clue the officers needed. In no time, the department had a new search warrant, and policemen were back to examine the crawl space that had been overlooked before. Then, one by one, the bodies were uncovered.

They were in no condition to be identified. Some had been there since 1975 and were completely skeletal. It was impossible to tell how each had died. But the exposure of the cache was too much for Gacy. Before long he was confessing, and explaining why Robert Piest's body had not yet been uncovered.

Gacy had been picking up and killing boys and young men, torturing and raping them over the previous three years at least. Some were employees, some were offered jobs, some were male prostitutes. Gacy would invite them to his home, and – using his expertise as "Pogo the Clown" – show them some conjuring

Gacy's house was eventually demolished, due to the extensive police excavations.

tricks. Eventually would come a trick which involved handcuffing the spectator. With his victim now helpless, Gacy put a rope round his neck and took him to the basement for sadistic sport. When he had finished with them, he would throttle those who had not entered willingly into the nasty games he devised to satisfy his perverted desires. He used two ligatures: a rosary, and a tourniquet he had made out of a board and ropes. He disposed of his victims by burying them in the crawl space. But so insatiable was his appetite that the space was all used up by the time of body number 27. (Actually, Gacy had lost count: 28 bodies were found under his floor.) So he used the garden for the next three. When that was full, he decided to use the Des Plaines River as a dumping ground. Five bodies ended up there, among them young Robert Piest's.

That was the sinister secret Gacy had been so keen to keep that he had given his police tail the slip. With Des Plaines police clearly not intending to pussyfoot with him over the lad's disappearance, drastic action was required.

Defence lawyer Sam Amirante entered a plea of insanity for his client. Gacy did not attend the preliminary hearing because of fears for his safety.

JEKYLL AND HYDE

John Gacy had, by his own confused confession, killed 36 people in six years. Yet the press, police and people of Chicago had no idea there was a serial killer in their midst, let alone the worst ever encountered in America to that date. Cook County medical examiner Dr. Robert Stein, in charge of the dreadful job of assembling whole cadavers from the rotted and mummified remains in the house, was overwhelmed by the task ahead of him. "It's frightening," he said. "That's the only word I can use. Frightening. Frightening."

Gacy tried to kill himself while he was in custody. He had to be restrained and watched continuously to keep him from damaging himself. While he was being questioned, the Illinois authorities contacted police in Texas, where Dean Corll and Elmer Wayne Henley had similarly entrapped, tortured and murdered adolescent boys in a boathouse. The way the victims had been abused and buried under the murder site seemed so similar that Des Plaines police wondered whether Gacy, like Corll, might have had an accomplice. But it seemed that Gacy had worked on his own, though he admitted having been influenced by what he had read about Corll and Henley.

In April 1979, 8213 West Summerdale Avenue was demolished as unsafe. The police had excavated in and around the house to such an extent that the decision was probably sound. But neighbours had stronger reasons for wanting to see it razed to the ground. Throngs of morbid sightseers came to look at the place and the evil reputation of the building was depressing local house values.

Guilty as charged, mass murderer John Gacy leaves the court at Des Plaines.

Pre-trial hearings were held before Judge John White, who ordered that Gacy must, for his own safety, be debarred from attending them. The parents of victims were only the spearhead of those who might have wanted to take the law into their own hands. Gacy was examined by a posse of psychiatrists, and their detailed reports determined the nature of his defence.

There would be little point in trying to deny the murders. Defence Lawyer Sam Amirante pleaded Gacy not guilty by reason of insanity. Stressing the extraordinary contrast between Gacy's public life as a pillar of the Democratic Party and a benevolent, up-standing citizen, and his secret life of sleaze, cruising gay bars, and torturing and murdering unwilling sexual partners, Amirante suggested that Gacy was a real-life Jekyll and Hyde figure. The two sides of Gacy were so radically different that he amounted to a split personality. "Despite what psychiatric terms you put on it," he declared, "he was so good and so bad, and the bad side of him was the personification of evil."

More impressive, perhaps, and certainly more legally relevant in a state which still accepted the McNaghten rules on insanity, four psychiatrists testified that Gacy was one of the most complex characters they had ever met; but undoubtedly psychotic and unable to differentiate good from evil.

The prosecution put all this insanity down to a bamboozling act Gacy was putting on for his defence. And the jury agreed wholeheartedly. John Gacy was found guilty on all counts and sentenced to die in the electric chair.

However, Illinois has a long appeals process, and has not judicially executed anybody since 1962. John Wayne Gacy, convicted of more murders than any other individual in America, is still on Death Row, and will probably die there.

TED BUNDY
DEADLY CHARM

On February 15, 1978, a Florida policeman stopped a stolen car. The driver called himself Chris Hagen. Later he claimed to be Kenneth R. Mizner of Tallahassee, but this name was as false as Chris Hagen. It was several days before the police realized who they had in custody – Theodore "Ted" Bundy, America's most wanted man. Bundy eventually confessed to 23 murders. Nearly all the victims were pretty, young girls who bore a resemblance to a girl who had once jilted him.

■

AT 7.16AM ON JANUARY 24, 1989, the switch was pulled on Ted Bundy, possibly one of the most prolific, probably one of the most cunning, and almost certainly the most enigmatic serial killer the USA had ever known. He didn't fit the pattern. He was good-looking. He was charming. He was intelligent. Yet in the view of some people Ted Bundy may have murdered 100 women.

In 1972 a woman walking home attracted the attention of a good looking young man and kindled a strange desire within him. Picking up a lump of wood, the man hid, waiting for the woman to pass by, intending to hit her and maybe even kill her. The woman turned into her house before reaching the place where the man was hiding. Undeterred, he later tried again. This time he struck his victim, but her loud screaming terrified him and he ran away.

In January 1974, the young man, whose name was Theodore Bundy, broke into the basement flat of a girl in Seattle, Washington. Her name was Sharon Clarke. Bundy struck her with a metal rod, then rammed it into her vagina. She lived, but her external and internal injuries were horrific and the attack left her brain damaged.

Later that month the good-looking, would-be murderer broke into another basement flat, where he found Lynda Ann Healy asleep in bed. He knocked the 21-year-old psychology student unconscious and stripped her. He hung her nightdress in the wardrobe and then remade her bed. Leaving the room to give the impression that neither he nor his victim had been there, he carried the girl to his car and drove her to some woods near Seattle. It was not until the evening of the following day that people became worried by Lynda Healy's continued absence and a more detailed examination of her room revealed blood on her bedsheets and night clothing.

On March 12, 1974, Ted Bundy met Donna Gail Manson as she walked to a jazz concert. She was never heard of again. Neither were Susan Rancourt, Roberta Parks, Brenda Ball, or Georgann Hawkins.

On July 14, 1974, two girls vanished from Lake Sammamish State Park, a popular location some 12 miles from Seattle and crowded on that hot day. A man with wavy hair and his arm in a sling approached Doris Grayling and asked if she would help him lift his boat onto his car. Going with her to the car, he said the boat was a short distance away, but Doris refused to accompany him any further.

A short time later Bundy approached 23-year-old Janice Orr with the same request. She invited him to sit down. He introduced himself as "Ted" and people nearby who heard him said he spoke with a Canadian or possibly an English accent. After some time spent chatting about sailing, Janice left with "Ted". She was never seen again. That same day, July 14, also at Lake Sammamish State Park, 19-year-

old Denise Naslund left a group of friends to visit a public lavatory. She never returned.

In September 1974, two miles east of Lake Sammamish Park, the remains of Janice Orr and Denise Naslund were

HE WAS GOOD-LOOKING. HE WAS CHARMING. HE WAS INTELLIGENT. YET IN THE VIEW OF SOME PEOPLE TED BUNDY MAY HAVE MURDERED 100 WOMEN.

Ted Bundy in court, examining one of the most compelling pieces of evidence against him.

found along with those of an unidentified third person.

The photofit pictures issued as a result of witnesses talking to the police, plus news that the killer seemed to be named or to call himself "Ted", brought a significant response from the public. In retrospect two calls were important. One

was from Ann Rule, a crime reporter and former policewoman, who had become friendly with Bundy when they worked together for the American equivalent of the British Samaritans organization. The other was from Meg Anders, a girlfriend of Bundy's. She noted that Bundy was never with her when one of the murders happened. She had also stopped playing sex games with Bundy when he almost strangled her during a bondage session.

But Theodore Bundy was only one of over 3,000 suspects and also one of the least likely. He was good-looking, charming, and "normal". He was also called "Ted", and detectives not unreasonably accepted that nobody would use their own name when attempting to abduct a woman.

THEODORE ROBERT BUNDY

On November 24, 1946, Theodore Robert Bundy was born near Philadelphia to a young, unmarried secretary named Louise Cowell. She never revealed the name of Bundy's father. She returned after the birth of her child to live with her parents and they maintained a charade that Ted was their son, a late baby, and Louise his sister. Ted Bundy wasn't let into this charade, though in 1950 he moved with his "sister" to Tacoma, Washington, where he took the name of her husband, John

Bundy. It was not until 1969 that Ted discovered the truth about his parentage.

When still young he seemed to grow ashamed of Louise and John Bundy, conscious of their lower class origins and status in society. However, he was intelligent, a hard worker and an enthusiastic sportsman. He developed an air of confidence and could be extremely charming, but he was also a fantasist, habitual liar and a thief.

In his late teens he met and became infatuated with Stephanie Brooks. They became engaged, but she found him immature and broke off their relationship. Bundy took the break-up very hard and began to behave strangely. He took a job as a waiter in a hotel, ran around with a drug addict and took to thieving in a reckless way, apparently not caring whether he was caught or not. But there was another, seemingly more caring, side to his character, the side that led him to become a political helper, work as a counsellor at a Crisis Clinic, and take a job with the Crime Commission and Department of Justice Planning.

Stephanie Brooks met Bundy again in 1973. He was not the immature young man she had dumped, but a confident, interesting man. The couple spent Christmas together, then Bundy dumped her. In January 1974 he began killing.

With the disappearance of Denise Naslund, the murders seemed to come to an end. What the police did not know, though they may have suspected, was that the murderer had left town. Ted Bundy had gone to Salt Lake City, to study law at the University of Utah.

Nancy Wilcox was 16 and a high school cheerleader. On October 2, 1974, she had a quarrel with her parents. On

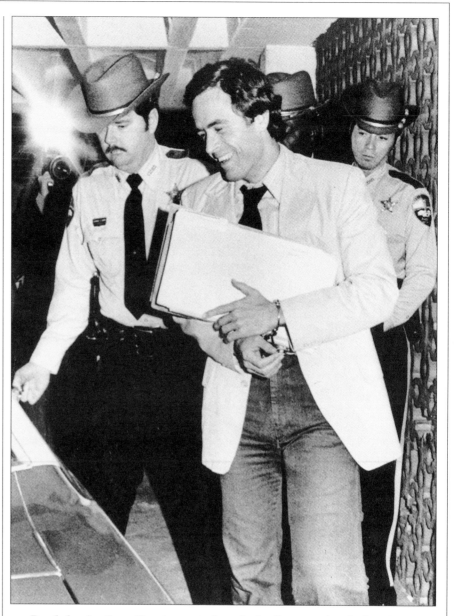

Bundy leaving Leon County court where Judge Cowart ordered a hearing to determine whether Atlanta attorney Millard Farmer could represent him.

October 3, she was seen in a yellow Volkswagen. She was never seen again (her body has never been found). Melissa Smith was the 17-year-old daughter of the police chief of Midvale, Utah. On October 18 she went to a pizza restaurant and left late. She began to hitchhike home. Just over a week later her body was discovered dumped in Summit Park. She had been abused, her face beyond recognition even by her family, and

strangled. On November 27, 1974, the body of 17-year-old Laura Aime was found in a similar condition to Melissa Smith. She had been missing since leaving a Halloween party on October 31, 1974, to hitchhike home.

Murray is a suburb of Salt Lake City. It was at a shopping centre in Murray that 17-year-old Carol DaRonch, looking in a shop window, was approached by Ted Bundy. He introduced himself as a policeman and asked questions about her car in the store car park. A man had just been apprehended breaking into the vehicle, he said, and could she go with him to see if anything had been stolen. Carol went with the man, but became a little suspicious because the policeman did not seem to know the way to the car. She asked to see some identification and was satisfied when Bundy flashed his wallet and showed what in the gloom of the damp November evening seemed to be a police badge.

Reaching the car, she checked it, relieved that it was undamaged and that nothing appeared to have been taken. She then accompanied the "policeman" to what he said was a sub-office where his partner and the would-be thief were supposed to be waiting. The door to the office – in reality it was a laundromat – was locked. The "policeman" apologized and said he'd have to drive Carol to the police station. In the car the girl now became even more suspicious as she noted the poor condition of the Volkswagen "police car".

The car sped off, in the opposite direction to the police station, and screeched down a side alley, coming to a stop. Carol began screaming as the "policeman" produced handcuffs. In the ensuing struggle, Bundy couldn't get the girl properly handcuffed. She pulled away and began to get the car door open. Bundy drew a gun and threatened to blow Carol's brains out, but bravely, or maybe desperately, she continued to open the car door. Bundy followed her, clutching an iron bar. Then, suddenly, there was a glare of headlights from an oncoming car. Bundy flung himself back into his car and drove away at high speed. Carol DaRonch was able to tell her story to the police.

Debbie Kent wasn't that lucky. Aged 17 and a student at Viewmont High School in Murray, Utah, she was watching the school play, unaware of the drama behind the scenes of the over-running production. Ted Bundy was there. He'd approached Jean Graham, the drama teacher, several times in an effort to get her into the car park to identify a car, but she had been too busy. As the play came towards its conclusion, Debbie left the theatre to make the short journey to the local ice-rink where her brother was waiting to be picked up. Nearby residents later reported hearing two piercing screams coming from the school car park that night. Police searching the area found the key to a pair of handcuffs, the same handcuffs that Bundy had left attached to Carol DaRonch's wrist. Questioning of the theatre audience soon led them to Jean Graham. Her description of the man she'd seen matched the description of the man given by Carol DaRonch. But too late to save Debbie Kent.

Ted Bundy's mother, Mrs. Louise Bundy, locked in despair after taking the stand to plead to the jury not to send her son to the electric chair.

On January 11, 1975, 23-year-old nurse Caryn Campbell went with her fiancé, divorcé Dr. Raymond Gadowski, and his two children to the Wildwood Inn, Snowmass Village, Colorado. While Dr. Gadowski attended the medical convention being held there, Caryn and the children entertained themselves, ski-ing and generally having fun. The following day they enjoyed dinner with Gadowski and a colleague. There was a friendly argument between Caryn and the colleague and on returning to the Inn, Caryn went off to fetch something from her room. On February 17 some cawing crows attracted attention to Caryn's naked body in the snow. She'd been struck with an iron bar and raped.

CAPTURE

It was in August 1975 that Sergeant Bob Hayward was driving through a quiet neighbourhood of Salt Lake City. It was very early in the morning, still dark in some of the side streets and Hayward switched on his car lights. The beams illuminated a battered old Volkswagen. The vehicle shuddered into life and drove off at high speed. Hayward followed, keeping up with the little VW as it drove through a couple of red lights and eventually stopped in the forecourt of a closed petrol station.

Ted Bundy got out of the car. Good-looking and well dressed, he sauntered over to the police car. He gave an excuse for driving as he had done and claimed that he had been to see the movie *The Towering Inferno* at a drive-in. Hayward knew this was a lie – the film had ceased playing at the drive-in.

On searching the car, Hayward found several pieces of incriminating evidence – a knitted ski balaclava, a mask, a strip of metal pipe and a pair of handcuffs. Hayward took Bundy in for questioning, but he was released later that same day. His possessions were certainly suspect and his behaviour in driving away from Sergeant Hayward indicated guilt about something, but there was no proof that Bundy had committed any crime.

A few days later, however, Detective Jerry Thompson of the Homicide Division was told about the arrest of Bundy.

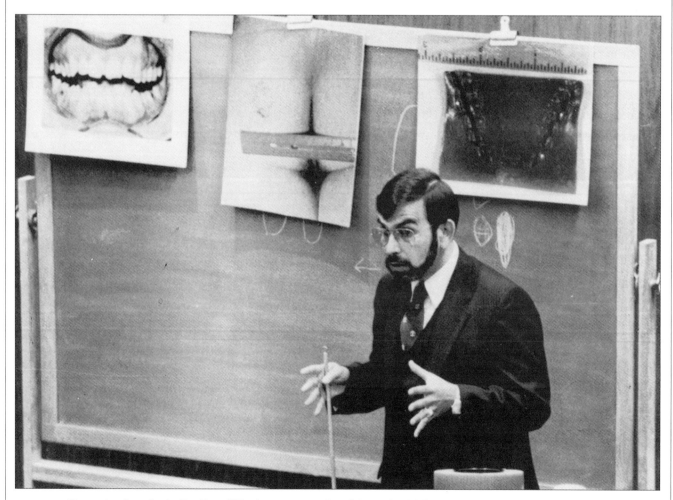

Forensic odontologist Dr. Lowell Levine compares Bundy's teeth with bite marks left on one of the victims.

The name rang a bell and on returning to his office he pulled a file sent to him by a detective in Seattle. The file read "Ted Bundy", a suspect in the Seattle serial killing case. And, Thompson realized, Carol DaRonch had been picked up by a man who drove a battered VW.

Bundy was rearrested on August 21, 1975. He was calm and confident. He gave his "good" reasons for possessing the items Sergeant Hayward had found in the car and freely gave the police permission to search his flat and his car. He denied ever having been to Colorado, but Thompson noted in the flat a number of holiday brochures for Colorado (which Bundy said belonged to a friend), one of which advertised The Wildwood Inn. Somebody had put a cross next to it. Thompson telephoned the Colorado police. Did The Wildwood Inn mean anything to anyone? Of course it did; Caryn Campbell had been staying there when she vanished.

Next Thompson learned that a credit card receipt he'd taken from a drawer in Bundy's apartment was for petrol bought in Colorado. In fact, the petrol had been bought in Glenwood Springs, no more than a few miles from where Caryn Campbell had been murdered, and the petrol significantly had been bought on January 12, 1975, the day Caryn Campbell went missing.

On October 1, 1975, the police held an identity parade. Three women, including Carol DaRonch and Jean Graham, picked out Ted Bundy.

Soon after his arrest the bodies of Lynda Healy, Susan Rancourt, Roberta Parks and Brenda Ball were discovered on a hillside some 20 miles from Seattle. It was obvious that the girls had been

Nita Jane Neary, a student at Florida State University, during her testimony against Bundy. She identified him as the man she saw leaving Chi Omega Sorority House.

abducted and taken to this lonely spot so that their killer could take his time sexually assaulting them. It created a horrible mental image. Ted Bundy made nationwide newspaper headlines. Yet by November 20, 1975, he was again walking the streets, released on bail.

For many people the disturbing thing about Ted Bundy was that he did not look or behave like a murderer. Good-looking, with a charming smile, he was a smart dresser, confident, outgoing and intelligent. His mother, of course, believed him innocent and stood by him. So, too, did his many friends in Salt

Lake City – it maybe says much for the reputation of the police in Salt Lake City that many of Bundy's friends were quickly prepared to accept that the police were framing him. But the case against Bundy was building almost daily. He was found to have the same blood group as Carol DaRonch's attacker, and hairs almost identical to Melissa Smith's were found in his battered car.

On November 23, 1976, the trial of Theodore Robert Bundy began in Salt Lake City. The evidence against him was circumstantial and Bundy's defence was to claim an awful series of coincidences.

Bundy (centre) drew on his experience as a law student to participate in his own defence. The trial was televised live to an increasingly interested American public.

was long gone. In fact he was in Chicago. Two weeks later Bundy, calling himself Chris Hagen, stepped off the bus in Tallahassee, a university town in Florida. The next phase of horror was about to begin.

CHI OMEGA

On January 15, 1978, Bundy committed the most daring and sickening of his crimes. Entering the Chi Omega Sorority House, he attacked roommates Karen Chandler and Kathy Kleiner. Margaret Bowman, a 21-year-old art student, was found dead, while 20-year-old Lisa Levy was alive but died while being rushed to hospital. Both girls had suffered vicious sexual abuse. Later, in a nearby house, police found Cheryl Thomas. Also brutally beaten, somehow she clung to life and survived.

On February 5, 1978, Bundy stole a white van. Three days later he tried to strike up a conversation with a 14-year-old girl named Leslie Parmenter, but his behaviour alarmed her and the arrival of her elder brother caused Bundy to retreat. The brother noted down the number of the white van. The following day, February 9, 1978, 12-year-old Kimberly Leach vanished – her body would be discovered two months later.

That night a policeman saw the white van and glanced into its interior. Bundy saw him and took off. He stole a Volkswagen and drove to Pensacola.

It was on February 15 that a policeman's attention was drawn to a VW by a moment's erratic driving. A quick radio call elicited the information that the

What let him down was his attitude in court. He was over-confident. The judge pronounced Bundy guilty of aggravated kidnapping and sentenced him to a maximum of 15 years in prison.

It was now widely recognized that Ted Bundy was probably the Colorado killer and the Seattle multi-murderer. Other courts wanted him, too. In 1977 he was transferred from Salt Lake City to Aspen, Colorado, and on June 7, 1977, appeared in court there, unmanacled and acting as his own defence counsel. At lunchtime he visited the library on the second floor of the courthouse. Far from wanting to consult the heavyweight legal tomes on the library shelves, however, he used the opportunity to escape, jumping out of the window. With an injured ankle, he limped away, and managed to get to the

mountains, where he holed up in a cabin for a couple of days. Unfortunately for Bundy, his luck ran out. He made a few stupid mistakes, got lost, and stole a car that was spotted by policemen who also recognized him. He was rearrested.

HE DEVELOPED AN AIR OF CONFIDENCE AND COULD BE EXTREMELY CHARMING, BUT HE WAS ALSO A FANTASIST, HABITUAL LIAR AND A THIEF.

His luck did not desert him for long. At the end of December 1977, Bundy escaped from Garfield County Jail in Colorado, cutting a hole in the ceiling of his cell with a hacksaw blade. By the time his escape was discovered, Bundy vehicle was stolen and the policeman, David Lee, forced the VW to pull over. Bundy seemed calm, but at the first opportunity he tripped the policeman and ran off. Patrolman Lee pulled out his gun and fired at the fleeing figure. Bundy collapsed to the ground. But as the police officer reached his prostrate body, Bundy swung a fist and connected with Lee's jaw. The two men struggled, Lee eventually snapping handcuffs around Bundy's wrists. "I wish you'd killed me," said Bundy as he was driven to the police station.

About 24 hours later Ted Bundy suffered a brief collapse. Exhausted, he began to admit to a series of murders, but the moment of demoralization soon passed. Bundy regained his composure and again assumed the air of self-confidence that had seen him through so far, defiantly declaring his innocence.

The trial of Theodore Robert Bundy opened in Florida on June 25, 1979. The core of the evidence against Bundy was a bite mark on victim Lisa Levy's buttock. This was found to match Bundy's teeth exactly. All the evidence, though circumstantial, was strongly against him. Bundy nevertheless won a number of points – getting his taped confessions to the Pensacola police declared inadmissible because they had been made without a lawyer present, for example – and he became adept at delaying tactics.

Whether or not he believed he would escape conviction is debatable. To many people in the courtroom, the evidence against him seemed overwhelming. On July 23, 1979, after seven hours of deliberation, the jury pronounced Bundy guilty and Judge Edward D. Cowart sentenced him to death.

It would be 10 years before Bundy's stalling tactics – which included trading victims' bodies for stays of execution – were exhausted. Finally, at Starke Prison, to the delight of hundreds of people outside the prison walls, many of them holding "Burn Bundy" parties, Ted Bundy was sent to the electric chair. He spotted his lawyer among those present to witness his execution and gave him a small nod of recognition and a brief smile. Moments later the switch was pulled and the electricity surged through him. Few mourned his passing.

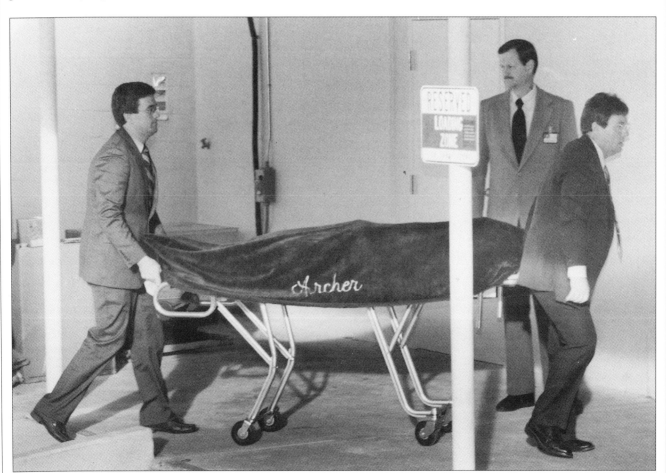

The body of Ted Bundy after his execution in Gainesville, Florida at 7.16am on January 24, 1989.

INDEX

ACKNOWLEDGEMENTS

Unless stated otherwise the photographs in this book have been licensed by Nugus/Martin Productions Ltd for the first series of *Great Crimes and Trials of the Twentieth Century*. Worldwide rights are fully reserved.

The Producers gratefully acknowledge the co-operation of the following:

ABC Capital Cities Inc.
Independent Television News Limited.
The National Film Archive Washington.
NBC News Inc.
Sherman Grinberg Film Libraries Inc.

Reuters Television Limited.
Topham Picture Library.
Metropolitan Police London.
New York City Municipal Archives.
New York City Public Libraries.

Dallas Historical Society.
Syndication International.
Library of Congress Washington DC

The publishers wish to thank the following sources for providing permission to reproduce additional photographs in this publication: The Associated Press; The Bettmann Archive; Camera Press; The Chicago Historical Society; Hulton Deutsch Collection; London News Service; The Municipal Archives N.Y; Peter Newark's Pictures; Popperfoto; Syndication International; UPI/Bettmann.